Also by Azadeh Moaveni

Lipstick Jihad

Iran Awakening (with Shirin Ebadi)

HONEYMOON *in* TEHRAN

HONEYMOON
in
TEHRAN

Two Years of
Love and Danger in Iran

Azadeh Moaveni

RANDOM HOUSE • NEW YORK

Honeymoon in Tehran is a work of nonfiction.
Some names and identifying details have been changed.

Copyright © 2009 by Azadeh Moaveni

Published in the United States by Random House,
an imprint of The Random House Publishing Group,
a division of Random House, Inc., New York.

RANDOM HOUSE and colophon are registered
trademarks of Random House, Inc.

Grateful acknowledgment is made to the following for
permission to reprint previously published material:

Arcade Publishing: Four lines from "If the Snake Is Domestic" by
Simin Behbehanit from *Strange Times, My Dear,* edited by Nahid Mozaffari,
poetry editor: Ahmad Karimi Hakkak, published by Arcade Publishing,
New York, NY, copyright © 2005 by Nahid Mozaffari. Reprinted by permission.

Daniel Liebert: "Why Cling" by Mowlana Jalaleddin Rumi,
translated by Daniel Liebert, from *Rumi: Fragments, Ecstasies* by
Mowlana Jalaleddin Rumi, translated by Daniel Liebert (New York, NY:
Omega Publications, 1999). Reprinted by permission of the translator.

ISBN 978-1-4000-6645-2
eBook ISBN 978-1-5883-6777-8

Printed in the United States of America on acid-free paper

www.atrandom.com

2 4 6 8 9 7 5 3

Book design by Dana Leigh Blanchette

For Arash

Why cling to one life
till it is soiled and ragged?

The sun dies and dies
squandering a hundred lives
every instant

God has decreed life for you
and He will give
    another and another and another.

—*Mowlana Jalaleddin Rumi*

HONEYMOON *in* TEHRAN

~✦

CHAPTER 1

Tell Them We Are Democrats

In the late spring of 2005, I returned to Iran to report on the country's presidential election. My career as a journalist for *Time* magazine had begun with an Iranian election in 2000, and though in the intervening years my reporting took me across the Middle East, it was in covering Iranian elections that I felt most at home. My real home, of course, was in northern California, where my parents still lived and where I had been born and raised, in a community of superlatively successful Iranian-Americans—doctors, lawyers, bankers, and venture capitalists—afflicted with émigré nostalgia. I visited California occasionally to attend friends' weddings, see my relatives, and fill a suitcase with Whole Foods products I could not find in Beirut, where I had lived since 2003. Situated on a glorious stretch of the Mediterranean, Lebanon for me was at the perfect geographic and existential distance from Iran. The proximity meant I could take a quick flight to Tehran for a few days of reporting, and then retreat to my calm, westernized life of Pilates classes and cocktail bars.

When I arrived in Tehran that spring, everyone in all my disparate worlds—from California to Beirut to Tehran—sent e-mails asking me to keep them abreast of my reporting. This in itself was unusual, as Iranian politics and its conclaves of mullahs did not typically elicit interest. But even the outside world understood that the upcoming election was of enormous import: it would indicate whether a crucial land of seventy million sitting atop one of the world's deepest oil reserves would ascend to the ranks of respectable nations, or would stay mired in the radicalism that had defined its past three decades.

As important as the election was, though, it was not my only reason for going back. My ulterior motive was to discover whether I could return at all. In the two years that had passed since my last visit, I had published a book about Iran that was, effectively, a portrait of how the mullahs had tyrannized Iranian society and given rise to a generation of rebellious young people desperate for change. *Lipstick Jihad* included depictions of drug-soaked underground parties, clerical hypocrisy, and the sort of criticism that had, in the mouths of other Iranians, led to prosecution and imprisonment. It was, in short, the sort of book that dictatorships never welcome and that one writes on the eve of permanent departure, a final, cathartic clanging of the door on the way out.

But being young and foolish, I had every intention of going back. I so desperately wanted Iran to be a place where you could speak truth to power that I decided to test reality. How wonderful it would be, I reasoned, if I could return unscathed. Then I could present myself back in the United States and say, "See, you were wrong. Iran is not such a dictatorship, after all. Unlike America's Arab allies, it tolerates criticism." And so I wrote breezy e-mails to friends saying things like "If I don't emerge from the airport, you can have all my shoes," and boarded the plane to spend two weeks in Tehran.

The portraits of the dour ayatollahs that hung above the arrival hall were so familiar to me that I didn't even look up. With enough time, I had simply stopped seeing them, their beards blending into the yellowing walls. It seemed entirely normal for a capital city in the twenty-first century to be covered with oversize images of turbaned clerics. For the briefest second, before I handed my passport over to the yawning female clerk in black chador, the nonchalance my therapist would call denial faltered, and I felt a flash of dread.

"Ms. Moaveni." She peered down at my passport. "This is highly irregular."

I said nothing. Perhaps I would be interrogated. Or maybe they would just confiscate my passport, a form of soft hostage taking. I began to feel nervous about what might happen to me, and about how foolish I would seem for having invited it.

"The stamp marking your last exit from Mehrabad is so light it is unreadable. In the future, please check and ask the passport official to use a fresh ink pad, if necessary."

I breathed in relief, and thanked her warmly. From there, it took scant minutes to collect my suitcase and sail through customs. This in itself signaled how much Iran had changed since the late 1990s. In previous years, the process of extricating oneself from Mehrabad airport had been a trauma in itself. When I visited Iran for the first time as an adult in 1998, customs officials roughly pried apart layers of my luggage. They triumphantly held up a dry academic book of Middle Eastern history and told me it could not enter the country without being vetted by official censors. They levied an outrageous sum of duty on a phone I had brought as a gift for my aunt, and left me to hastily repack the contents of my suitcase, struggling to keep bras and other such intimate belongings out of sight. By the time I reached the point where I would be inspected for proper Islamic dress—a headscarf that suitably covered my hair, long sleeves, and a coat that reached my knees—I was a sweaty, enraged mess eager to reboard the first plane to the civilized world.

But this time, I found Iran treated its returning citizens with less arbitrary abuse than ever before. Mehrabad bustled with crowds of excited relatives greeting their kin, the acrid smell of sweat mingling with the perfume of giant bouquets. In the past six years, Iranians living abroad had begun returning in significant numbers for the first time since the 1979 revolution. The homecomings overwhelmed the modest capacity of Mehrabad, built in the late 1940s, and on nights like this, everyone ended up pressed up against everyone else, an intimate, jostling throng in which men and women embraced and veils slipped off entirely.

I reminded myself to e-mail my father later and describe to him how comfortably I had made it through the airport. Like many Iranian residents of the United States, my parents traveled to Iran infrequently and had little sense of how much had changed in the past six

years. They came to the United States in the late 1960s to attend university, back when the Iranian government was closely allied with
Washington and believed it needed a generation of western-trained
professionals to modernize the nation. They returned to Tehran with
their American degrees, got married, and went about applying their
expertise until the mid-1970s, when they followed my grandmother
to California, intending to keep her company for a few short years
while she received cardiac treatment at Stanford.

The revolution of 1979 dashed any hopes of return to Iran, and my
family ended up, along with the great influx of Iranians who fled on
the eve of the uprising, as immigrants to America. For years they did
not visit Iran, save one short trip when I was five, and I grew up with
the émigré child's ambivalent yearning for homeland. I encountered
the real Iran only as a young adult, when I visited in 1998 during a
Fulbright year in Cairo. During that brief trip, I discovered the fascinating debates over Islam and democracy that were under way in
Iran, and concluded the country had more to offer than just pistachios
and Islamic militancy. I packed up and moved there in 2000, to report
for *Time,* convinced that Iran was somehow a part of my destiny. I
had imagined I could teach journalism, helping young Iranian reporters write clean, coherent news stories instead of the wordy, obscure,
overlong prose that filled newspapers, which still often functioned as
mouthpieces for political factions. As I pursued such idealistic dreams,
I recounted all my experiences to my parents, encouraging them to
visit Iran and find out for themselves how dramatically the country
had changed.

Outside the arrival hall I found a taxi, rolled down the creaky window, and lit a cigarette, gazing at the enormous, sloping white marble
façades of Azadi Tower. The Shah had built the monument to commemorate the twenty-five-hundredth anniversary of the Persian empire; like everything else in Tehran it had been renamed after the
revolution—fortunately though, not after a martyr.

These late-night taxi rides from the airport were particularly special to me, a wordless journey during which the city felt as intimate as
my own skin. I had spent most of my adult years in Tehran—it was
my home from 2000 to 2002, and the place I spent most of my time

in the years that followed—and, though I had never anticipated it (New York, Cairo, other cities had always seemed more likely), Tehran had become the backdrop of my life. I was a single woman, and Tehran provided all the sparkling memories a young person could want—summer parties where brilliant musicians played under the stars until dawn; sophisticated dinners where the country's premier intellectuals debated Iran's past and future; and a diverse, lovable array of friends, from Spanish diplomats to the rebellious children of high-ranking clerics. No matter its shabby murals of ayatollahs, no matter that it was run by inhospitable ideologues who preferred to keep women at home—the city, I believed, had eluded their grasp.

As the taxi sped north toward my aunt's house in the neighborhood of Elahieh, I gazed at the billboards advertising Teflon rice cookers, which vied for attention with murals glorifying the Iran-Iraq War. The unsightly profusion of squat apartment blocks abated only when we swung into Elahieh's narrow streets, turning around corners that still contained magnificent, faded examples of classic Persian architecture canopied by the slender branches of sycamore trees. Not far from my aunt's house, we passed a columned villa that stood reclusively at the back of a vast, overgrown garden, behind high gates of lacy wrought iron. I could hear the clang of workmen from the construction site across the street, laboring illegally at this late hour on what would surely be a tacky "luxury" apartment tower built without regard for earthquake safety—a common practice of the "build quick and sell quick" developers, who ignored the fact that at least a hundred known fault lines ran under Tehran. Such lax construction was taking over the city, its aesthetic chaos and structural weakness suggesting Tehran was stumbling toward an ill-understood, inferior future.

I rang my aunt's bell and was admitted to the quiet courtyard of her building, the familiar figure of the Afghan doorman emerging from the shadows to help me with my bag. "Welcome back," he said softly. "Inshallah this time you will stay with us long."

"I still can't believe you're here," my friend Nasrine said, tapping her nails against a bowl of carrot jam. She was also a journalist, and we'd

worked together often during my trips in the past three years, crossing the city for press conferences and demonstrations. Sometimes we
held conversations of great seriousness, discussing how the Islamic
Republic cultivated the loyalty of its citizens through networks of
subsidies, low-interest loans, and mercurially dispensed social freedoms. More often, we holed up with a refrigerator full of chicken
schnitzel and watched Merchant Ivory films, comparing nineteenth-
century and Persian styles of courtship (the two bore marked similari-
ties, chiefly in the pursuit of the advantageous marriage). Together we
also indulged in a secret pastime, which we called, rather sheepishly,
our portable disco. This meant piling into Nasrine's Korean hatchback,
turning the music up loud, and cruising Vali Asr Boulevard—the wide,
tree-lined artery that runs north–south through the city—listening to
the Tehrangeles-based pop duo Kamran and Houman. This activity
was deeply shameful, considering our age (we should have been at dinner parties with other thirtyish professionals, making polished remarks
about Iranian cinema and the government), but it was how thousands
of young Iranians entertained themselves, and it made us feel at one
with Tehran's Thursday nights, which belonged to the city's youth.

The phone rang, interrupting our breakfast chatter.

"*Salaam,* welcome back," a familiar voice greeted me. It was
Mr. X, I realized uneasily. I pointed to the receiver dramatically, trying to communicate to Nasrine who was calling. I had called his mobile the previous day, the first day of my arrival, wishing to hurry
along our inevitable contact. He had not picked up, but had likely
deduced from the number who was calling. As reluctant as I was to
see him, I did not want to begin working without his permission. As
my official government minder, Mr. X was perhaps the most important person in my Iranian life. The regime charged him with maintaining a file of my conduct as a journalist, alerting me to the red lines
of coverage (marking subjects as taboo or discouraged), and attempting to secure my "cooperation." This euphemism meant that during
times when the security-obsessed regime felt particularly vulnerable, I
would, so it was hoped, report the opinions and behavior of journalist and diplomat friends to the government, and disclose the identities
of anonymous sources.

Though Mr. X occupied such a central place in my work life, the institution ostensibly charged with dealing with foreign reporters belonged to an entirely different branch of government. The foreign press office of the Ministry of Culture and Islamic Guidance issued journalists' credentials and handled the numerous bureaucratic details involved in writing even the simplest story. If I wanted to visit a seminary, meet the foreign minister, or travel to a sensitive border region, I would need the press office's approval and assistance. During especially busy times, reporting an election or a cover story, for example, I might call its staff as many as ten times in one day. But although the press office—run by sensible, hardworking people who understood the news business—nominally handled journalists' affairs, it was really Mr. X and his employer, the Ministry of Intelligence, who had final say over whether a reporter was permitted to work. Even I had a hard time understanding the balance of power between the two, and perhaps they did as well.

When I lived in Tehran during 2000 and 2001, my relationship with Mr. X was a complicated dance of avoidance, in which I would refuse to do any of the things covered by "cooperation," and he would try through alternating tactics of intimidation and persuasion to bring me over to his side. We met quite regularly, perhaps every two months, and for a long while he behaved like a controlling husband. He wanted to know every last detail of my life—where I went, who I met, what I heard and said—and grew suspicious and nasty when I could not recall (or would not disclose) information with sufficient accuracy. He knew all about my friends, and would sometimes drop their names casually ("Wasn't it Jon who introduced you to Simon?") to convey just how much he knew about my social life. Once, for no particular reason I can remember, he went so far as to make a macabre joke about my committing suicide. I was stunned. I hadn't expected such malice from Mr. X, whose immaculate plaid shirts and close-cropped hair made him look harmlessly preppy.

The physical locales of our meetings—secluded, anonymous apartments, empty hotel rooms in unmarked establishments—created the theater of intimidation Mr. X so cunningly used to his advantage. He knew that it frightened me to meet in such places, and also that I could not refuse to go. If I screamed, no one would hear; if I called on my mobile phone for help, it would take forever to describe where I was. I could easily be transported elsewhere against my will without anyone noticing. The first time one of my journalist friends met Mr. X in an unoccupied, furnished apartment, she arrived before him and, terrified, rushed about finding all the kitchen knives and hiding them under the furniture, so that she would be prepared once he arrived.

Though his presence was undeniably creepy, Mr. X strove to be more than just a menace. Sometimes he behaved almost sociably, softening the expression in his brown eyes and asking politely after my family. He had on occasion actively facilitated my reporting, going out of his way to clear some bureaucratic obstacle to a trip, or authorizing an outing whose permissibility seemed in doubt. If anything went wrong, he said, I could always call him. Once he even suggested I help him assess foreign correspondents who applied for visas to Iran, blackballing those whose work I considered biased. I demurred, of course. The chance to keep my journalistic rivals out of the country was bait, a message that I could stand to gain if I put my scruples aside.

In late 2001, in the aftermath of September 11 and President Bush's labeling Iran as part of an "axis of evil," Mr. X demanded to vet my stories before publication and insisted on knowing the identities of my anonymous sources. He threatened to revoke my press credentials if I refused. Unable to elude him any longer, I chose to stop reporting from Iran and move to New York.

I had written openly about Mr. X in my book, violating many taboos at once: I revealed that such meetings took place (most journalists in Iran had a government minder, though they never admitted it), disclosed their content, and, perhaps worst of all, described in a book of nonfiction the secret thoughts I imagined he harbored. Part of me felt relief at having exposed him, voiding the insistent admonitions that "*no one* must know of our meetings." Mr. X now existed on the page, and this somehow took away the power of secrecy he had always cultivated. But surely he would be furious and seek to avenge himself.

"Yes, this afternoon is convenient for me." I hoped that my dread didn't show in my voice.

We spoke only long enough to plan our meeting. Nasrine volunteered to take me, and I coached her in the code that I had used with my former driver, Ali, who had taken me to so many of these meetings. After ten minutes, she was to call my cell phone. If I answered, "Yes, I'll be back in time for lunch," it meant there was no cause for alarm. "I'm going to be late, don't wait for me," meant something had gone terribly wrong, and that she should immediately start making emergency calls and try to rescue me.

Nasrine stopped the car at the top of the street, and pressed my hand before I stepped out. My heart beat swiftly as I searched for the hotel Mr. X had described, and my mind whirled with grim possibilities—Mr. X could permanently ban me from reporting in Iran; he could confiscate my passport and bar me from leaving the country (even the state equated an overlong stay in Iran with incarceration); send me to a court that might then send me to prison; or, in my direst imaginings, immure me in the room and inflict unspeakable punishments.

I passed up and down the street's length twice more, and even asked two passersby, but no one had heard of the apartment hotel. Suddenly I remembered that Mr. X had given me a building number as well as the hotel's name, and with that I quickly found it—six stories of unmarked white cement. What sort of hotel was this, unknown to the neighborhood and mysteriously unlabeled? Its anonymity seemed to confirm my most hysterical suspicions. My hands began to shake, and before I summoned the courage to climb the stone steps, I breathed deeply and told myself young women from California were not typically victims of political murder.

Someone buzzed the door open from inside, and I entered a small lobby presided over by a young man in sandals. I never knew what to say in such situations. In the past, Mr. X had often summoned me to meet him at secluded (though clearly marked) hotels, with instructions no more precise than "Be there at two P.M." The truth—"Hello, my name is Azadeh and I'm here to meet a government minder whose name I've been told never to repeat aloud, although we all know it's a pseudonym anyway"—sounded awkward.

"They're waiting for you in apartment five on the second floor," the young man said, sparing me. I said thank you and gazed at him with a winning expression, one that I hoped radiated innocence and established me as a productive, indispensable member of the global community, the type of person he should definitely try to help, should he hear screams from apartment five.

The elevator door opened onto the second floor, and I adjusted my headscarf before a hallway mirror, tucking strands of hair away, as though such attentions might somehow influence what would happen to me. Mr. X opened the door and ushered me inside. Such empty, furnished apartments—the type of place where Japanese businessmen would stay to negotiate oil deals that Washington would later veto— lent a bizarre, corporate coziness to the setting.

"Would you like tea or coffee?" Mr. X asked, busying himself in the kitchen. He poured us both tea, and then took a seat at the dinner table across from a plate of cream puffs. Eating pastry under duress was another hallmark of my meetings with Mr. X. During our initial encounters I had refused to eat anything, reluctant to provoke the nausea I usually felt. But this caused him offense, and I began to accept whatever I found on the table, eager to win his good humor.

His shirt was buttoned to the top, and his hands, hairy and blunt, fiddled with a pen.

"I have read your book," he began. "And the question I have is this: what is this *ash-e gooshvareh* [earring stew] of which you write? We have no such stew."

It was a dish I had mentioned my grandmother once made while visiting California. Like so many Iranians, perhaps a third of the country, she belonged to the Azeri ethnic group, whose cuisine included many unusual, laborious recipes distinct from Persian cooking.

"It's Azerbaijani," I replied.

"Okay." He looked unconvinced.

Someone knocked at the door, and Mr. X opened it to admit his partner, whom I had described in my book as Mr. Sleepy. In our meetings he was usually either asleep or menacing, the bad-cop foil to Mr. X's slithery inducements and intimidations.

We spoke very briefly about my book tour. Mr. X offered me a cream puff. And then he made a gesture of wrapping up his papers.

"We would like you to know that we consider your book worthy of appreciation," he said.

I sipped tea silently, waiting for the condemnation that would surely follow. But Mr. X and Mr. Sleepy began smiling openly, as though they were having tea with a favorite aunt.

"So didn't people ask you, if Iran is so repressive, then how do you write these critical articles and travel back and forth?"

"Yes, I was asked this all the time. And I told people that Iran tolerates some measure of dissent, that this is what makes Iran so special." I went on to describe Iran as an island of Persian practicality in a sea of brutal Arab dictatorships.

I could tell from their expressions I had replied well. It occurred to me that just perhaps, they both enjoyed appearing in a book, albeit as henchmen of a repressive regime.

"It is true, we are enlightened people, and we believe in democracy, freedom of expression."

"Of course."

"So do not be worried. Go back to America, and tell them we are democrats." He leaned forward, and began gathering his papers in a sign that we were finished. "You are yourself proof."

"Thank you," I said, picking up my bag. Then I said goodbye, walked out the door, and ran out into the sunny street. I inhaled the diesel fumes, the waft of fried herbs in the breeze, and felt triumphant. This country, my sad, troublesome homeland, perhaps it wasn't altogether as bad as everyone thought.

On the way back to the car I stopped at a headscarf shop and bought Nasrine and me pretty cotton veils in celebration. As I recounted the conversation to her, though, it sounded entirely too easy. Perhaps Mr. X really was as accepting as he'd seemed. Or perhaps my book had angered him, and he would punish me in time. For the moment, I simply accepted his approval as a blessing. When I got home, I phoned everyone I knew to gloat.

That evening, I shared my good news with my aunt's neighbors Lily and Ramin Maleki. Mr. Maleki was Iran's most accomplished translator of English literature, a gentle, erudite man who in the fantasy Iran of my imagination would hold the post of minister of culture. Lily, his beautiful wife, was a publisher and writer of considerable charm. Their home was a salon for writers, directors, and intellectuals, as well as a place where you could discuss Samuel Beckett, smoke indoors, and be offered all manner of delicious sweets, from fresh macaroons to walnut-studded nougat. They were as excited about my nonpariah status as I was.

They invited me to stay to dinner, one of the quick, delectable meals Lily fashioned out of a quintessentially Iranian cookbook, *Ashpazi az Sir ta Piaz,* an exhaustive collection of recipes—from Indian curries to Persian puddings—compiled by an Iranian writer who cooked his way through a long prison sentence under the Shah.

Our dinner conversation touched on the upcoming election, but just barely, for although the outside world was interested in its outcome, the race had generated little excitement among Iranians. In the two previous presidential elections, 1997 and 2001, the moderate cleric Mohammad Khatami drew Iranians to the polls with his cheerful magnetism and broadly attractive promises of political and social liberalization. His landslide victories were widely interpreted by Iranian analysts and the outside world as mandates by the people of Iran for building a more democratic society, one more at peace with and accepted by the international community. But the conservative establishment—fundamentalist clerics and bureaucrats influential within the regime's myriad institutions—blocked Khatami's liberal policies. People grew disillusioned with the regime as a whole, and with the electoral process as a means of reform. By now, many Iranians had come to view elections as a ceremonial act, an empty practice that lent a veneer of democratic consent to the mullahs' absolutism. By boycotting the race altogether, many believed, Iranians could reject the entire system of Islamic rule.

The lackluster ballot also contributed to this widespread apathy. The three top candidates were equally lacking in personal charisma and fresh vision: Akbar Hashemi Rafsanjani, a former two-term president, was a graying mullah notorious for his personal corruption, as well as for institutionalizing graft within the regime; Mohammad

Ghalibaf, the former national police chief, came across as untested and vaguely junior; Mostafa Moin, a former minister of education, reminded most people of a librarian.

Although I opposed a boycott—the differences between the candidates were meaningful enough, I felt, to warrant making a choice—I understood the lure of opting out. The reformists, mired in internal squabbles, had failed to agree on a single candidate, and were fielding two, equally gray and uninspiring. The presumed leader, Moin, though outspoken on human rights and democracy, was worryingly silent on economic matters. Rafsanjani, a crook with a record of failure as president, was a catastrophe wrapped in a disaster. To understand how Iranians felt about him, you must imagine him as the equivalent of a Richard Nixon who also happened to sink the American economy. And the conservative—well, hardly anyone took him, or any conservative candidate for that matter, seriously. Khatami's 2001 landslide, in which he took 80 percent of the vote, was interpreted by most Iranians as a loud rejection of Islamic conservatism in politics. Public support for his policies—dialogue with the United States, democratic governance, and cultural and social reform—indicated that the majority of Iranians wanted an open society run by a secular government. As one prominent conservative told me that year, "We need to go out into the wilderness for a long time, and figure out how we can one day return."

This was the disappointing array of choices Iranians faced in the spring of 2005, which is why that evening, rather than discussing the future of our country, we talked about novels. Before long, we were engrossed in a discussion popular in Iranian literary circles: had Ayatollah Khomeini's fatwa crushed or kindled Salman Rushdie's talent?

"Azi *jan,* what would you like to do this Friday night?" My aunt Farzi poured me coffee at breakfast, and began her attempt to fill my precious two weeks in Iran with social activities. My reporting trips in the past had often lasted a month or longer, and she was accustomed to planning multiple dinners for me with all her friends.

"I'm going to be very busy this time, so please don't make any plans for me," I said. I hurried my way through a chewy piece of *barbari* bread, and went to dress.

Certain I would be pressed for time, I had begun scheduling appointments the first day of my arrival, assuming I could keep or cancel them pending the outcome of my encounter with Mr. X. That foresight meant I already had two full days of interviews arranged and could start working immediately. My editor at *Time* had assigned me only one piece, a long essay illustrating how young Iranians lived and how they saw their futures on the eve of this important election. Given the striking apathy I had already encountered, this kind of article seemed to me the real story, a gritty look at what young Iranians actually cared about, since they didn't care about politics at all. I would spend two or three days talking with young people, and then stitch their stories together.

I rifled through my suitcase and pulled out a wrap dress, which I pulled on over a pair of jeans. I slid on a pair of sandals, kissed my aunt goodbye, and ran out to the waiting taxi, arranging my headscarf in traffic. The Khatami government had eased restrictions on women's dress so thoroughly that I gave little thought to what I should wear. When I first visited Iran as an adult, back in 1998, I spent the entire stay in a shapeless black manteau (literally, a coat, after the French word for the same) that reached my knees. I was twenty-one at the time, and wearing baggy folds of black made me keenly unhappy. By 2000, however, the women on the streets of Tehran had shed their dark robes for slim, fitted manteaus in brilliant colors and chic styles, simple tunics, and clingy ensembles of halter dresses worn over turtlenecks. This development, though perhaps superficial, brightened my spirits considerably. It was one of the myriad small things that when stacked together made daily life lighter and more livable. Back in 1979, Khomeini had urged Iranians to procreate wildly to bolster the revolutionary nation, creating a demographic bulge; the millions of young Iranian women in their late teens and early twenties shared my sentiments. That was one reason why they reelected Khatami in 2001 with such a wide majority.

Although the permissiveness mattered deeply, Iranian women were concerned about far more than their head covering. Not a single one of my Iranian girlfriends would have said her life was more meaningful simply because she enjoyed more flexibility in matters of fashion. The loosening of strictures on dress, however, reflected the Khatami government's tolerance of women pushing for equitable legal rights and access to public space. Women had begun doing aerobics in parks, petitioning for equitable legal rights in parliament, and organizing around issues from polygamy to domestic abuse. In short, the government that tolerated the pink veil also tolerated a grassroots women's movement of considerable vigor. It was this that women cared about, rather than whether their veils were now brighter, transparent, pushed back on the head, or designer.

But I, like so many women, took for granted what had changed under Khatami. This was for two simple reasons: I didn't know Iran at the height of the revolution's repression, in the 1980s; and it was not nearly enough. It was not enough for a society with 90 percent female literacy, whose women received 60 percent of the college degrees awarded each year. They considered themselves entitled to all the freedom and opportunity women enjoyed in the world's most advanced countries. The gap between their expectations and reality still loomed so great that a few millimeters of progress, on most days, hardly seemed to merit notice. When I arrived at Café Naderi in downtown Tehran for my appointment that day, for example, I sat by myself in the central room, lit a cigarette, and leafed through an independent newspaper that provided a reasonably balanced window onto both Iran and the world. Back in 1998, when I first tried the café's Turkish coffee, a girlfriend and I, dressed in our black sacks, were relegated to the back room, reserved for women unaccompanied by men.

Now I sipped my coffee and scanned the room. Bookish young men with goatees occupied nearly half the tables, but nowhere did I see the student activist I was there to meet. The café, situated on a crowded stretch of Revolution Street, still attracted artists, professors, émigrés, and freelance intellectuals, drawn to its rose-colored walls, vaulted ceilings, and leafy garden, as well as its literary legacy: Sadegh

Hedayat, Iran's foremost modern novelist, had frequented the place in the 1940s, back when they served perfectly thick Turkish coffee, and the United States had an embassy nearby.

"Ms. Moaveni, I'm sorry I'm late." Mr. Amini sat down opposite me, arranging his hands formally on the table, and assumed a resolute expression.

We ordered slices of buttery tea cake, and talked about how the student movement—once influential enough to spark the student riots of 1999, the most serious wave of unrest since the revolution—had fizzled out, its leaders terrorized by the security apparatus into abandoning their activities, or going abroad. Mr. Amini, like my relatives and so many other Iranians, had passed through the cycle of hope, anger, and boredom that these days characterized people's attitude toward politics.

He described friends who had spent time in prison, how they endured solitary confinement and modern forms of torture—weeks' worth of sleep deprivation, mock executions, heads stuck in vats of sewage, fake newspapers that reported the arrest of Khatami himself.

"I'm not voting," he said flatly, stubbing out a thin Bahman cigarette, named after the Iranian month in which the revolution "became victorious," in the regime's parlance. "I want to give a signal to the reformists. I want to tell them that they no longer reflect what people want. Not voting shows that I don't accept a system where the president doesn't even have the power to direct a budget."

As we stepped out into the street, pausing near a tree where a hawker sold contraband DVDs of American and pre-revolutionary films, Mr. Amini turned to look at me. "Do you realize how impossible it is to compete in Iran, in a place with no rules? Everything in this country is based on connections, on your relationship to people in power. People like me, we can't even compete in this game. Do you realize that at the current salary of a university graduate, it would take me eighty years to buy a flat in a decent part of town?"

I didn't know what to say. I only wished that I had paid for our coffee, though he had refused. Mr. Amini was right about his prospects. A modest flat was now beyond the budget of the average middle-class couple; only Iranians supported by their parents, or those few who belonged to the upper middle class, could afford to own their own place before their forties. I wished we had spent more time discussing this, a matter that most young people thought about every day and that was surely more pressing than the question of Islamic reform.

Mr. Amini waved goodbye and disappeared into the bustle of Revolution Street, a yawning thoroughfare north of Islamic Republic Avenue. In the ten minutes it took to find a taxi, the polluted air seemed to coat my contact lenses with a grainy, oily film. As we drove north, I could scarcely see the Alborz Mountains before me, for the city, as usual, was trapped beneath a noxious brown haze. The Alborz range runs like a wall across the north of the country, and its lofty peaks include the world's fifth highest ski resort, complete with gondola lift and rustic stone hotel. While the mountains mitigate the ugliness of the endless expanse of low-rise apartment blocks, they also block the Caspian winds blowing from the north, producing a thermal inversion of pollution that annually kills thousands of Iranians from respiratory diseases.

We idled in traffic near Argentine Square, whose adjoining boulevards reflected the worst of Tehran's haphazard, lowbrow architecture—buildings modeled after the Parthenon sat awkwardly alongside business complexes that resembled Transformer toy robots. The taxi sped through a tunnel that had just opened after years of construction, its impressive Persepolis motifs capped by an overwrought tribute to the Prophet Mohammad's daughter: "Would that my heart had a route to hers! Would that Fatemeh too had a shrine of her own!"

The tunnel knit a major expressway into a busy central avenue, and I wondered whether the roads I was traveling on were those mapped by my paternal uncle Khosrow and his cousin Mansour. They were among the chief architects of modern Tehran, responsible for the city's master plan before the revolution; the roadwork constructed later followed their original lines, which were intended for a population of 6.5 million, not the over twelve million who inhabited the city today. The modern, western city my relatives designed, with wide avenues and properly located and zoned residential, commercial, and industrial areas, had been transformed after the revolution into a haphazard sprawl of unappealing suburbs.

On a secluded side street just south of the new tunnel, I found the office of Emadeddin Baghi, a former pro-reform journalist and prominent dissident who had spent time in prison for his political writing. That experience had convinced him that Iran needed basic respect for human rights before it could benefit from political journalism. As the author of some twenty books and innumerable articles that advocated secularism and revealed the regime's brutal treatment of its opponents, Baghi considered himself a "religious intellectual"; this meant he was devoted to Islam, but believed the faith could accommodate democracy and should be removed from politics.

In 2000, when I had last seen Baghi, he was lying prostrate in a hospital bed. During his trial for apostasy, the judge had kept Baghi on his feet for long hours, which worsened a preexisting condition he delicately avoided naming. I remembered the sweaty evening vividly, how a young woman in chador, a student activist, found her way into Baghi's hospital room and pressed a bouquet of flowers into his hands. Student organizers considered him a hero, and the emotional young woman asked him, "Why do you write these articles, when you know it is like holding a gun to your chest?"

"If Iran takes one step in the direction of democracy, isn't that a precious thing? Precious enough that my ceasing to exist is a very small price in comparison," he told her. The young woman choked up and ran out of the room. It occurred to me that in 2005—only five years later—you surely would not find college students loitering outside the hospital rooms of political dissidents. That short, breathless period during which change seemed possible and Tehran felt as intellectually and politically animated as Prague in the spring of 1968, was resoundingly over.

"I can't believe how apathetic young people are these days," I said. Baghi agreed that the Tehran spring had petered out, and that most Iranians now coveted Bosch vacuum cleaners more than freedom. "Politics has become like a soccer game: people just watch and applaud from the sidelines. They don't actually do anything." He looked dejected, running a hand across his black seminarian's beard.

In the past, Baghi and I had often discussed his mentor, Grand Ayatollah Hossein Ali Montazeri, once Khomeini's favorite and designated successor, who was cast aside by the revolutionary leadership for speaking out against its human rights abuses. The octogenarian cleric lived under virtual house arrest in the holy city of Qom, but remained a guide and inspiration for Islamic intellectuals like Baghi. His name did not come up once that day. Instead, we talked about home appliances. I asked him what he thought preoccupied young people these days, and he said getting married. He told me about the government's marriage loan scheme, a low-interest advance of about $1,000 that covered a wedding dress and a middle-class wedding party.

Just as it had transformed so much of Iranian life, the revolution had changed how and when Iranians married. Inflation and the lack of viable jobs had pushed the marriage age up by nearly a decade. Now couples found it took until at least their thirtieth birthdays before they could approach financial independence. Young people tended to blame their leaders for the economic straits that put early marriage out of reach, and the government's marriage payment was designed to curb this resentment. "Lots of couples use the loan to buy appliances for their new life, or the first month of rent for an apartment.

"Are you following this pyramid scheme business?" he continued. "The newspapers are full of stories warning people to stay away from them. Parliament is trying to outlaw them altogether. This just shows how desperate people are to get rich without effort, because making money legally requires connections."

The clock on the wall announced I needed to leave for my next interview, so I gathered my things. Baghi asked whether I could help him submit an "opeedee" to some American newspapers, and it took me a second to realize he meant an "op-ed." I corrected him gently and promised to try. We exchanged e-mail addresses and I rushed off to find a taxi and sit in the stagnant traffic.

I arrived a few minutes late at Café Shoka, a coffee shop where the ex–student activist Amir Balali had suggested we meet. But Amir sent a text message to say he would be late, too, so I ordered a milk shake and watched young couples whisper over banana splits, as the speakers purred French lounge music. At least two couples had their heads bent closely over the table, whispering intimately and oblivious to their surroundings. Young people desperate to be alone together often resorted to spending time in coffee shops, among the few public places where they could sit tête-à-tête without drawing attention or being harassed by police. In fact, a whole genre of dimly lighted coffee shops tucked away in the city's numerous mini-malls catered exclusively to this young clientele.

Amir strode in half an hour later, dropped his mobile phone on the table, and sat down with arms crossed across his Umbro soccer jersey. Most student activists were painfully shy young men from the provinces who could barely look a woman in the eye, but Amir was clearly more urbane. He explained that he was semiretired, and that activism no longer interested him very much. This was not, he insisted, because of his 2002 imprisonment, during which he was kept standing—sleepless, facing a wall—for seventy-two hours straight, and beaten. I must have looked very grave as he described this horrific experience, for he looked up from his latte and said, "They didn't pull out my nails or anything." Nor, he said, was the imprisonment the reason for his withdrawal from political life. He did not say what the reason was; I inferred, from his other comments, that he saw no use in trying to reform a system that needed to be rebuilt from scratch.

Earlier he had called Iranian society a "social catastrophe," so I asked him what he thought was the greatest social challenge facing young Iranians.

"This sick double life we lead," he said. "Everyone wears masks, and no one trusts each other. This whole society is a lie. You realize, I can buy liquor at the pharmacy or get tabs of E at the juice stand."

I knew pharmacies sold a mysteriously expensive brand of rubbing alcohol that was intended as a base for drinks, but I was slightly scandalized to hear a popular chain of juice stands might also vend a party drug. "You mean Juice Javad sells Ecstasy?"

He nodded knowingly. My ignorance of this important fact apparently signaled a lack of information about the degenerate ways of Iranian youth, and Amir wearily set about enlightening me.

"At this very moment, there are thousands of *garçonnières* [bachelors' flats] across Tehran. Young men save up their money, pool their resources, and share the keys. The marriage age has gone up, and no one can afford to get married. Young people have needs, of course. The regime has no answer to this crisis, so young people find solutions themselves."

Given how busy they must be coordinating their *garçonnières* and buying illicit drugs from Juice Javad, I wondered if the young people he knew were going to vote. "Nah, not really interested. I thought about organizing around one of the opposition candidates, thought maybe we could pull a sort of Ukraine-style thing here. But then I decided against it. No one cares about anything besides their own prospects right now. Their idol isn't Che Guevara anymore, it's Bill Gates."

We chatted a while longer about this new self-centeredness, and then headed our separate ways. It was nearly six o'clock, and it would take me an hour to get back to my aunt's house in traffic. That would leave me just enough time to shower and change before her dinner guests arrived. As I stood on the crowded street shouting out my destination to passing taxis, disjointed thoughts flitted through my mind—why were Tehran buses painted in such peculiar sanatorium shades of powder blue, buttercup, and tea rose pink? When had young Iranians started to care more about home appliances than freedom of speech?

I wondered whether the authorities had successfully stanched young people's despair by purposefully dispensing more social liberties. After all, the regime had never seemed less able to control young people's lives than it did today. Perhaps this explained why the political rage I chronicled back in 2000—the impulse that brought that young chadori woman to Baghi's hospital bedside—seemed to have evaporated.

My aunt's dinner party that evening did little to illuminate these matters. Her friends were mostly in their fifties, and their twenty-something children had already been dispatched abroad, to western universities. Nearly all Iranian parents—from the affluent to the financially strained working class—shared the ambition of sending their offspring to peaceful societies where they could live meaningful, evolved lives of material ease. Of my aunt's friends, one (an oil executive married to an aristocratic heiress) had managed this with little trouble, another (a documentary filmmaker) with great hardship. I sat on the couch among them, selected a ripe peach from the fruit bowl, and asked whether they planned to vote. Most, convinced that eight years of reform government had failed to improve their lives, said they had no intention of voting at all. Two said they would vote for Rafsanjani, in hopes that he would balance the regime's warring moderate and right-wing factions, and perhaps even improve ties with the West. The discussion petered out rather swiftly, and my aunt summoned us to eat *kookoo,* a sort of frittata dense with herbs, walnuts, and barberries. I took this opportunity to drift away from the living room unnoticed, eager to organize my notes from the day's interviews, and refine what I would ask Iranians, my eternally unsatisfied people, tomorrow.

CHAPTER 2

To Vote or Not to Vote

On my fourth day in the city, I was sitting in a soundproof room the size of a minivan, hidden in the back of a greenhouse. Nasrine had fetched me earlier that morning and escorted me to a rehearsal by the underground band 127. Next to me, a young man in a tasteful plaid shirt and faded Converse sneakers was offering Nasrine a cigarette and explaining how in Iran dictatorship could not quash creativity. "It's like in Soviet Russia, all the writers just kept writing, right?"

One of the most surprising aspects of Iran in 2005 was its alternative music scene, the explosion of bands like 127 whose music the government considered a symptom of toxic western culture but tacitly tolerated. Of the many cute bands whose music carried tame political undertones, 127 was a particular success. Its members labored to cultivate an audience over the Internet (a difficult feat in a country where YouTube and MySpace were banned), and its inspired act, fusing jazz with Iranian music, was the first in Tehran to attract attention in the West.

The members were most excited over their newest single, "My Sweet Little Terrorist Song," in which the vocalist airs a sentiment perhaps universal in Iran ("Legally I'm nobody, but when I cross the border I'm somebody new") and complains in English that he should be granted a U.S. visa to visit his pretty cousin in California. He promises that if let in, he will "not fly into the Pentagon alive." Before they began rehearsing, I tried to get Sohrab, the band's lead singer, to describe how he felt living in Iran. He would not oblige me, though. "Life abroad also seems very sad, and not all that much better," he said. "People in the West seem to pop Prozac day and night, and it's not as though we're entirely cut off here. We're connected to the world, in our own way."

The band was composed of art students and the children of moderately well-off Iranian intellectuals. Yet, although they were not fighting off poverty, or shackled to parents who rejected their sideburns and choice of artistic pursuit, their music resonated with a very contemporary Iranian despair, the frustration of living in a nation with the world's largest brain drain: "As the new sky's falling, no one's running. No one's running but me."

As the musicians began tuning their instruments, I whispered to Nasrine that she should ask for the guitarist's phone number. "He looks about eighteen," she sighed.

"No, he's twenty-six! I asked all their ages while you were parking the car."

The theme of Nasrine's love life, her dire mismanagement of all affairs of the heart, dominated most of our conversations. By the base calculations of the Tehran dating scene, she should have been a highly desirable partner—she had a successful career and was financially independent; she was fluent in two western languages (English and French); and she was willing to date before marriage. Her wide smile, sensuous proportions, and penchant for tight clothing made her appealing to a wide range of men, and I could never understand her catastrophic choices. Partly, I suspected, she believed a sound relationship would mean the end of her lively youth, of all those Friday nights she spent drunkenly tossing her long black hair around on party dance floors. Partly, she just seemed lost, uncertain of how someone of her middle-class background might negotiate that party scene, dominated as it was by worldly, upper-caste Iranians. Nasrine had recently discovered the phenomenon of Bridget Jones—the novels and films whose protagonist, a female journalist, celebrates her romantic haplessness—and concluded there was no shame in her single plight.

Nasrine wouldn't approach the guitarist, and when the band was done practicing we filed out of the soundproof bunker, blinking in the glare of the midday sun. She headed off to run an errand, and I retired to Café Mint, a coffee shop on Gandhi Street that served "frippucino," to wait for my next interview. Kambiz Tavana, a hyperverbal young journalist in black wire-rimmed glasses, had worked for the reformist newspaper *Etemad* ("Trust"), which like more than a hundred other publications had been shut down by judicial decree since 2000. While the assault on independent journalism had inspired a would-be democrat like Baghi to dip his toe into "civil society," it seemed to have propelled Tavana into the Rafsanjani camp. I wanted to know how a liberal who reported on student uprisings had ended up serving a heavyweight mullah, despised by most intellectuals for his brutal record of harassing dissidents.

"Let's be realistic here," Tavana said, in the unruffled, confident tone of someone whose boss partly ran the country. "Rafsanjani has a dark history, sure. But he has power, and power can achieve things. What is the lesson of the U.S. invasion of Iraq? That quick change is not possible in the Middle East. We need to adjust our expectations to fit reality. Things have improved here. Ten years ago, you couldn't take a test in jeans. There were no shopping malls in Qom. Now look at how much more open life has become. There are openly gay areas in Mashad, teenagers on the bus listening to rock music on their mp3 players."

When I asked whether this was not just the result of a demographic wave, the regime softening before the pressure of an immense generation of young people, Tavana disagreed: "Rafsanjani is the architect of all this. These changes were a strategy, and just look how it's bought everyone's consent. Once, they asked him at a university speech what was wrong with men and women sharing notes. He said, 'Nothing,' and they gave him a standing ovation. Rafsanjani realizes everyone's top priority is himself. Comfort, normalcy, a decent economic life."

Tavana told me he did not see much point in pursuing an open society or holding the powerful ayatollahs accountable for gutting the
economy of an oil-rich nation. "Civil society, democracy, human
rights, these are all just buzzwords. You can't do human rights unless
you teach people what rights are, and right now that's not part of the
curriculum."

The Rafsanjani strategy of Islamic dictatorship lite—of buying
young people's acquiescence by doling out more social freedoms,
while hounding pesky critics who demanded political change—did
not disturb Tavana. He neatly outlined how the U.S. invasion of Iraq
had ended young Iranians' dreams of being rescued by tanned and polite American soldiers, who would deliver a shiny latest-model democracy. Forced to accept a grim yet stable future in the arms of their
ayatollahs, he said, people were making the best of their disagreeable
situation. Tavana's summation depressed me, but he remained in good
spirits, energetically poking a straw into the dregs of his iced mocha.
I could imagine him in ten years' time as the speechwriter for an Iranian president. Young people like Kambiz Tavana seemed curiously
able to mold themselves to the demands of the political moment: one
day, a disgruntled democrat; the next, a pragmatic, pro-regime hack.
He embodied for me the state's own inability to define its postrevolu-
tionary identity. Was Iran destined to become a model of Islamic democracy? A regional player with superpower ambitions? Or would it
just remain a shabby dictatorship stuck between East and West?

On the way to Naziabad, a working-class district in south Tehran
where I would finish the day's reporting, I mulled over Tavana's pronouncements. I wondered whether his preoccupation with social freedoms would be echoed in this neighborhood, where young people
tended to be poorer and lacked such westernized habits as the afternoon iced espresso drink.

The huddled brown apartment blocks were interspersed with fruit
sellers, butcher shops displaying forlorn heaps of raw chickens in
their front windows, and kiosks adorned with portraits of the Shia
Imam Ali appearing as tanned and handsome as a Brazilian soap
opera star. In north Tehran, such kiosks would sell imported Euro-

pean chocolates and Zippo lighters, but here they peddled the Iranian version of Kit-Kat (Tic-Tac), *tasbeeh* (prayer beads), and special pillows that murmur the Koran. The murals extolling revolution and martyrdom that adorned the sides of Naziabad's buildings had clearly not been touched up in years, the faded ayatollahs still frowned sternly and the artwork still bore the raw touch of Maoist propaganda. Though the city had yet to deliver its twenty-first-century billboards to Naziabad—central and north Tehran were treated to sleek black-and-white portraits of beaming revolutionaries; gorgeous, graffiti-inspired renderings of Persian calligraphy—the neighborhood's power is still considerable. Its Basij militia commands units across the city. Many of the city's influential politicians have risen to prominence from Naziabad's side streets, and mayors of Tehran, along with senior clerics, often pay visits to its main mosque.

Nasrine and I had agreed to meet at a busy intersection; waiting for her to arrive, I peered into the window of a bridal shop filled with mannequins wearing décolleté gowns adorned with feathers and sequins. Their finery in no way contradicted the black-clad figures of the neighborhood women striding past, plastic bags heaving with summer fruit. The brides from this culturally conservative neighborhood would most likely celebrate in the company of only female relatives, so they could dress as seductively as they pleased. Nasrine handed me a plain veil of navy cotton, which I pulled on in place of my thin scarf, and we set out toward the neighborhood mosque, in search of its mullah. It was three in the afternoon, an hour when many Iranians go home for a siesta. Most shops and doctor's offices close in the mid-afternoon, in the old European style. A gardener spraying enameled tiles till they sparkled in the sun directed us toward the mullah's house.

We rang the mullah's bell, and only when the iron door clicked open did I notice I had forgotten to bring a pair of closed-toed shoes. If the Iranian press corps had had a prize for Most Unsuitably Dressed Reporter, I would have won easily, year in, year out. Most female journalists kept alternative manteaus, headscarves, and shoes in their offices, for reporting trips to more conservative places like mosques and universities. Without an office to speak of, I often ended up as I did that day, suitably modest from head to ankles, with one forgotten detail, in this case a crimson pedicure, ruining the effect.

Hajj Agha (Iranians referred to most clerics over thirty this way; it literally designates a man ["agha," or mister] who has performed the hajj) invited us into his spare living room, empty but for a machine-woven carpet and a few cushions for furniture. He cast a bemused glance at my toes, but said nothing. Nasrine, in her most honeyed voice, addressed him with a string of gracious Farsi formulas: "How is your health? May your hands not hurt for agreeing to see us. I hope we are not disturbing the family, who I hope are well . . ." Then she began explaining our reporting needs. She was skilled at eliciting information from men, an indisputable aid to her reporting, and one of the reasons why I had asked her to join me.

Hajj Agha adjusted his blue-gray robes and invited to us sit down. Even he expected little to change with this election, he explained. When he heard that I worked for an American magazine, he stiffened slightly, but said we were welcome to talk to the Basij of his mosque. Like most of the militia, he said, they tended to be underemployed, occasionally borrowing a motorbike to work as messengers outside the Tehran bazaar.

The origin of the Basij as a frontline militia during the Iran-Iraq War is one of the saddest stories of the Islamic regime. Comprising volunteer soldiers too young to serve in the regular army, the Basij were used as human mine sweepers. The government dispatched them onto the border plains to certain death, supplied with plastic keys meant to open the doors to heaven. When the war ended, the Basij was transformed into a paramilitary force with the hazy, worrisome mandate of "promoting virtue" among young people, nominally accountable to the country's chief authority, the Supreme Leader, but run unsystematically out of local mosques. Depending on the bias of the news source, the Basij today are variously described as an Islamic version of the Boy Scouts, a voluntary militia, or a thuggish street gang. Really they are all these things at once. Basijis carry official cards; some carry weapons (from the classic AK-47 to the more medieval mace, depending on the task at hand); and they operate both independently and in coordination with what human rights groups call the state's "quasi-official organs of repression." The murky origins of the Basij's authority lie in the government's mix of Islamic and secular law, an unworkable amalgam that produces only lawlessness.

I suppose most Iranians would favor the description that reflects their particular history with the Basij, either as the recipients of its happy largesse or as victims of its unofficial but vicious authority. In the short time I had spent in Iran, my experiences with the Basij included being thrown out of a mosque because a lock of hair peeked out beneath my scarf; being arrested at a checkpoint because I was in the company of a male colleague; being pulled over on the freeway for sleeping in the backseat of the car (I had just traveled overland from Baghdad to Tehran and had nodded off in exhaustion; "Is *sleep* now also illegal?" I asked in exasperation); and being chased with a club for attending a soccer rally. If I had endured all those run-ins in the course of just five years, I could only imagine what those who had spent their whole lives in Iran must have suffered.

Western reporters tended to view the Basij only through the lens of social class, writing that they were well received in low-income neighborhoods and shunned in the affluent suburbs of north Tehran. While this captured the element of class frustration in the Basij running checkpoints in north Tehran, it missed the dislike of middle-class and working-class Iranians for the Basij's strong-arm tactics. They often acted like mafia enforcers in ordinary neighborhoods, demanding bribes from store owners for letting them sell contraband music and films and raiding private parties to confiscate alcohol that they would later resell for profit. They abused their privileges within the university system, intimidating other student organizations and crushing student protests.

But regardless of the Basij's reputation for enforcing a Taliban-esque morality, they also happened to be far more representative of Iranian society than most people realized. In 2001, a majority of their ranks had voted for Khatami.

As dusk settled and the call to prayer echoed from the mosque loudspeakers, the men of the neighborhood gathered inside to kneel in the direction of Mecca. After prayer they filtered out, disappearing into the narrow back alleys or the produce shops, and the nineteen-year-old head of a Basij unit joined us on the lawn outside the mosque. His name was Hossein, and the gel that slicked back his hair glinted under the orange of the street lamps.

We began by discussing television.

"I only watch Fox News," he said.

"Fox News?" I repeated.

"Yes, it is important to know what the military Americans are thinking."

When I asked if he was pleased with Khatami, he responded quickly.

"He is a good man. But he has allowed the atmosphere to get too open. Worst of all, he has melted before the West. At night we sit with my father, and we discuss. Why should Iran have to curtail its nuclear program? We who control the Strait of Hormoz."

Hossein was eager to show us that despite his nationalist views, he was a thoroughly modern young man. In our thirty-minute conversation, he managed to mention that he met friends on orkut.com (Google's social networking site), owned a complete collection of Eminem, considered *A Beautiful Mind* the finest movie ever made, and enjoyed weekend trips to the Caspian subsidized by the Basij. He said he would vote in the election, for a conservative candidate with close ties to the Supreme Leader.

"What about your friends?" I asked, nodding toward the young men in untucked shirts and shabby shoes who were congregating near the front of the mosque.

"Them? It hasn't really come up."

After our talk, Nasrine and I bought potato chips for our journey back to north Tehran, a trip that took two hours in traffic. On the way we debated how the Basij might vote in this election, whether they might take another chance on a reformist candidate, or favor the conservatives whose more austere campaigns resonated with their traditional sensibilities. We both felt that Hossein did not entirely represent the Basij's wider cadres. His status in life—as a college student, reasonably well trained in English, who owned a mobile phone—suggested he was the son of a well-off conservative bureaucrat, pushed forward to speak to us by his less educated Basij peers, because he could articulate his views. In fact, Hossein was something like a voluntary fundamentalist. He did not *need* the Basij; his ties of loyalty to the force were hereditary, traditional, and optional. He could afford university and weekend trips to Mashad and the Caspian Sea without the militia's help. But his low-income friends, the ones who had spoken reluctantly when Nasrine and I approached, self-conscious about their unrefined answers to our questions, relied entirely on the Basij for the very minor perks that brightened their otherwise bleak, impoverished lives.

Were the Basij a problem or a benign sociological reality? Their existence reflected the fact that a portion of the populace still believed in Khomeini's legacy, but to my mind, this was not necessarily pathological. Compared with those youths in other Muslim countries who considered Osama bin Laden a hero and were signing up to be suicide bombers, the conservative Basij were tame, even manageable. They became a threat only when they ceased to be a civic organization for traditional youth, and became a tool in the hands of militant ayatollahs hostile to democratic change. I had spoken to many Basij members during my years in Iran, during demonstrations and at universities, and it was obvious they were not an independent movement, but a private force operated by remote control. Men who wanted to maintain active membership—and enjoy those trips to the Caspian, those bus rides to Imam Reza's shrine in Mashad—had to show up for duty; that sometimes meant breaking up lectures by progressive clerics and beating students during sit-ins. The Basij, in short, did not mobilize themselves, but were mobilized by others.

This distinction mattered deeply to Iran's future. It meant the difference between a core of fundamentalists who would die to prevent change, and a core who might not embrace democracy, but who could be convinced of its merits. In the 1997 and 2001 elections, the Basij were permitted to vote freely, and they cast their ballots for a moderate who advocated an open society and rule of law. Somehow, though, I could not imagine them voting for a reformist this time around. The Iran of 2005 was not the Iran of 2001; the notion of reform now rang empty, and the reformist candidates had not risen to the challenge of convincing people otherwise. Would they vote for Ghalibaf, the conservative police chief? He was a natural candidate, but so far the style of his campaign did not resonate with the youth of Naziabad; everything from his choice of poster attire (chic shirts and glasses) to his sponsors (one was a maker of nonalcoholic beer) seemed to cater to a more secular, middle-class constituency. That left only Ali Larijani, the respectable but somber director of state radio and television, and Mahmoud Ahmadinejad, a relative unknown whose only record of public service was an undistinguished term as the mayor of Tehran. Perhaps, as the reformists hoped, the conservative vote would be divided among these various candidates, and in the end someone reasonable—pragmatic and open to the West—would win.

⌇

CHAPTER 3

The It Girl of Tehran

A week into my trip to Iran, I felt vexingly uncertain about my big Iranian youth story. The only thesis I could come up with—that young people were unhappy but also disinclined to revolt—struck me as limp and obvious. It occurred to me that I could test the theory of Kambiz Tavana, the Rafsanjani hack, who argued that the regime was easing young Iranians' discontent by loosening social strictures. While that sounded reasonable enough, especially considering young Iranians' rebelliousness and their taste for western culture, I felt the point needed refining. I decided to investigate further by spending some time with a twenty-eight-year-old professional race car driver named Sonbol, Tehran's reigning It Girl and a symbol of the regime's new tolerance.

Nasrine had suggested right away that I interview Sonbol, but I had resisted. Every foreign correspondent in town covering the election had already written about her, using her as an example of how Iranian women were among the most sophisticated in the region. In Saudi Arabia, women were forbidden to drive altogether, while in Iran they were literally racing ahead. It was a useful point to make, given that many in the West saw the situations of Iranian and Saudi women as comparable, but I was more interested to know whether such liberalism was winning over restless young Iranians, or at least keeping them quiet.

We planned to meet Sonbol one evening at Parkway intersection, one of north Tehran's busiest interchanges. Nasrine idled her car near where Vali Asr Boulevard tangled with multiple cement overpasses, and we watched cars pause to pick up discreetly dressed prostitutes. Though it was difficult to tell from a distance, what with the women's thick makeup and the homogenizing effect of their veils and man-teaus, the average age of the city's prostitutes had fallen to about twenty, by the government's own published calculations. Young girls who ran away from home often resorted to selling their bodies, as did drug addicts, who numbered in the hundreds of thousands in Tehran alone. The rush hour traffic of early evening was the prostitutes' busiest time; indeed, there was nothing any woman could do to avoid being propositioned, if she found herself walking outdoors between five and eight P.M.

Half an hour after our appointed time, Sonbol screeched up along-side in a silver BMW. She had pouty, collagen-enhanced lips and a nose job better than most, and seemed to be wearing a velvety hunt-ing manteau, if such a garment existed. She leaned over the passenger seat, raising her voice above the din of traffic. "I forgot my riding les-son! Follow me out to the stables." With that command, she must have floored the gas pedal, for in seconds she was lengths ahead of us.

We sped in the direction of Behesht-e Zahra, the sprawling ceme-tery on the southern outskirts of the city, where the approximately 500,000 young men who had died in the eight-year war with Iraq were buried. Somewhere in the vicinity of the Imam Khomeini's shrine—its ornate gold and turquoise domes designed to convey the ayatollah's divine status—she called Nasrine's mobile phone. "Do ei-ther of you ladies want a drink? Hurry up and catch me!"

The speedometer on Nasrine's Kia quivered as she yanked the wheel right and left to avoid the slow-moving Peykans on the high-way.

"This is ridiculous," I said, unable to look ahead. "What's wrong with you two?" Since Nasrine had met Sonbol the previous month, they had become party friends. Sonbol was clearly a bad influence, a point I would make as soon as their obnoxious race concluded. Nasrine pressed on, and soon we were speeding alongside Sonbol, who stretched her arm out the window, waving a plastic cup of honey-colored liquid. We barreled down the highway side by side, swerving to get close enough to pass the drink, so close that I could hear the insipid Lebanese pop song Sonbol was playing. (In our car, you could hear only the dignified bass rumblings of Shaggy.) Tehran, with its "I Love Martyrdom" murals of suicide bombers, Versace billboards, and rickety buses adorned with portraits of Shia saints, slid by in a smoggy blur. As we veered close, I looked down at my lap, too nervous to watch. "You can't do this properly if you keep closing your eyes," Nasrine snapped.

At last we got close enough. I grabbed the cup and leaned back in my seat with great relief. I tasted the liquid. "Something alcoholic with mulberry juice," I announced. "Is that a good mix?" Nasrine grabbed the cup and nearly emptied it. I was aghast.

Fortunately, we were not far from the stables. Within a few minutes, we pulled up beside the barn, parking near an old Toyota Land Cruiser.

"Is that his car?" I said. For weeks, Nasrine had insisted I meet a close friend of hers, a man named Arash. She had invited him along to the interview with Sonbol and had phoned him en route to the stables with directions. "You're perfect for each other," she had insisted. "Both of you act like you're already retired, always stuck at home reading books."

In anticipation of the meeting, I was wearing a new sea-green manteau and a cashmere shawl. "You look like a grandmother," Nasrine said, yanking it off.

Sonbol was already in the ring, lit by fluorescent lamps, cantering a sleek mare. A long plastic table bore mezze, olives, chips with yogurt, and falafel, and her instructor and a few friends were smoking and mixing drinks. Arash sat slightly to the side of the group, legs crossed, listening to the frivolous chatter with an amused expression. He wore a dark red plaid shirt, jeans, and leather sandals, all of which immediately conveyed long years spent in the West—the luxury of being casual, of not having to impress anyone. His black hair, wavy and nearly to his chin, complemented his relaxed bearing. Though I found him quite attractive in general, his eyes were his finest feature. They were immense, rimmed with a sweep of dark lashes and set under elegant, winged eyebrows, their expression both playful and serious. His skin was olive, like my own, and his slender fingers tapped rhythmically on the table. Nasrine introduced us, and I liked him from that first moment. As we made introductory small talk, I noticed the deep timbre of his voice, and a formality that seemed a cover for shyness.

"Nasrine says you've just been to Tajikistan. Was that work-related, somehow?" I asked, fishing for something interesting to talk about.

"It was meant to be a trekking trip, actually. But most of the routes I had in mind were blocked by snow, so I spent a week in the capital, instead."

"And how was it?"

"Frankly, totally depressing. And nothing at all like I had expected. Lots of run-down Soviet architecture, all cement of course. I don't think Tajiks are very accustomed to western-style tourism, and twice I was called a spy for writing in a journal." He went on to describe how the Tajiks seemed to consider all Iranians sex tourists and crudely plied them with women.

His experience reminded me of Afghanistan, and soon we were engrossed in a lively discussion about the ethnic mélange and violent ways of Iran's neighbors, the post-Soviet 'stans.

"Aren't you supposed to be working?" Nasrine nudged me, glancing toward Sonbol, who had dismounted and was now striding toward us.

Maybe I could get the interview over with quickly, and go back to talking with Arash. I pulled out my notebook and asked Sonbol whether her ability to have a racing career made life in Iran more palatable, hoping to direct the interview toward the subject of youth frustration. She evaded this with a bored mention of the upcoming Istanbul Grand Prix, and then dispatched one of her friends to the stable's kitchen. "Egg rolls please!"

Constantly batting her eyes and holding side conversations with

the others at the table, Sonbol seemed as impatient as I for our interview to be over. I asked her whether she had always wanted to be a
race car driver; mistaking herself for a head of state, she sighed loudly.
"I've been asked that *so* many times, can't you just read what I've said
on the Internet?"

Though annoyed, I explained politely that I couldn't filch material
about her from other news stories, which she interpreted to mean
I was done bothering her with intellectually taxing questions. She
launched into a wandering aside about her hobbies, especially her
heartfelt wish to go trekking in Nepal. It finally occurred to me that
all the eyelash batting, the dreams of roaming through the Nepalese
mountains, were directed at Arash. "She's using my interview to flirt
with him!" I whispered to Nasrine. "She probably thinks Nepal is a
mountain."

A question about state television's refusal to broadcast images of
her receiving winner's ribbons caught Sonbol's attention, and she finally warmed to the topic of women versus the Islamic state. Curiously, her sympathies lay with the latter. She told me that Iranian
women had somehow been too lazy to push for equitable rights—that
if they had sufficient courage, like her, they would find that it was actually quite easy to secure new freedoms.

Her comment reflected how little she knew about the women's
rights movement and its long history in nearly every domain of Iranian life. If women had made too few inroads, this spoke to the im-
mensity of the challenge, not a deficit of courage. But Sonbol was a
twenty-something party girl, full of herself and indifferent to such
context. If she had been a more important contact, a senior official or
an influential cleric, I would have circled back only at the end of the
interview to probe what she had said. Since I doubted I would ever
need her expertise again, I decided I could challenge her right then.

"Sonbol *jan*," I interrupted, "I'm surprised to hear you think Iranian women aren't using sports to pursue access to public space." The
ruling clergy forbade women to attend sports matches, ostensibly because the unruly atmosphere was unfit for them but in reality because
they frowned on women and men mixing in public and on women
participating in sports. Earlier that spring, a group of about a hun-

dred women had blocked the entrance to the Azadi soccer stadium before a match with Bahrain, chanting "Freedom is my right, Iran is my country." They scuffled with police and chanted for five hours before finally managing to storm the stadium gates in time to watch the second half of the game, the first women to openly enter a sports stadium since the revolution. The breakthrough had taken place under Khatami, who was present at the game that day and ordered that the women be given seats. Perhaps only a handful of Iranian women were drawn to auto racing, but hundreds of thousands were passionate lovers of soccer, and having fought their way into the stadium was a significant achievement.

"Nothing that happens to me here is affected by the outcome of an election," Sonbol said, munching on an egg roll. Arash followed our exchanges with twinkling eyes.

Night had fallen, and mosquitoes were preying on my exposed ankles under the table. I leaned toward Nasrine and suggested we head back to Tehran. Sonbol seemed not to notice our move to leave, though Iranian hospitality demanded she attempt at least twice to detain us.

"I should be getting back, too; I have guests waiting for me at home," Arash said, rising from his chair. Sonbol suddenly remembered she had brought lamb kabobs to grill, but the three of us insisted we really could not stay, and began walking toward the parking lot.

Nasrine asked Arash to join us for dinner, but he said he actually did have houseguests he couldn't abandon. After conferring over the best route back to Tehran, we shook hands and parted ways. I was pleased enough with the evening. As I saw it, Iran might have its own Danica Patrick, but this fact mattered little outside Sonbol's privileged world. Even she, who should arguably have been grateful for the state's magnanimity in letting her race, seemed not to consider her career meaningful. If, as Kambiz Tavana argued, Rafsanjani's strategy for Iran was to toss young people scraps of liberalism—a female race car driver here, a female deejay there—I saw no great hope for his candidacy. Most young Iranians considered the revolution an abject catastrophe, and sought to leave for other lands where they could have a future. Convincing them otherwise would take much more than any ayatollah would be willing to give.

The next morning, I went to see someone who understood Iran better than almost anyone. Shirin Ebadi lived in Abbas Abad, the neighborhood in north-central Tehran where my mother had grown up in the 1950s. Back then, fruit orchards and two-story houses covered most of the district. Now, like the rest of the city, Abbas Abad featured many oversize apartment towers unsuited to its narrow streets. The unfinished minarets of Mosallah—the city's colossal ceremonial mosque, forever under construction—loomed over the neighborhood. I jumped out of the taxi a block ahead of Shirin khanoum's street, near the local pizza shop that borrowed its pizza descriptions and menu graphics from Domino's.

In 2003, Shirin khanoum won the Nobel Peace Prize for her work defending human rights in Iran, and two years later she and I began collaborating on her memoir. I had been familiar with her efforts before she received the Nobel, as she had represented the families of the victims in Iran's most recent, prominent trials—the notorious 1998 murder of a dissident couple by state agents, a 1999 police attack on a student dormitory, and a brutal child abuse case that highlighted Iran's terrible custody laws. In 2005, the year we met in New York and began working together, Shirin was in her late fifties. She wore her dark hair, tastefully highlighted with streaks of golden brown, practically short, and her rounded eyebrows emphasized her soft, pleasant features. She was a small woman, but her assertive stride and intense manner lent her a more sizable presence.

I found her mercurial, constantly shifting between the many facets of her complex life and persona: she could be warm and winsome, radiating the inviting grace of an Iranian hostess, or as tersely combative as a seasoned trial lawyer. At times the depth of her humility moved me, while on other occasions I found her almost arrogant, prone to over-swift judgment of people and their circumstances. With time, I came to understand her better, and realized she had grown into precisely the person her work demanded she be. If she was tough, it was because she must be to fight against her everyday opponents, the unscrupulous, brutal authorities of Iran. If she was a touch paranoid, it was because she had been hounded by the regime for nearly two decades. Despite all the edges of her personality, Shirin khanoum was also deeply generous and lots of fun.

In the long hours we had spent together tracing her fascinating, rich life, from her early years as one of Iran's first female judges, to the loss of her judicial career after the revolution and her emergence as a defender of human rights, our relationship had deepened. I looked to her for guidance in many areas, especially those confusing junctures in Iranian political life where the wise choice and the ethical choice seemed entirely at odds. These moments were Shirin khanoum's specialty, and she handled them decisively and swiftly, with great skill.

She opened the door looking more rested and animated than usual. The last time we met, she had been suffering from all the stress and exhaustion of her work—padded braces had encased both her neck and wrists (pinched nerves), and she was on medication for high blood pressure. I was relieved to see the braces gone, and the comfortable way she padded around in her house slippers. We needed to work on her book's final chapters, and I pulled out the questions I had prepared.

I felt we hadn't explained quite fully what drew her, a young woman in her early twenties, to become a judge. "Did you have any role models, anyone you looked up to?" I asked.

I could tell from her impatient expression she thought this was a silly question. "I've never wanted anyone to be my role model, because that's close to hero worship, something I've always been wary of," she said sternly.

"But is there no one whose work you admire?"

"I suppose I can't hide my affinity toward people like Indira Gandhi," she conceded. "She was defeated once, but she didn't withdraw. She pulled herself back up and returned to the ring."

I sped through the rest of my easy questions, and gathered my thoughts for what I knew would be difficult.

"I think we need to help readers understand better what kind of democracy you envision for Iran, and how you see Iranians getting there. You've talked so much about Islamic democracy in the early pages, but later you tell us that because Islam is forever open to interpretation, it's difficult to use religion as a foundation for legal rights. How do you square these views? Also, if the Iranian government has shut down most of the legal avenues for criticism, how are Iranians supposed to bring about an Islamic democracy, anyway?"

Shirin shook her head impatiently. "Do we really need to get into this? This is supposed to be a book about my life. I'm not a political scientist; why should I have to explain something even political analysts can't figure out?"

"Because people look to you for guidance," I said gently. "You symbolize the possibility of peaceful change, and they expect to hear your thoughts on what they wonder themselves."

"Well, I just don't know what you expect me to say. Should I say armed struggle? That's all that's left when peaceful movements go nowhere. But obviously I don't think that. Iranians are ready to go to prison, to be killed for dissent, but they're not ready to pick up weapons."

"I've heard you say many times that change is going to take a long time. Why don't you just explain both the limits and importance of working within an Islamic context, and be honest about your own frustrations?"

She nodded in assent, and I could tell by the glint in her eyes that she was already honing her thoughts, that I had convinced her. Often she felt she had to respond to my questions with answers—with the solution to a complex, unworkable situation—when all I wanted were her candid thoughts.

We paused for a break mid-morning; Shirin poured us coffee and cut slices of a moist swirl cake with creamy icing and raisins. I asked whether she was still planning to boycott the election, and whether that might not backfire as a strategy. I already knew why she had no intention of voting. The Guardian Council, a powerful, unelected clerical body charged with vetting elections and legislation, had intensified its interference in domestic politics, barring many reform-minded candidates from the last parliamentary elections. In this election, it had approved only eight of the thousand people who had applied to

run, and disqualified every single female candidate. Shirin khanoum
believed that such interventions in the process rendered Iran's elections a sham.

"But what about the consequences of not voting at all? Would that
not be abandoning the fight, leaving the political theater open to unpopular radicals?" I asked.

"My daughter asked me the same thing," she said. "They held a
debate in her college class, and decided that it's better to vote, if only
to prevent Rafsanjani from being elected by a wide margin." Almost
everyone believed that Rafsanjani would win, and a common concern
among liberal Iranians was that he not win with a landslide. They believed he should win in a manner that reflected the ambivalence of the
electorate, the fact that he was primarily an alternative to the conservatives. If we all agreed that was important, her daughter had wanted
to know, then why was it right for Shirin khanoum not to vote? "Not
voting is also right, as an act of civil disobedience. The world is not
black and white, and some choices are subjective," she explained to
me. "From my perspective, something may be entirely right, but from
yours it will still be wrong. What I happen to think is that by voting,
I add another drop to the bucket of the regime's legitimacy. You, of
course, are free to think differently, for it is in this way that we represent different aspects of reality."

Our discussion about the election drew to a close, and I gathered
my things to leave. On the way back to my aunt's, I reviewed what we
had talked about and tried to piece together my thoughts. By instinct,
I found myself closer to Shirin khanoum's daughter's opinion, inclined
to shape the outcome by active choice rather than by abstention.
There was something to be said for staving off the greater evil—a position shared by many in Muslim societies. But the clarity of Shirin
khanoum's moral position also resonated with me, and though she
had never said so outright, I felt there was a rare dignity in choosing
not to vote, particularly in not voting for Rafsanjani, a man who had
presided over Iran during an era that had witnessed numerous extra-
judicial killings, as attested to by files Shirin khanoum had seen with
her own eyes.

If I had lived Shirin's life, perhaps I too would refuse to vote. Her work involved daily entanglement with unimaginable evil, and that had shaped her judgment of how best to deal with Iran's rulers. Earlier that year, when we were in New York working on her memoirs, we sat facing each other in her hotel's breakfast room, for twelve hours each day, poring over her life. We sorted through the details of cases she had defended, and events in Iran's history about which she held special, privileged information.

She told me about the hundreds of young people the revolutionary regime executed in the early 1980s, most of them members of the Mojahedin-e Khalgh. This group, which opposed the leaders who had taken power, had targeted top officials for assassination. Many believed that the Mojahedin's campaign, together with the state's brutal response, actually enabled the regime to consolidate its power. In the years that followed, survivors and families of victims had sought out Shirin in numbers; she had more information than I could ever have imagined. They told her about how women were raped before execution, a brutality the state justified by its belief that virgins cannot go to hell (a final condemnation these women, they felt, deserved). They told her about how the authorities even forbade relatives from holding funerals for their dead kin. Much of this testimony we did not include in her memoir: we would collaborate again in the future, Shirin told me, and talk about these things "another day."

But she wandered through the painful memories all the same, recounting the story of her young brother-in-law, who numbered among the executed. The prison wardens used to call his mother and inform her of injuries he had suffered during interrogation—once a broken jaw, another time a fractured arm—so that she could send money for his medical treatment. "What had he done? His only crime was selling newspapers. There wasn't any law anymore. . . . People's lives had become so cheap." Shirin's eyes filled with tears. So did mine.

On another of those days in New York, she told me about how the government recruited and trained special teams for assassinating dissidents. "They usually didn't kill people the same way. Some were killed in car 'accidents,' others in fake robberies. . . . Others were stabbed; some were gunned down. One other method was to inject them with a drug that would later result in a heart attack, a seemingly natural death." The assassins, of course, belonged to the Ministry of Intelligence, Mr. X's employers. That night I had nightmares of being stabbed as I left a meeting with Mr. X, of being chased down dark alleys.

She told me many stories of prison torture, of inmates being blindfolded and led to mock executions. But these did not terrify me as much as her account of Zahra Kazemi, an Iranian-Canadian photojournalist who died in 2003 of injuries sustained while in police custody. I had heard she had also been raped, but had dismissed it as a rumor. Police rape was Iran circa 1989, not 2003. This was my denial at work, of course. Zahra Kazemi—the holder of a western passport, a resident of North America—could have been me. Shirin had represented the family in court.

"Zahra's mother visited her in the hospital," Shirin told me. "She saw her under an oxygen mask, and realized she was being kept alive by machines. She pulled back the sheets and saw dark bruises all over her breasts, her arms, and her thighs."

I put down my pen, and bit down hard on my tongue, to hold back my tears. We went downstairs, so I could smoke a cigarette on the street outside the hotel.

Since those days, I had come to view Shirin as a repository of the regime's darkest secrets. Her decision to boycott the election arose partly out of this history, but for most Iranians, the impulse to boycott reflected more prosaic concerns. By 2005, the status quo permitted considerable space for criticism in the cultural sphere. Those who felt the need to comment on their society did so by producing films, becoming activist photographers, and pursuing other cultural endeavors that reflected and commented on the country's dire reality. Frustrated young people started underground bands like 127 and penned lyrics that ambiguously communicated their despair. Though rock music was still semi-taboo, they often managed to hold small concerts on university campuses or other closed venues. A few years earlier, young people had had no such outlets for artfully expressing the dark, complex reality of their lives. That they were able to do so now made Iran more tolerable. The government denied them many things, but it permitted them to articulate their deepest selves in ways that actually encouraged their creativity.

It seemed as though Iranians had reached a tacit accommodation with the government over which taboos might be reconsidered. Women novelists dominated the best-seller lists with personal tales of romance and sex, topics that a few years earlier they could not even broach. The government still censored more literary fiction, especially novels by western writers such as Flaubert, but this had resulted in a minor renaissance of literary journalism. Journals and magazines flourished, creating an outlet for accomplished writers to publish essays and criticism and exposing Iranians to international literary figures like Orhan Pamuk and Umberto Eco.

Meanwhile, entrepreneurs with some capital found society ripe for new forms of consumption. Seemingly overnight, the ice cream chain store called Ice Pack, which served American-style milk shakes, had established itself across the city. The numbers of Internet providers across the country continued to grow, striving to keep up with a population that despite government censorship used the Internet at astonishing rates (by various accounts, Farsi numbered among the top four languages used in the blogosphere). Bootleggers provided alcohol with unprecedented ease, dispatching cases ordered by callers to their mobile phones. When one of Tehran's top liquor dealers decided to retire, he sold his mobile phone number for a reported ten million toman, the equivalent of ten thousand dollars.

The last three years of living outside Iran brought 2005's contrast with the past into sharper focus. Today, it seemed to me, Iranians accustomed to a bland, mullah-controlled existence lacking in entertainment and retail prospect had never faced so much choice. There were more novelties than ever to buy; there was more to watch, more to do. I had never seen so many ads for household products as on this trip, had never seen couples so tranquilly bent close over milk shakes. For the culturally inclined, there were more galleries than ever to attend, more magazines to read, more plays to see. On the whole, it did not amount to a great life, but it was less miserable than before. And for the religious—well, it was their country, after all. They were as pleased as ever with the stability of living under Khomeini's legacy, in

God's grace. Scarcely anyone considered this state of affairs precarious, or thought of it as attributable to a set of political variables subject to change. Iran still left so much to be desired in the hearts of its citizens (the acknowledgment of basic human needs for a lawful society, a functional economy, real social and political freedoms) that it occurred to no one to fight for this status quo. Surely what was just decent, the bare minimum, hardly good enough, did not, could not, require upkeep.

CHAPTER 4

The Right Man?

I had been in Iran for over a week, and would spend my last few days writing my story. One afternoon, I took a break to have lunch with Nasrine. We met at the kabob restaurant Nayyeb, whose creamy, pillared edifice evoked the residence of a Roman emperor. The taxi driver dropped me off half a block away, beyond the chauffeured BMWs and Mercedes double-parked outside the restaurant. A footman in tails admitted me into a sumptuous space painted in golds and pastels, its walls adorned with the gilded paneling of an eighteenth-century French palace. The people who could afford to eat at Nayyeb clearly aspired to royalty. The crowd inside, a mix of young men in tight designer shirts, slim, tanned women bearing status handbags, and businessmen with Islamic stubble and chador-draped wives, all ate the same thing: tender lamb kabobs with fluffy saffron-and-butter-infused rice.

When I lived in Tehran during 2000 and 2001, the branches of Nayyeb numbered fewer than five. Now they were opening across the city. At lunchtime, the wait was over an hour, a fact that told you the number of people who could afford a ten-dollar plate of kabob was on the rise. "There is money sloshing around this country," I said to Nasrine as we jostled to reach the hostess. The restaurant's patrons came from the country's middle and upper classes, estimated at about

8 to 10 percent of the population. Though the vast majority of Iranians struggled increasingly in the country's decrepit economy, this small group had somehow managed to increase its wealth. Many of the affluent belonged to the higher echelons of government and amassed fortunes through graft. The rest profited from the three lone areas of the private sector that thrived—housing, construction, and consumer products. In Iran, there is no middle class as we understand it in the West. If you try to carve up society in terms of income, you're left with a handful of affluent Iranians (ranging from the comfortably well-off to the obscenely wealthy) and everyone else, who is poor (ranging from the strained to the destitute). The sorts of people who would be automatically middle class in the West—college professors, engineers, graphic designers—earn only enough to cover expenses like rent and school tuition. People who hold those jobs in the West can usually afford regular holidays and restaurants, but in Iran few have any meaningful chance to improve their lot. They are, however, educated, modern, and worldly—the attributes you'd associate with the middle class in the West; to call them anything else, like working class, would be misleading. For clarity's sake, I call this sizable population of Iranians as middle class in these pages. I do this to capture how these Iranians would define themselves, and to emphasize how much influence they wield in Iranian society. As you read on, I ask you to please bear in mind this one caveat: in Iran, middle class means something different than two big cars parked in the driveway.

I wondered whether Nasrine and I—wearing little makeup and simple linen manteaus—would even manage to get a table, but after half an hour, we were seated in the back corner of the second floor. We chatted with a twenty-nine-year-old waiter, who was sweating in the silly uniform of frock coat and tails. When I asked how he felt about the Khatami era, he leaned against one of the restaurant's magnolia columns almost as if to steady himself. "What do I have to be content with? I work from eight A.M. to midnight, commute an hour each way, and manage to see my wife and child for half an hour before falling asleep exhausted. It took us a whole year to manage to get married, I'm still paying off the marriage loan, and since we had a baby immediately, supporting us all has gotten even harder. I almost regret it."

In a society where people traditionally married in their early twenties or younger, the staggering costs of housing and of holding a conventional wedding had wrought nothing short of a social crisis. Young people were living at home longer, and premarital sex was becoming more common; both conditions strained the ties between parents and children as never before. To ameliorate the situation, the state offered marriage loans, but these one-off disbursals of largesse tended to thrust low-income young people from one predicament to another. Instead of being poor at home with their parents, they become poor married couples, left to fend for themselves in an inflationary economy. Often they had children immediately, only to discover that they had rushed into a life they could not afford. The waiter's complaints mirrored those of my former driver, Ali, who at twenty-four rarely saw his daughter and regretted his rush to early fatherhood. Now employed by an oil company that offered him longer shifts, he no longer worked for me, but his bitter fights with his wife, conducted over a mobile phone as he swerved through traffic, still rang in my ears, a reminder of how unpleasant it was to be young, poor, and responsible for a family. It all convinced me to start my own family late, in my thirties, only once I had lived my youth to its fullest and become financially independent.

I thought of Ali as the waiters rushed past carrying platters of glistening grilled meat, tending to the clipped calls of bearded businessmen and of women in Hermès headscarves. I asked the waiter whether he would vote in the election, just over two weeks away. The waiter said he didn't know much about the candidates and wasn't sure he would bother. We finished our lunch, unwrapped the sticks of banana gum that came with the check, and prepared to leave.

That day marked the start of the official campaign period, the eighteen days candidates legally had to make themselves known to voters ahead of the election. One of the most perplexing aspects of covering an Iranian election was the official scheduling, which essentially gave the nation—its citizens, its media, its pollsters, and its candidates—a bit more than half a month for a process that in other countries takes months or even a year. This made public sentiment notoriously difficult to predict.

Rafsanjani launched his campaign that evening on a busy, tree-lined corner where street vendors usually sold fresh walnuts and sour green plums. The seventy-year-old mullah's grinning face was plastered across the hood of a new Mercedes-Benz, while dandyish young men and made-up young women in snug, bright tunics leapt into traffic to slap Rafsanjani stickers on passing cars.

I was packing my bags to return to Beirut as my two-week trip neared its end. I had not intended to stay through the election itself; *Time* would run its big election package, including my story, that same week. The actual results would appear as a small news update in the following issue, as was *Time*'s custom for elections in which no surprise was anticipated. As we drove around the Rafsanjani campaign corner that evening, Nasrine tried to coax me to stay another week. We hadn't had time for any fun, she complained, and besides Arash was having a party over the weekend and had expressly invited me. I was tempted, especially by the prospect of seeing Arash again.

"Tell me exactly what he said."

"He just said he would be *very* happy if you would come, and that I should *definitely* make a point of bringing you," she said, adding what I assumed was her own emphasis.

"How many people are invited?"

"About fifty, I think."

I thought about it for a moment. Arash and I hadn't met since our first brief encounter, and a party seemed like an ideal chance to get to know each other. But I hadn't made arrangements to be gone any longer, and felt bad asking my Beirut friends, for the umpteenth time, to pay my rent, cancel my Arabic lessons, and tend my other details.

"I don't think I can do it, Nas. You have to tell him very nicely that I wanted to come. Explain that I had lots of work."

I pledged to return early that summer for another round of work on Shirin khanoum's book, thus consoling Nasrine as well as myself.

On a Thursday evening, I boarded the weekly Iran Air flight to Beirut. As usual, I was the only woman on the flight with a bright headscarf, a lone fleck of color among the women in black chador and the turbaned mullahs in their muted robes. About ten minutes after takeoff, during which the entire cabin chanted loud salutations to Allah and his messenger, I pulled my headscarf off. Iran Air regulations demand that women keep their veils on throughout all flights (international law holds that aircraft can impose the laws of their own nation). But in the past three years, the airline had relaxed this code. The flight attendant politely served me tea and saffron pudding, and I unfolded a Lebanese newspaper, curious to read about Iran's vote through Arab eyes.

The next morning, I resumed my Beirut routine as usual. First, I had breakfast—a thyme croissant and cappuccino—with my Lebanese friend Kim at the local patisserie. We did not spot any celebrities that morning, though usually you could count on at least one pop star or Robert Fisk. As this was Beirut, a city with a French attitude toward comportment, we had dressed carefully for breakfast, even though we were headed straight to the gym. We both worked out with our personal trainers (mine commended me for not eating too much rice in Iran), and then lay by the pool overlooking the Mediterranean. The poolside terrace had been damaged a few months prior, when a massive bomb killed Lebanon's prime minister along the stretch of road below. But from where we were reclined, you could see no traces of that event. I told Kim all the important details of my trip, from Mr. X's reception to meeting Arash, and wondered aloud whether I shouldn't have stayed longer after all. Kim said the comforting things girlfriends say at such moments, and we parted ways to run errands and spend a few productive hours writing, before reconvening that evening for dinner and cocktails.

My first week back in Beirut passed quickly. The sybaritic whirl of Levantine socializing for which the city is legendary—seaside nargileh (water pipe) sessions, vineyard lunches, and nightclub openings—made the Iranian election seem as distant as Tibet. To bridge this sense of disconnection, I stayed at home on June 17, 2005, the day Iranians went to the polls, to read that week's *Time* and follow the results. The magazine had put Rafsanjani on the cover with the tag "The Return of Rafsanjani" as "the man likely to be Iran's next president." The story recounted his political rise, fall, and reemergence. I had not contributed, preferring to focus on my own essay, which ran alongside, about how the regime was seeking to buy off discontented young people. The people I had met on my trip—the Basiji in Naziabad, the former activist Mr. Amini, Sonbol the racer, and even the Nayyeb waiter—all appeared. I had detailed their diverse frustrations, as well as the state's ineffective efforts to address them.

That Rafsanjani would win was taken for granted among strategists in all camps. Everyone, reformist and conservative alike, shared the underlying assumptions: that he spoke to the perceived desires of the young electorate and offered a bridge between factions; that without him, the country was much more likely to move toward radicalism. Rafsanjani was the only candidate who could slaughter the revolution's sacred cows. He understood the importance of restoring ties with the United States and of cutting Iran's support for militant groups, such as Hamas, that opposed peace with Israel. The eternal pragmatist, Rafsanjani offered the promise of subtle change while the fundamentalist old-timers died out. Two days ago, I had read online a column by one of the country's most important conservative strategists declaring "It's over . . . we have no chance."

As had been expected, Rafsanjani came first, with 21 percent of the vote, but he was trailed closely by an obscure candidate, the former mayor of Tehran Mahmoud Ahmadinejad, with 19 percent; Mehdi Karroubi, a dark-horse reformist candidate, took 17 percent. I shook my head at the television in Beirut, confused. Not a single person I had spoken to in Tehran the days before the election had uttered the name Ahmadinejad. It wasn't simply a matter of not being a favorite; the man was unknown. In describing whom they preferred, many Iranians had referred to other candidates, explaining why they would not be voting for them. But Ahmadinejad might as well not have been on the ballot, so little did he seem to figure in either the calculations of strategists or the minds of everyday Iranians. In truth, I had little sense of him, apart from half-formed impressions of a religious fundamentalist. As mayor, he had focused on Islamic gender segregation schemes, and rumor held that he had attempted to bury war martyrs in all of Tehran's public squares.

I did not at first believe that the election had been fixed. The regime had its characteristic ways of distorting the democratic process, but in the recent past outright vote fixing had not been one of them. The mullahs believed such measures would destroy the government's legitimacy, so instead they carefully vetted candidates, keeping those they considered undesirable off the ballot. It was a far more subtle form of political corruption. In the most recent presidential and parliamentary elections, the authorities had permitted a substantial number of reform candidates to run. These elections were fiercely competitive; outside observers considered Iran's electoral process more open than many of its neighbors'. But this time around, everyone in Iran wondered whether the vote had been fixed. The concern was not that ballot boxes had been stuffed, but that, as a spokesman for the Interior Ministry put it, people's votes had been "orchestrated and organized."

Much has been said and written since about what happened that fateful day, but this much is clear: at the very last minute, the top leadership of the Iranian state chose to back Ahmadinejad with all its considerable institutional weight. The Revolutionary Guards and the Basij, both accountable to the Supreme Leader, mobilized their networks of tens of thousands, spreading the word throughout their obedient constituencies that Ahmadinejad was the man to vote for. This campaign began after I had left Iran, scant days before the vote, and journalists who picked up on the activity underestimated its scope. Basij members received phone calls and text messages "persuading" them to vote for Ahmadinejad, and instructing them to pressure others. At Friday prayers on election day, Ahmadinejad's supporters appealed to the most faithful, pleading for their votes despite the official ban on campaigning on election day.

The unsuccessful candidates leveled more serious charges: Basij members verbally pressuring voters at polling stations; some voting twice with duplicate or false ID cards. Because the regime chose not to investigate the irregularities, the charges will forever remain unsubstantiated.

Karroubi, the aging reformist, dispatched a terse letter to the Supreme Leader, Ayatollah Ali Khamenei, after the first round. He cited "a great deal of very odd and strange interference" in the election, suggesting that "a great deal of money has changed hands." He charged that the tampering had been planned in advance and approved by the highest echelons of the Islamic leadership. Four newspapers that printed his letter were banned from publication by the hard-line judiciary. I did not bother calling any of my sources in Iran, certain they would not speak openly over phone lines that were surely tapped. But I did speak to journalist friends covering the election, and I surmised from their descriptions that this was the dirtiest vote in Iran's recent history.

In the week between the first and second rounds of the election, Iranians marveled at the Ahmadinejad surprise, but the moderates still did not imagine that he would ascend to the presidency. I certainly never considered it possible; I was blindly convinced that the regime itself considered Rafsanjani the sensible candidate. Still, however poor Ahmadinejad's prospects seemed, his presence on the ballot alarmed reformists. They realized many things too late: that their inability to unify and support one promising candidate had left the field dangerously open; that the highest echelons of the regime opposed Rafsanjani and were organizing his defeat; that the pairing of the notoriously corrupt Rafsanjani with an unknown populist made for unpredictable voter behavior. It was no longer clear at all who was driving events, and the imperative of getting Rafsanjani elected, however distasteful his record, became a shared cause. The reformists found themselves trying to resurrect a man they themselves had ruined.

On June 24, 2005, I was watching the early results on CNN, getting ready to go out for cocktails at Beirut's newest rooftop bar perched above the Mediterranean. I remember the moment exactly—the strawberry juice I was drinking, the taxis honking in the Christian quarter—the way people often recall precisely where they were, what they were doing, when the unthinkable occurred. The phone rang. It was Nasrine calling from Tehran, her voice tearful. "He's ahead . . . he's ahead by thirty percent," she said. "Go vote now." I dialed the number of the Iranian embassy in Beirut, a place not known for its dutiful participation in the democratic process. "Would it be too late, please, for me to come vote?" "Voting finished at two," the attendant snapped, before hanging up. Frantic at being away, I called everyone I knew in Tehran, ordering them to the polls. But by six P.M., it was obviously too late. I put down the phone, feeling terribly alone and misplaced. The world seemed to be falling apart, and Beirut, going about its shimmery summer evening, scarcely took notice.

In the week that had passed since the first round of voting, I had researched Ahmadinejad's tenure as mayor. He was an unabashed religious conservative, and his work as mayor showed a disturbing tendency to inflict his own hard-line values on a more progressive population. He had sought, for example, to turn back into mosques the many cultural centers that had been created in Tehran. These centers figured importantly in the lives of middle-class young people, being among the few places they could go to socialize, borrow books, and freely cultivate their minds. The impulse to shutter these centers and replace them with mosques signaled a sinister disregard for young people's modern needs. Even clerics spoke openly about Iran's spiritual crisis, how years of stern Islamic brainwashing had alienated young people from the faith. When even senior clerics admitted that mosques were more empty than ever before, how could Iran choose a president who wanted to build more?

We had all been wrong. Desperately, fatally, irretrievably wrong. The election had mattered after all, and so had voting. A fundamentalist former mayor with no record of leadership at the national level, whose major efforts as mayor of Tehran were to turn the capital's squares into cemeteries and segregate the elevators in government buildings, had become president of Iran.

CHAPTER 5

Days of Wine

In July, a month after the election, a number of Iranian officials conveyed to me directly and via intermediaries that they had been displeased with my article. It had run under the headline "Fast Times in Tehran," and it opened with a scene in which friends of mine drank alcohol while driving down a Tehran freeway. The officials' disapproval, in fact, revolved entirely around this passage. In my years of reporting on Iran, I had always wondered what story would eventually get me into trouble. Perhaps it would be an investigation into regime corruption, I had thought, or a clandestine interview with a dissident under house arrest. That I could be reprimanded for mentioning the public consumption of cocktails had never crossed my mind. I couldn't believe that such a trifling scene—amid far more damning descriptions of how young people despised the mullahs— could provoke the ire of so many. What I considered an example of some of my best reporting, a wide-angle portrait of a despairing generation, was reduced to "the article in which Ms. Moaveni's friends drink on the freeway."

I tried to make a case for my story with one official, an Iranian diplomat I kept in touch with by e-mail and had met on a brief trip to Europe. "But don't you think it shows how sensible the Iranian government has become? That it tolerates the natural behavior of young people?"

He did not agree. I asked why this one depiction rankled so much, when Tehran's underground party culture had been documented in enough articles to render it almost a cliché.

"Yours was so . . . unsubtle," he said. But his offhand tone did not suggest *he* actually minded. It seemed as though scolding me was a duty, as if he needed to be on record registering disapproval.

"Do you actually think that people around the world believe Iranian young people don't drink?"

"That's not the point. There are limits in an Islamic country, and this crossed them."

I left feeling irritated at myself for not having anticipated such a reaction.

More upsettingly, another official conveyed this message through a friend of mine: "Efforts were made to ensure Ms. Moaveni's safe return to Iran after the publication of her book. We read her story with disappointment. We had not expected this of her."

While it all seemed quite irrational to me—my first book contained many instances of people drinking, after all—it was clear I would need to make amends to the Iranian authorities. Fortunately, the timing could not have been better. That summer, Lebanon was a dead news story, and my editors were eager for me to return to Tehran and parse Ahmadinejad's victory. My work on Shirin khanoum's book also required some time in Iran, for one more round of in-person interviews. And, truth be told, I was impatient to see Arash again. I had been thinking about him, remembering the witty, insightful way he had described Tajikistan. I booked an open ticket to Iran, where it seemed I might spend a more productive summer all around.

Upon arriving in Tehran, I made my obligatory phone call to Mr. X, who greeted me rather indifferently. "Welcome back, keep in touch," he said briefly, without asking further about the purpose of my trip. Neither did he mention my article, which I found strange, given the widespread censure it had managed to provoke. Since I wasn't about to bring it up myself, our conversation ended quickly.

The first thing I did, before even alerting my friends that I was back, was to write a sober article about the Basij for *Time*. My article, I hoped, would humanize the militia's rank and file, explaining how they were partly compelled by poverty to become members. Given that the militia organized the get-out-the-vote effort that propelled Ahmadinejad to victory, the Basij offered a legitimately current subject. More important, the story would be placed in my government file, and I could always invoke it to argue that I covered the Basij as forthrightly as I did tipsy Iranians. The story only took a couple of days to finish, as my notebooks were already full of research and interviews. I concluded that Ahmadinejad won the Basij's loyalty by promising to relieve the grinding poverty and joblessness that afflicted most of its members; ultimately, they would judge him on whether he was able to improve their daily lives.

Next, I sought an interview with one of my best sources. I wanted to understand Ahmadinejad's surprise win, and this government official was both well connected and candid. His assistant set up a meeting for the following day at one of the Shah's former palaces in north Tehran.

I arrived early, and an attendant escorted me through a spacious, sunlit foyer to what must have been a drawing room in the Shah's day. A chandelier composed of a thousand delicate crystals hung over the empty room, whose walls were covered in intricate paneling. I much enjoyed meeting government officials in former palaces. The opulent backdrop offered a striking contrast to the mullahs' turbans and Islamic rhetoric, and I felt privileged to be watching one of history's truly great revolutions unfold. Sooner or later, though perhaps not during my lifetime, the Islamic Republic would evolve into a normal country, and college students would study the revolutionary mullahs along with Robespierre.

Usually a bearded male secretary arrived to interrupt these musings before they blurred into visions of Marie Antoinette. But that day, the cleric I had come to see was especially busy and kept me waiting longer than usual. I could hear him trying to explain to foreign reporters, in between cryptic, hushed phone conversations with senior officials, the fateful outcome nearly everyone had failed to predict. Perhaps Ahmadinejad's election affirmed stereotypes that many held about Iran. But for those who knew the country well, Iran was a nation of moderate, educated young people receptive to the West. Their election of an avowed hard-liner demanded explanation.

Seeing the Al Jazeera logo on a camera inside the room, I realized I would be waiting for a long while yet. The officials of the Islamic Republic granted Arab journalists special access, more time, and precedence whenever possible. The regard was mutual, for Tehran's Arab press corps—composed mostly of journalists who sympathized with Islamist ideology—often covered the country as though the revolution were an unmitigated success, ignoring student protests and reporting on stage-managed marches in a manner befitting *Pravda*. Underlying all this was the fondness of Iranian officials for all things Arabic, including the language, of course, in which the Koran had been revealed, and the longing of Arab journalists from secular dictatorships for an Islamic dictatorship. And so I waited another half hour, wondering whether anyone would notice if I poked around the drawing room. I took a few steps inside, and discovered the grand piano was less out of tune than I had expected. I ran my hands across the keys, warming up with a Chopin exercise I learned when I was twelve and then turning to an old Persian melody I had played as a child, "Golden Dreams." Many displaced families nostalgic for Iran favored it especially.

After a few moments, an assistant called out, "Hajj Agha will see you now, Ms. Moaveni."

I hurried toward him, rehearsing all the questions that had vexed me since I'd first heard of Ahmadinejad's victory. In the first few days, while still in Beirut, I had reread my notes obsessively, trying to understand how this had come to be, how everyone had misread what was about to happen. I tore the sheets out of my notebook and spread them across my desk, attacking the sentences with a highlighter, in search of recurring themes and clues. As I struggled to decipher my handwriting, slowly the signs started to appear, as though written in an invisible ink only now being dusted so that its message might be re-

vealed. Over and over, the words stared back at me: "marriage,"
"loans," "jobs," "salaries," "pyramid scheme," "unemployment,"
"rent." These were the concerns of most of the Iranians I had talked
to, and only at the eleventh hour had they been linked to Ahmadinejad's promises of curative economic justice.

I sat down opposite the official across a coffee table covered in
newspapers and a platter of raisin cookies. After we had exchanged a
few pleasantries, I was ready to pose my first question. But Hajj Agha,
a tall, fidgety man whose graying hair peeked out beneath the sides of
his white turban, put in:

"Ms. Moaveni, if you were to grant me permission, it would make
me very happy to provide you with a piano."

"A piano?" I said.

The lustful mullah is a classic figure in modern Iranian culture, as
archetypal as the hypocritical clerics of Molière. When I first began
reporting in the Middle East, I imagined that clerics who espoused political Islam were devout ideologues, too busy pursuing Islamic government to pursue women as well. Experience soon overturned this
naïve belief.

"That's very kind of you, but I don't really play anymore. I'm sorry
if I disturbed you earlier."

The assistant carried in cups of tea.

"Not at all. You play very beautifully," he said. This was untrue.
Even in my adolescent prime, my exasperated teacher had advised my
mother to consider tap dancing lessons for me instead.

"Please allow this as a gesture from a friend," the cleric continued,
once the door closed. I did not know at the time that many clerics
frowned upon even classical music, and that the proposal was theo-
logically, as well as professionally, inappropriate.

"Should I find myself in need of a piano, I'm certain my father
would be pleased to buy me one," I finally said, reaching for a cookie
and breaking it in two with what I hoped signaled closure.

I asked how he saw the future, and we turned to a discussion of
whether the country was going to fall apart, now that a fundamentalist (or a more-fundamentalist-than-most) had mysteriously taken
over. Many factors had been at work, the mullah explained. Ah-

madinejad had emphasized day-to-day problems and focused on the poor, an appeal he made effectively in a television interview after the first round, portraying himself as exclusively preoccupied with improving people's economic welfare.

"It is true," the cleric admitted, fiddling with a bowl of sugar cubes, "that the reform movement's disorganization is truly to blame. If the moderates had banded together, chosen one charismatic candidate, and run a platform that stressed *both* social and economic reform, people would have voted for them in droves.

"On the other hand," he mused, "the top leadership wanted a subservient president, a yes-man, and it made sure it got one."

This was a coded way of saying (to be more blunt in a certainly bugged room would have been unwise): Ayatollah Khamenei, the Supreme Leader, wanted a weak president who would not challenge his leadership or make him look fusty, so he colluded to get Ahmadinejad elected.

"I'm confused," I said. "I thought I understood Iranian society. I thought most people wanted more secular government, wanted freedom and reform, and now they've gone and elected a man who considers cemeteries decorative."

The mullah put the sugar bowl down and looked at me very seriously. "Do you think the people who voted for him even knew that? He spoke only about jobs and the economy." He paused. "But still, don't make the mistake of thinking that only class drives politics. Iran, as you should know by now, is more complicated than that. Eight years of failed political reform disappointed people. It made them indifferent to politics. This time around, they figured that if they could not have real freedom, they might as well have more manageable rent, better jobs. How old are you, by the way?"

"I'm twenty-eight."

"So when you voted for Khatami you were in your early twenties, like the rest of the young people who elected him. In those years, the college years, human rights, listening to music, holding hands on the street mattered. Now that you're almost thirty, and thinking of getting married inshallah, you may have realized how difficult it is for the average Iranian your age to start and support a family. It is a simple truth that in a country this wealthy, that is unjust. Redressing that, providing justice, is what this man promised. And as you know, we have a long historical tradition of demanding just that."

It was an honest answer, one that admitted an uncomfortable truth: as long as reformists sought change within the system, they would be tainted by its inherent shortcomings. Its failures would be seen as theirs, and before long, their promises of a more open society would be considered as empty as the conservative promise of piety. Taken together, the last three presidential elections had not contradicted one another: Iranians wanted a more liberal, democratic society, *as well as* job opportunity and an easing of economic hardship. They had simply never been offered a candidate who emphasized it all. Voting for Khatami did not imply a disregard for the economy, just as voting for Ahmadinejad did not indicate a lack of concern for freedom. Slowly, my bewilderment lifted, and I could see this election for what it was—a natural pendulum swing between fixed priorities, the movement itself illustrating that neither side alone sufficed.

I called Nasrine as soon as I arrived home from my interview with the mullah, and she came over promptly after work. I told her to buy a toothbrush on the way, as my aunt was away in California and we had her apartment to ourselves. Nasrine tended to trudge loudly when she was unhappy, so I could tell by the lively clack of her heels up the steps that she was in bright spirits. She dropped her laptop bag on the couch, handed me a bag of carnelian cherries, and kissed me on both cheeks.

I poured us tea, and we settled into the L-shaped sofa, where we would spend the next several hours talking about the latest stories we were reporting, watching satellite television, and checking our e-mail.

"You're here just in time," she said. "I have a blind date tomorrow night, and I need you to come with me."

"Don't be silly. With who? I hope not with one of those Internet guys."

The latest stage in Nasrine's quest for love involved trolling Iranian websites for dates. Though the men she met were inevitably second-rate, she maintained that there were eligible types to be found if one was patient. I had no wish to tag along.

"I mentioned to Arash that I could really use some moral support, and he's agreed to stay for the beginning at least," she said, innocently.

I had to laugh at her connivance. In the end, though, Nasrine managed to convince me that the evening would be fun. As her chaperones, Arash and I would have plenty of time to chat. And should the young man prove unsuitable, we could help extricate her from the date.

The next evening, as Nasrine and I headed to pick up Arash, I admitted to myself that this was an ideal second encounter. Nasrine's suitor provided instant material for conversation, and as co-chaperones we were paired without being on our own date. All of this made me relieved, and at first sight of him, I felt the same pull, the same deep attraction, I had in May. He got into the car, leaning forward to shake hands. "It's lovely to see you again," I said.

Nasrine steered her Kia into the slow-moving traffic of Niavaran Street, the main thoroughfare of north Tehran that ran into the Shah's summer palace. She and her date had arranged to meet near Book City, one of Tehran's most popular bookshops, and they traded coordinates by mobile phone. He suggested that she find a parking spot on the street, and that we proceed in his car to a nearby park, where we could stroll and have coffee. Before long, he pulled up alongside us in a gray Peugeot, double-parking so that he could alight and introduce himself properly. He wore a tight white T-shirt that outlined his premature paunch; there was a heavy gold chain around his thick neck, and he smelled powerfully of an unpleasant, overly spicy cologne. From the moment he opened his mouth, we bit our tongues, dug our nails into our palms, to keep from laughing. Nasrine managed to whisper before we climbed into his car, "Are my eyes deceiving me, or is he wearing *foundation*?" Arash had already scrambled into the backseat, and with a beseeching, hunted look, Nasrine hopped in beside him.

Forced into taking the front seat, I realized with my closer vantage that he was indeed, unfathomably, wearing a thick layer of foundation. He had told Nasrine that he lived in Los Angeles and was only in Tehran to visit family.

"Where do you live in L.A.?" I asked.

"Sort of central."

"Do you mean Westwood? The Valley?" I prodded, growing suspicious.

"Yes, around there."

It took me about twenty more seconds to ascertain that he did not in fact know that California is situated on the West Coast. While I attempted to make small talk, Nasrine was whispering furiously to Arash in French about how to abandon her date. The opportunity presented itself not long after we arrived at the park, when he ran back to his car to retrieve his mobile phone. We all felt a twinge of guilt at leaving him that way. But as we hurriedly crossed to the other side of the park, we agreed he deserved to be abandoned, given the foundation and his false biography (likely meant to attract women with the prospect of a green card). Nasrine's mobile began to ring.

"What should I do?" she asked.

"Just turn it off. What can you possibly say to him?" I said. "He'll get the message soon enough."

We retreated to a nearby coffee shop, ordered *cafés glacés,* and laughed until our stomachs hurt. Once we finished recounting her date's worst qualities, Arash and I scolded Nasrine for her antics. He advised her to start trying to meet people through friends, an approach that would at least weed out the foundation-wearing charlatans. I told her to have the decency to take the front seat when she enlisted her friends to come along on disastrous dates.

Our conspiratorial escape from Nasrine's date seemed to seal us as a threesome intent on finding her a decent relationship. Before disbanding that evening, we agreed to meet the next day for lunch. Arash casually asked for my number, and entered it into his mobile phone.

Later, when we were alone, Nasrine said, "See, I told you he fancies you."

"I'm not so sure. He has such lovely manners that I think maybe he's just being polite." I was sincerely uncertain, and preferred not to be too hopeful, lest I be disappointed.

"Whatever. You'll find out for yourself soon enough. Did I tell you Sonbol's been calling him ever since they met? She wants his father's company to sponsor her next race."

"No, you forgot to mention that."

"But he hasn't paid her any attention. Not even polite attention."

"Good." If Nasrine was right, I couldn't wait to find out.

Shortly after noon the next day, my mobile phone beeped with a text message from Arash. "Are you all right? Yr phone appears off. Worried." I was meant to meet him and Nasrine for lunch, but not for another hour. I called him back.

"Nasrine says you could be arrested any minute. So when your phone didn't answer I thought maybe something had happened."

"Her imagination is overactive," I said, laughing. "Of course I'm not going to be arrested." I was annoyed at Nasrine for telling Arash such a thing. Overly dramatic by nature, she had surely embellished some aspect of my work—perhaps my interactions with Mr. X—and convinced him I had one foot in prison.

"I was just visiting a cousin, and their house doesn't get cell reception," I said. Nasrine called a few minutes later to tell me she would be delayed at work (matchmaker contrivance, I presumed), and so the two of us went to lunch alone, feigning surprise at her unexpected deadline. Arash suggested we go to Café 78, a coffee shop in central Tehran popular with writers, artists, and musicians. Such coffeehouses, the kind that carefully listed the contents of the salads on the menu, were still novel. Most restaurants, in the Soviet manner, listed only the one word, "salad," as though only one type existed and the desire to know its ingredients was somehow westernized and decadent.

The authorities frowned on establishments that provided thoughtful people a milieu for conversation, so they often needled Café 78's owner with petty zoning edicts. One week the café had to stop serving lunch, since she had been told that cafés serving coffee were not permitted to also offer food (the state apparently considered lingering a danger). The next week, the café resumed serving sandwiches and salads, but customers found the coffee page of the menu crossed out with a large X and covered with an inleaf suggesting a restorative herbal tisane. Such nuisances were still annoying, but compared with the mid-1990s, when the police would storm cafés and round up women for improper Islamic dress, they were tolerable, even laughable.

Such repression, the kind that sought to serve Islam by preventing the serving of coffee, provided rich material for satire. Like most people who suffer under such regimes, Iranians coped by honing a subversive, mordant humor. When I first moved to Tehran in 2000, this love of irony struck me as one of the most charming aspects of Iranian life, though I knew its purpose was to ease the pain of being ruled by heartless, inept, and hypocritical mullahs. During one of my first afternoons driving in the city, I struggled to execute a three-point turn across lanes of chaotic traffic. Halfway through the turn, my veil slipped off, and I froze, uncertain whether to clear the road or adjust my covering. As a man passing by surveyed the traffic jam I had caused, he noticed me fumbling with my scarf, grinned, and yelled, "Islam is in danger!"

Though the corruption and fundamentalism of Iran's present rulers was unparalleled in the country's history, Iranian writers had a long tradition of holding their leaders to account through satire. During the two years that I lived in Iran, I spent many evenings reading aloud to my aunt and uncle the columns of Ebrahim Navabi, the country's premier satirist. These sessions, during which we laughed, proclaimed him a genius, and repeated certain passages until they were committed to memory, seemed to dissolve the layers of accumulated resentment, providing the resilience that enabled us to make it through the next day.

Though scarcely a month had passed since Arash and I had first met, the Tehran summer had grown unbearable. The dry heat beat down powerfully and the café's air-conditioning sent out only meek, occasional puffs of cool air. I looked about our surroundings carefully, trying to commit the details to memory. I felt certain that this lunch would matter, and that I would later wish to recall what he wore, what I ordered. We dipped tall spoons into glasses of cool *sekanjebeen,* a sugar syrup of mint and vinegar over grated cucumber, and began a conversation that would go on for hours.

I started by asking about the photo on his mobile phone, of a little girl in pigtails with a lovable smile. I knew already from Nasrine that Arash had a daughter from a previous marriage, and wanted to create an opening for him to talk about her. "Her name is Amitis and she's almost four," he said, gazing at her photo with clear adoration. He told me that she lived in California with her mother, and described the time they spent together on his visits. "She loves the children's rock-climbing gym. She's always saying, 'I want climb big mountain!' because she knows I go mountain climbing, and wants to come too." The tender way he talked about her charmed me, and I could tell he was a doting, engaged father.

He then asked about my parents, who lived in California as well. Our lives, we discovered, paralleled in their disjointed swings between Iran and the West. While my family's stay in California was made permanent by the revolution, it was the Iran-Iraq War, which began in 1980, that displaced Arash's family to Germany.

"Did you miss Iran?" I asked.

"In a way. But more because of how we left," he said, describing how the family decided to stay in Germany while on what was ostensibly a holiday visit. Arash was nearing fourteen, the age when Iran's draft laws would prohibit him from leaving the country. "We stayed almost on a whim. My mother was scared that if we went back, I'd have to be smuggled out later. So I never had the chance to say good-bye to my friends."

At the outset of our discussion I felt thrilling flashes of recognition and imagined that our families and psyches must face similar struggles—fitting in as an Iranian in the West, finding a balance between two cultures. But soon it became clear that being an émigré in California was a different matter entirely from being an émigré in

Germany. The émigrés in Europe could travel to Iran more frequently, which helped them stay emotionally and physically connected with their homeland.

"It just seems to me that in Europe, Iranians have a more realistic picture of what Iran is actually like, and how much they actually want to be connected to it," Arash said, musingly. "Even their homesickness is different, more grounded somehow."

The diaspora in America had less vacation time and a longer physical distance to cover, and many belonged to the various groups (the persecuted Baha'i minority; former political dissidents or officials) whose members could not return at all. These conditions fostered a culture of nostalgia and longing that in turn shaped how Iranians in America assimilated. The exiles in America also had the fraught history of Iranian-U.S. relations to contend with; the fresh memories of the hostage crisis meant most Americans associated Iran with hysterical violence. Iranian Americans often coped with this by either distancing themselves from their background or retreating into it defensively.

Although our experiences as Iranian immigrants in the West had hardly overlapped, Arash and I had shared the impulse to return to Iran as adults. We were both motivated partly by that longing for contact with homeland, that inevitable curiosity that seems to lurk in the heart of most immigrant children (a breathless circuit of thoughts, from "Could I manage?" to "Would they accept me?" to "Would it feel warmer/kinder/*homier*?"). But more important, both Arash and I believed, perhaps naïvely, that our professional expertise could and should contribute to the country's development.

Arash, for his part, had sought to bring the world of open-source software to Iran. I had no idea what this meant, so, over our lunch of crepes, he explained.

Free software, as opposed to proprietary software, he said, serves as a framework for sharing intellectual capital. In practical terms, this means a country's information and communications industry can attend to its needs without expensive licensing.

"When I moved back to Iran, I was hugely enthusiastic about open source," he said. "I knew that developing countries were embracing it, and almost immediately profiting, both economically and socially. I thought it would be good for Iran, and good for me."

"What makes it so special for developing countries?"

"Take Iran's case. Iran has never signed international copyright treaties, and basically endorses pirated software. Before Iran can join the WTO, for example, it needs to clean up its act. It needs to ban pirated software and run a legitimate technology bazaar. This sounds easy enough, but it's actually a huge challenge. For one, licensed software like Microsoft's is tremendously expensive, especially in a country where people are used to buying pirated Microsoft Office for a dollar. Even worse, U.S. sanctions mean Microsoft can't sell to the Iranian market. Even if Iranians had the means to buy a licensed product, there'd be nothing to buy. Why should Microsoft produce a Farsi version of Windows when it can't sell to the biggest Farsi-speaking market in the world? It can't and won't. Open source would bypass all of these problems. You'd have a Farsi platform for computers, it would be inexpensive, and it would be legal under international copyright. Iran could participate in the international community, on international terms, without the pressure of copyright."

He explained all this so convincingly, with such fluid gestures, that I only nodded for him to continue.

In the first year of his return, Arash and his colleagues had managed to produce the first Farsi version of KDE, the desktop environment that runs on top of Linux, the operating system of the open-source world. They attempted to set up a training center that would certify Iranian software engineers in Red Hat, the largest commercial distribution of the Linux operating system in the world. But because Red Hat is American, and the United States had imposed economic sanctions on Iran, the firm canceled the Iranian project the moment it went online.

"Half the story is about U.S. sanctions, and how awful they are," he said.

"But don't you think the Iranian government deserves to be sanctioned?"

"That's not the point, really. Who suffers as a result of sanctions? Not the government. At the time, Red Hat certification basically guaranteed you a job in Europe. We wanted to bring that certification process to Iran. All these Iranian young people were going to places like Kuwait to get certified, and paying twice as much. That put certification out of so many people's reach. On top of that, the money went out of Iran and into some sheikh's pockets. It's the Iranian engineers who suffer, not the government."

Next, the Iranian government stepped in to offer resources for an umbrella project charged with oversight of Iran's open-source activities. Arash's firm found itself competing for bids with organizations that entirely lacked IT background but were connected to the regime and saw the initiative as a lucrative opportunity. The regime's aim, as usual, was to control and oversee a realm where it had no place.

I told Arash that his story, its technical aspects aside, sounded overwhelmingly familiar. Many Iranians who had returned from the West seeking to introduce a concept premised on the existence of civil society could relate to such an experience. In these instances the regime usually co-opted the initiative and steered it into the hands of incompetent but loyal cronies.

"I know exactly what you mean," Arash said. "I was once asked to advise a senior official on open source. He told me very frankly, 'Mr. Zeini, I don't believe in technological independence, Farsi-language software, or open source.' We debated. I told him, 'But Microsoft won't do Farsi Windows because of sanctions, and that means Farsi speakers—especially old people, children—can't use computers.' He just shrugged at me. Two months later, the same guy was all over the media claiming to love open source."

It was in such episodes that one could identify the real pathology of the Islamic Republic. Obsessed with security, it preferred to sabotage the future prospects of its young engineers, its own IT sector, than to experiment with endeavors that sounded somehow suspect.

After this, Arash told me, he began working for his father's textile business. While the work did not inspire him, it was important: textiles had once been the great hope of Iranian manufacturing. "It was always expected that I would work with him someday," he said slowly. "But fulfilling my duty, that wasn't really my objective."

Outside, the sky had begun to darken. Reluctant to part, we decided to drive north to Niavaran Palace, the Shah's summer complex, for an open-air concert of classical Indian music.

I've kept the ticket stub from that evening, a violet slip bearing a bejeweled elephant, for it marks the day we became inseparable. We met again the next day, and the day after that, for weeks. We set out at dawn to climb in the Alborz Mountains, hiked through rugged valleys dotted with springs and waterfalls, and camped overnight under the cover of pine trees (camping was common, but not so much for unmarried couples). On Fridays we explored the dilapidated neighborhoods of south Tehran, the capital's historical center, dotted with faded turquoise tiles and arched doorways dating to the nineteenth-century Qajar dynasty. We sifted through the Friday antiques bazaar in search of Turkoman tunics and Afghan string instruments, often finding rare treasures hidden among the dusty junk. We spent a week in Beirut, where Arash charmed all my friends at dinner parties and they whispered in my ear that I was lucky. It was a perfect summer.

No particular conversation or moment determined our plans. We had slipped into each other's lives seamlessly, as though we had known each other for years. I took his husky for walks through the quiet side streets of Tehran; he covered the Salman Rushdie novel I carried around with newspaper out of concern for my safety, and deleted the ironic call-to-prayer ringtone (installed by a teenage cousin) from my cell phone. By the end of the summer, being children of the western diaspora, we did what came most naturally, un-Iranian though it was: we moved in together.

Up until that point, our relationship had followed the conventions of mainstream Iranian dating. We went out for lunch, attended parties and dinners together as a couple, and once a week drank tea with each other's relatives. Our decision to live together, however, permanently separated our course from that of our peers. Though nearly all of our friends, and a solid portion of Tehran for that matter, engaged in the behaviors associated with living together—dating, premarital sex—actual cohabitation remained taboo. I had lived in Iran long enough to understand why. While many of my girlfriends might have sex with their partners, this was not a reality their parents (or the boy-friend's parents) openly acknowledged. Some parents even pretended their children did not date. On many occasions, I had watched mothers boldly lie when visitors asked whether their daughter was "socializing with any prospective suitors." Such discretion, or deception if you like, enabled Iranians to maneuver between their society's traditional mores and their children's modern urges.

Living together was far too unsubtle, and none of my friends in Iran had even considered the idea. The enraged parents, the dashed marriage prospects, the perhaps vengeful backlash from a culture still hung up on the "honor" of its women aside, living together was also financially out of reach for most couples. Part of the reason young people uniformly lived at home until marriage, even if they married in their thirties, was to save money for an apartment. Very often couples who wedded late still needed help from their parents to start an independent life, and the notion of living together unwed . . . well, it just contravened sensibility and practicality too much to be considered by even the city's most notorious playboys and party girls.

Arash, like most Iranians who had returned from the West as adults, lived alone. But his apartment was on the third floor of a building in which his parents and sister also lived. After the revolution, when single-family houses were razed in favor of apartment blocks, and traffic made the city unnavigable, many families opted for such living arrangements. Most of my married friends lived in family buildings or at least on the same block as their parents.

Neither of us really took our parents' reactions into consideration when we decided to cohabit, probably because I was twenty-nine, Arash was thirty-five, and we were both westernized enough to think this meant we were beyond parental oversight. His parents, though far more traditional than my family on the surface (they spoke undiluted Farsi at home instead of English, were fond of Iranian culture, and did not affect the lifestyle of the international elite), took the news with rather elegant composure and warm acceptance. His mother invited me to lunch as though it were the most natural thing in the world, noticed my favorite things to eat, and wordlessly added them to her shopping list and cooking menu, as though she had overnight acquired a third child who deserved to be doted upon.

My parents reacted less sanguinely. "They will hunt you down in the street and throw acid on your face," my father warned ominously over the phone from California. "You will be disfigured for life." He had only visited Iran once since 1979, a brief trip during the grim 1980s. He thought Tehran was overrun by Taliban-esque fundamentalists who had nothing to do but detect and purge sinful living-together couples. My mother's concerns, predictably, focused on propriety over safety. "I warn you, Azadeh, his parents may *act* like they don't have a problem with it, but deep down they consider you *loose,* a girl of easy virtue, and they will never, ever permit their son to marry you."

Though my mother had spent the majority of her more than sixty years in California, and though she was at home driving to and from the organic grocery store on its spacious freeways, she had never quite come to terms with the essential Americanness of her personality. Her identity remained a puzzle to many who knew her, and probably to herself. In some respects, her biography was American in its show of independence. She asked for a divorce when I was only a few months old, launched a second career in psychiatric nursing when I started elementary school, and lived with seeming disregard for everything that was expected of her as an Iranian woman. She did not keep house with particular tidiness and she failed to match her china, preferring instead to visit the local ashram and participate in a local peace network that promoted better ties with the then Soviet Union. She might have been a character in a Woody Allen film, so thoroughly did she embody the neurotic charm of a hypereducated, urban American.

I told my parents they were being absurd and paranoid and, worst of all, were cloaking their own disapproval in safety concerns and worry over the hypothetical, imagined disapproval of Arash's parents. "It's really very amusing that after three decades in California, after attending Berkeley and studying gestalt and becoming American enough to obsess about food, you are still as conservative as the most conventional Tehrani parents," I said during one conversation. They maintained their stony, long-distance censure, and I ignored them, preferring to concentrate on do-it-yourself sponge painting, my antique kilims, and other elements of apartment décor.

Although neither Arash nor I had any reservations about our decision, we were well aware that it was something we should disclose only selectively. We told our very closest friends and relatives, but hid our living arrangements from the rest of the world—our colleagues at work, the officials we both dealt with professionally, the neighborhood merchants. This involved a rather small degree of subterfuge. I maintained the pretense of living with my aunt in Elahieh and asked most work contacts to call me on my mobile phone. My aunt, a sympathizer and confidante, pretended I was out when I received calls at her house, and relayed messages punctually.

The only problem was, Mr. X never left messages. I had returned the mobile phone I'd been using, on loan from my uncle, and was still waiting for the mobile line I had bought in 2000 to be reconnected. Meanwhile, it would be unthinkable for Mr. X to call my aunt and say, "Please let your niece know that her minder at the Ministry of Intelligence called." I assumed that when anyone besides me answered the phone, he simply hung up. I worried that he might grow suspicious if I never picked up the phone at my aunt's. To ward off any problems, I made a point of calling him more frequently myself. Either the ministry was less paranoid than usual or Mr. X was busy with more important charges, for our conversations were shorter and more procedural than ever before. My side often went like this: "Hello . . . Are you well? . . . May you not be tired. I'm calling to say that I'm reporting a story on the election results. I will be speaking to the following analysts. . . . You don't want to know anything else? Very well then. May God protect you. Bye."

With Mr. X thus taken care of, hardly any obstacles remained. For the most part, no one noticed or asked questions. It was common for dating couples to be publicly inseparable, at least in middle-class and affluent neighborhoods, and everyone assumed they retreated to their separate homes at the end of the evening. And so, with very little apprehension and much delight, I took up residence in Darrous, a neighborhood of north Tehran just below the hills of Qeytarieh. The area had changed significantly since 1979, its story in many ways the story of how Tehran was transformed by the revolution. Eshrat khanoum, Arash's mother, grew up in Darrous, and during her girlhood in the 1940s, the quarter was composed of villas surrounded by orchards of mulberry, apple, and plum trees.

The neighborhood's location, its shady avenues and gardens, made it a desirable place to live. Before the revolution it became popular among foreigners, perhaps also because it was where the American community in the city built a sort of country club for tennis and socializing. In the 1990s, the mayor of Tehran, Gholamhossein Karbaschi, oversaw the city's large-scale transformation, permitting the razing of old villas and the construction of apartment towers and high-rises. Within a few years, Darrous's population quadrupled, as pious merchants from the bazaar (*bazaari*s, as they were known) and other affluent religious families took up residence in the new towers. Despite their piety and ostensible disregard for western culture, *bazaari*s were afflicted with a deep inferiority complex. They envied the social eminence of more worldly Iranians and they wanted the status that living in Darrous afforded. They brought with them a culture of religious observance entirely new to the quarter. The new buildings were often columned monstrosities adorned with Koranic calligraphy, a style that illustrated what happened when piety, class anxiety, and large bank accounts collided.

The influx of such residents had gained the area a special reputation among the clerical and administrative elite. Once, when an official overheard me asking a messenger to send some documents back "home" to Darrous, he nodded his head in solemn approval. "A very fine neighborhood, indeed," he said. "Home to the very *aseel* [noble] families, the very best people." The neighborhood's old families and merchants, however, were of different opinion. The new residents, while respectable enough, behaved with a sort of vulgar hauteur, like social climbers abusing their servants. Eshrat khanoum, for example, treated the merchants in Hedayat Square, the neighborhood's central shopping area, as colleagues. Her children had grown up with theirs and all had respectfully shared space for decades. By contrast, the chador-clad wives of the new residents tended to burst into the small shops barking orders, waving their hands about, insulting the produce, and shrilly issuing demands ("Give me parsley! Mint! Don't you have anything better than that, it's *wilted*! Where do you keep your good tarragon? Give me the good herbs, do you hear?"). The merchants bowed their heads, said, "*Chashm* [Certainly], Hajj khanoum," and glared as their heels clicked in retreat.

Naturally it did not escape the attention of the merchants in Hedayat Square that Arash was associating with a new woman. They craftily tried to deduce the nature of our relationship by calling me "Mrs. Engineer" or "Mrs. Zeini" so that I would correct them. When I refused to oblige, they turned their efforts to Arash: "Your fiancée likes strawberries; why don't you take a kilo for her?" To shop with a girlfriend or boyfriend in Hedayat Square was tantamount to announcing one's courtship to the entire neighborhood, and I found myself buying fruit elsewhere, hoping to maintain a sense of relative anonymity.

Because all the merchants in Hedayat Square recognized me, I circled around its backstreets when walking Inuk, Arash's husky. The government, in keeping with strict Islamic tradition, considered dogs ritually unclean and banned them as pets. Secular Iranians considered this absurd, like so many of the government's laws, and acquired toy poodles and other small dogs as pets. For some years, it had become trendy for women in north Tehran to travel about the city with their lapdogs as accessories. This incensed the regime, whose clerics bellowed against short-legged dogs at Friday prayer, and also led to dognapping for ransom as a new genre of petty crime. I kept to the backstreets partly to hide Inuk from the view of Hedayat Square, whose merchants might think less of the family for keeping a dog as a pet, and whose shop clerks, with knowledge of our address, might hatch dognapping plans.

Sometime that summer, perhaps in early August, Mr. X contacted me to request a meeting. Though nearly all our interactions are etched in my memory, for some reason the physical details of this particular encounter elude me. I suspect this is because he neither tried to intimidate me, blackmail me into revealing information he wanted, or warn me of his ministry's displeasure with my work. As our meetings went, it was remarkably civil, almost benign.

Though I cannot say exactly where we met—surely an empty hotel room like the others across the city where we had convened in the past—I do recall our conversation.

"How do you see Iran's future these days?" he asked. Mr. X was always keen to know how the press corps viewed the country's prospects. It was as though he needed to fill out a form each month at the ministry: "Please tick one of the following. In [blank for the month], do journalists view Iran as: ❑ a failed theocracy ❑ a rising regional power ❑ a nascent Islamic democracy ❑ an oil-rich Third World mess."

I replied blandly, explaining that we needed to wait and see what the Ahmadinejad era held in store.

From there, Mr. X subtly turned the subject to Shirin khanoum. He asked about her safety; had she been receiving threats recently? I mentioned her state-appointed bodyguards, since she herself spoke publicly about them.

"Does needing to have these guards scare her?"

"Shirin khanoum doesn't scare easily," I said. This was untrue—I had seen her almost terrified on certain occasions—but the truth was nothing Mr. X needed to know. He looked at me expectantly, as though waiting to hear more. "She seems to be handling things very professionally," I added.

He asked nothing more, and we spoke briefly about other matters. Before long, after perhaps just thirty minutes, he began wrapping up his notes. Usually our meetings lasted an hour and a half, but that day Mr. X seemed especially relaxed. Perhaps the ministry, suspended between the outgoing administration and the new, lacked a particular mandate. Pleased to be released earlier than usual and without having suffered any emotional distress, I waved goodbye and hurried out into the Tehran sunshine.

My memories of that summer bear so little connection to the days that were to follow that they seem almost of a different Iran. As peculiar as it may seem, the nation's politics hardly seemed to matter. Perhaps that is not entirely right, for surely they mattered, but that summer they remained unchanged. This interregnum allowed us to imagine life would simply limp along, the status quo of the past few years in place: an economy whose failings were buffered by subsidies and manageable inflation; cultural life that was controlled by philistine censors but that permitted creativity on the edges; social permissiveness that made the pursuit of happiness, in the form of dating, outings, and parties, fraught but possible. Iran was not yet at peace with the world, but neither was it at war. It was a time, in short, when Iranians had the luxury of tuning out the factional squabbles of their ruling mullahs and focusing on their personal concerns, as if the two bore little relation to each other.

For many, in the month of July, no concern mattered quite as much as making wine. Since the regime outlawed alcohol, Iranians who drank—a not inconsiderable portion of the population—coped in a variety of ways. Most were content to consume homemade *aragh,* a hard liquor made easily from raisins. Beer lovers fared worse, for beer was hard to make at home and expensive to buy from the bootleggers who delivered orders door-to-door. But for the many Iranians who drank wine, the prohibition offered up an opportunity they may never have contemplated otherwise: making their own. The state permitted the 400,000 Iranians of Armenian Christian origin, one of the country's biggest though dwindling religious minorities, to produce and consume wine, and most Muslim Iranians had for years bought their wine from trustworthy Armenians. Some housewives who still made their own jam and pickles simply added winemaking to their seasonal labors.

One day in high summer, when grapes reached their peak, we set out in search of the *shahani,* a grape whose dusky purple skin and pink flesh produce a full-bodied, deep red wine. The *shahani* grape did not enjoy an international reputation like its cousin, the grape of

Shiraz—which is thought to be the ancestor of the French syrah and before the revolution had been exported to vineyards across the world—but we enjoyed its flavors nonetheless.

"Aren't you thankful for the Islamic Republic?" I asked Arash as we left for the main produce market of the city, Maidan-e Tareh Bar. Farmers from throughout the country sent truckloads of summer fruits and vegetables to the sprawling expanse of parking lots. There, wholesalers sold to produce merchants serving the capital's fourteen million inhabitants. "If this were a normal country, we would probably live our whole lives without once making our own wine," I said.

We were directed to the lot where the grapes could be found, and began threading our way through the stalls, covered in piles of crates overflowing with grapes of myriad variety. I noticed other Iranians dressed in city clothes—distinct from the produce wholesalers and retailers—picking through the fruit. It was a practice as old as the revolution, it turned out, to go shopping for wine grapes. The wholesalers smiled conspiratorially, selling their grapes with the ease of shrewd businessmen aware they sat on the dominant end of the supply-demand equation.

This open-mindedness was an inadvertent effect of nearly three decades of repressive, Islamic rule. By intruding upon people's private lives in the name of religion, the regime had managed only to make its own petty meddling unpopular, creating an unprecedented, deep-rooted appreciation in the most conservative pockets of Iranian society for the rights of the individual, however at odds with Islamic sensibilities. I had not witnessed such tolerance anywhere else in the Middle East, and I suspected it was one reason why Iranian immigrants in the West tended to assimilate more seamlessly than those from other parts of the Islamic world. For most Iranians, Islam had become a matter of intensely private importance, not a prism through which you negotiated personal identity or cultural anxieties.

This more evolved, salutary relationship with religion arose partly also from the regime's haphazard imposition of its strictest codes. The grape hall of the produce bazaar was just one of many corners of Iranian life that the regime had neglected to infiltrate. It had simply forgotten to dispatch its agents to intimidate the wholesalers into stricter oversight of their sticky clusters. I imagined ways in which it could do this: "Mr. Qazvini grape merchant, do not sell grapes to anyone whose clothes do not bear produce stains, who is using a sedan or other noncommercial vehicle for transport, and, in cases where you are not certain, ask for a *ta'ahod,* a signed promise, that the grapes will be used only for fruit bowls, vinegar, or juice."

As I envisioned such interventions, we trudged among the stalls, bending down to squish grapes whose skin resembled the dark purple of the *shahani,* checking to see whether the flesh and its juice were red, as the variety is meant to be, or white, which marked a variety similar in appearance that produced a blush wine.

"You've come too late," a vendor told us, as we made a second circuit with hands that were sticky but disappointingly unstained. "The *shahani* usually finish by eight. If you want *khomreh* [meaning jug, the traditional vessel in which Iranians store wine] grapes, you need to arrive early." So we drove that same day to Qazvin, a city about 165 miles northwest of Tehran, and in the recesses of its cozy bazaar found enough crates of *shahani* to yield the equivalent of two barrels. By the time we loaded the trunk, we were covered with dirt and ravenous, and finding all the restaurants in the city already closed, bought a loaf of fresh *barbari* and some salty white cheese, and drove out to nearby Alamut, a mountain fortress on the central plain.

It was from here that the mystic-militant order of the Assassins had emerged in 1090. Little remained of the original citadel, just a jagged gray rock slung low on the landscape. We reached it after passing through a village and crossing a nearly dry stream. As we climbed the citadel's steps, I told Arash what a shame it was that he hadn't read *The Da Vinci Code* yet. We'd made this stop at my behest: I was immersed in the novel and enthralled with the Templars and the Crusades. This fascination now filled my evenings, and I stayed up late reading books of Templar history and watching films like *Kingdom of Heaven,* which made the religious conflict at the heart of the Crusades seem like a page out of the day's newspapers.

The Assassins' story runs as a fascinating subplot through the history of those times. They were best known for striking poisoned daggers into the hearts of viziers, kings, and others they viewed as impious usurpers. Though the Assassins are notorious for targeting Crusaders, they directed most of their strikes against the Muslim elites—viziers and sultans who, in the Assassins' eyes, had strayed from the true faith and condemned the doctrine of the Ismailis, the Islamic sect founded by Hassan-e Sabbah, to which they belonged. One reason the Assassin legend has endured throughout the ages, capturing even the modern imagination in novels like *The Da Vinci Code,* is the lore surrounding Alamut itself, their fabled castle-citadel. Marco Polo, in the thirteenth century, described breathlessly the "largest and most beautiful garden ever seen . . . [containing] palaces the most elegant that can be imagined and . . . conduits, flowing freely with wine and milk and honey and water."

We ate our bread and cheese on the dusty steps, our conversation interspersed with contemplative silences. My eyes roamed across the distant valleys, and I thought about the Assassins. In reporting on Islamic militant groups and the Islamic Republic, inevitably I wrote and contributed to stories about the roots of violence in the Middle East. Did the Koran sanction assassination and suicide bombing? Did Shiism somehow make special allowances for the use of terror as a political weapon? Though the Assassins had disappeared in the thirteenth century, many journalists and Middle East experts drew a neat arc between the era of the Assassins and the present, arguing that modern militancy—manifested in groups like Hamas, Islamic Jihad, and Hezbollah, and even states like the Iranian Islamic Republic—descended from the Assassins. This was lazy logic, a shortcut way of explaining complex political problems. It did not help explain why the streets of Tehran today bore the names of famous assassins (from the man who killed Anwar Sadat, to an Iranian cleric who targeted secular statesmen and historians). Nor would it help one understand the motivations of men and women today who bombed shopping malls and buses. This had never been more evident to me as that afternoon, sitting amid the ruins of Alamut.

The uneven stone ledges and crumbling dirt slopes reaching up to the citadel's peak evoked nothing of the castle's twelfth-century splendor. But I could see the genius in the castle's position: it afforded panoramic views of the snowcapped mountains in the distance and the mossy valleys below, but was neatly enclosed and made easily defensible by the rock's steep face. As the afternoon grew cool, we began making our way down, our grapes still requiring transport to Arash's family home in Lavasan.

Lavasan had previously been a village outside Tehran, but it was becoming a full-fledged town where middle-class and wealthy Iranians could escape the toxic pollution and traffic of the city. The house was built of red brick from Tabriz and was situated on acres of apricot, walnut, cherry, and willow orchards. The next day we would begin crushing the grapes, but that evening we sprawled out on the Persian-carpeted terrace, staring up at the stars in the summer sky and listening to the frogs croak. "Did you know eighty-six different varieties of grape grow in Iran?" Arash asked lazily, not really expecting a reply. Too worn out from the day's journeys to play backgammon, explore the gardens, or undertake any of the other pursuits that usually filled our idle time in Lavasan, we drifted off to sleep outside, dreaming of castle strongholds, daggers at the bedsides of sultans, and other twelfth-century manifestations of what the mullah I had interviewed called "our historical compulsion to seek justice."

CHAPTER 6

The View from Dubai

Not long after our wine-making adventure, sometime in August, something very peculiar happened. While visiting a well-known jewelry store on Jordan Street, I decided, on a whim, to buy my mother a ring. The purchase being unplanned, I did not have enough cash on me; like most stores in Iran, the shop did not accept credit cards. I asked them to hold the ring while I phoned my aunt to see if she had enough cash in the house. She did not, but said a close family friend had an errand to run near Jordan Street and could probably pick it up for me. The friend stopped at the jewelry store and purchased my ring, for which I promptly repaid him. The next day, the jeweler called him and asked him to return to the store. When asked why, the jeweler only said elliptically, "Some gentlemen would like to speak to you." These "gentlemen" met him in the jeweler's private office and introduced themselves as security agents. They began interrogating him as to the nature of our association; why was he buying me jewelry? He explained. They demanded to know how I could afford such expensive gifts. The ring was not, in point of fact, particularly expensive for someone who earned an American dollar salary. But the friend felt this was not a tactful thing to say, and instead noted that I had worked for many years and likely had savings I could draw upon.

Wondering whether the agents had been Mr. X and his colleague,

I asked the friend to describe them. His vague account could have applied to half the men in Iran under fifty, so there was no way to know
for certain. I might have confronted Mr. X directly, but this could easily backfire. When it came to Mr. X, it was always a matter of staying
one step ahead in the dance. If he had not been responsible, he would
suggest trying to find out which security body had sent the agents, and
perhaps he would report back that they belonged to the scary, shad-
owy intelligence branch of the judiciary. He might tell me that they
were also monitoring me, and that I had best cooperate more fully
with him, so that he could protect me against this more nefarious, independent security cell. All this might be absolutely true, or a pack of
lies. I would have no way of knowing, but would be beholden to him
nonetheless for acting on my behalf. By not telling him, I risked losing
his protection against a sinister arm of another branch of government.
But how meaningful was the protection of one questionable institution against another? Not very, I reasoned; probably I was better off
saying nothing to Mr. X, and maintaining my current position in our
fraught relationship. I deliberated telling Arash, and decided not to
say anything to him, either. Unaccustomed to the creeping presence of
state agents in his life, he would worry too much.

I called Mr. X the next day to discuss another matter.

"I thought you might like to know that I am being criticized by
Iranian émigrés in Los Angeles for my latest article," I told him.

Often my work inspired the squawks and condemnation of Iranian
exiles in California, mainly those who were badly out of touch with
daily life in Iran and ascribed their own beliefs to a distant people
with other concerns. These armchair revolutionaries believed, for example, that Iranians should rise up immediately and overthrow the
mullah regime (they would applaud from Beverly Hills), reinstall the
Pahlavi monarchy, and embrace the United States. When my reporting intruded on these fantasies, when I wrote about how the United
States had lost political capital in Iran after the botched invasion of
Iraq, they sniped that I had become an apologist for the authorities, a
traitor. They had castigated me on Persian radio call-in shows, and in
person at lectures. Many of them despised Shirin khanoum, the country's only Nobel laureate, for pursuing change within the confines of

the regime. This made her a great nuisance to them, as a symbol of peaceful change from within. Her vast popularity hindered their calls for a U.S. military ousting of the mullahs. Our association had further blackened me in their estimation. My mother had friends among these out-of-touch monarchists, and they often called her to complain about my stories. I used these grievances to boost my position with Mr. X. It was important that he and his superiors realize that while my reporting might appear insulting or unwelcome from their vantage, it registered among some as regime propaganda.

"That is very interesting. What has been said?" Tales of my persecution at the hands of the L.A. exiles always fascinated Mr. X. He liked to hear about how they reconciled their black-and-white views of the government's repressiveness with its tolerance for my critical stories and a book that disparaged its rule. "Did they ask how you can come and go, even after the publication of your book?"

Though Mr. X appeared to enjoy these exchanges, even seemed to appreciate the fact that tolerating me enhanced the government's image abroad, I could not measure whether I was seeing signs of his private opinion or a reflection of the government's practicality. Despite his job as a security agent, Mr. X seemed to view Iranian society with level-headed reason. He had fought in the Iran-Iraq War, and like many veterans had experienced firsthand the government's fickleness and the hollowness of its ideology. The regime embraced the soldiers who fought in the war, as long as it required their sacrifice, glorifying martyrdom and the "sacred defense" of nation. But as memories of the conflict faded, so too did the regime's dedication to its veterans. The special privileges they had once enjoyed throughout the system, from loans, to government posts, to special access to university, slowly dried up. Their loyalty to the state faded, a sense of betrayal set in, and many became fiercely critical, able to see the regime's failings with special acuity. Often I noticed such perceptiveness in Mr. X's conversation, when he derided the bureaucratic inefficiency of government offices and the corruption that had grown rampant throughout the system.

Mr. X was the final link in a chain that included the head of domestic security and the minister of intelligence. My attempts to describe him and the nature of our interactions to Arash had made me realize how much about Mr. X still eluded me. Though in his effect on my life it was only he who mattered, he represented more than just one agent's opinion. Sorting through his allusions, his vague administrative language, his metaphors, to deduce what that opinion actually was, though, was often beyond me. On some days, Mr. X seemed to me a prudent, insightful functionary, trying to nudge a dictatorship toward openness. On other days, he seemed a narrow-minded bully.

Perhaps it was a touch morbid to follow the deathbed vicissitudes of a perfect stranger with such avidity, but Akbar Ganji was a dissident on hunger strike and would have appreciated the attention—or so we told ourselves. Over two months had passed since he had launched his strike in late May, in protest against his imprisonment.

"How is Ganji?" my friend Lily asked most afternoons, as we quietly sipped tea in her book-lined living room. Often I had updates: today he refused his intravenous feeding tube; his doctors are warning his kidneys will fail within the week; the state hospital has threatened to operate on his arthritic knee. These developments cast a pall over that summer, especially because it seemed we were the only ones who cared, or, for that matter, who knew. Independent newspapers had been tacitly warned to avoid coverage of Ganji and his hunger strike. But I suspected that even had that not been the case, few Iranians would have paid much attention, so disenchanted were they with politics, the reform movement, and its symbols.

Shirin khanoum was serving as Ganji's lawyer, and as we met frequently to complete her book, her anxiety about his condition infected me until I, too, began to feel that his health somehow embodied that of the nation. As the country's most important political prisoner, Ganji had served five years and three months of the six-year sentence he received in 2000, his punishment for articles linking powerful officials to the murders of dozens of intellectuals in the mid- to late 1990s. I met him once, back in 2000, before he went to prison, and we were mobbed on the street in Haft-e Tir Square, for in those days, back when Iranians cared about politics, Ganji was like a pop star. His book on the murders, whose title might be translated as *Dark House of Ghosts,* was a best-seller, and its success profoundly shook the Islamic Republic, in a manner not unlike the Watergate scandal.

Ganji was a repentant former revolutionary; his conversion into a modern-day democrat was an intellectual journey to which most Iranians, who once had supported the revolution but had been disappointed by its slide into authoritarianism, could relate. Despite having spent the last five years languishing in prison, Ganji had kept himself at the intellectual and tactical forefront of the drive for change. He published a taboo-shattering book calling for a full separation of mosque and state, and was the first to declare publicly that Islamic reform was yesterday's debate, that the reign of the ayatollahs must give way to representative democracy. The establishment, of course, detested him, for he was the most legitimate voice to call the entire system into question.

The letter he released that week from his sickbed, relayed over the Internet, had shocked me with its boldness. "Mr. Khamenei must go," it read, evoking memories of the last time an opposition figure uttered such a call, back when the Ayatollah Khomeini from his distant exile in Paris declared "The Shah must go!" That same week, the authorities transferred Ganji to a state hospital, where they proclaimed they would operate on his arthritic knee, despite the wishes of his family. Given his badly emaciated state, and the certain wish of the establishment to do away with him, it seemed plausible he might die of "complications" in surgery. Two days prior, Shirin khanoum had attempted to visit him in the hospital, and a hard-line newspaper accused her of conspiring to kill him (her own client!) to stain the reputation of the Islamic Republic.

I saw her just after the newspaper story came out, and in the nervous tension of those days I noticed again the physical toll her work was taking on her. The stress had drained her face of all its color, exacerbated her high blood pressure, and caused pinched nerves in her neck and wrists. Some afternoons, as she whispered into her cell phone and disappeared into her office with colleagues, she seemed almost to wither under the force of her worries, as though the ugliness of what she confronted each day was somehow collapsing her diminutive frame.

"They haven't asked you anything about me, have they?" she asked, referring to the agents of the Ministry of Intelligence. Everyone in Iran whose profession made them relevant to the security-obsessed regime—professors, writers, translators, musicians, journalists, and people in a plethora of other seemingly benign trades—was preoccupied with the question of who might be disclosing information about them to the authorities. At times, this could produce an almost Soviet atmosphere that tainted friendships and families, making people distrust one another—which was, in all likelihood, the whole point.

In fact, Mr. X had asked me about Shirin during our last meeting.

"Yes," I replied truthfully. "They wanted to know if you were scared."

"What did you tell them?"

"I told them you seemed to be handling things very professionally." It occurred to me that I had also told Mr. X that she didn't scare easily. But now, sitting before her, I wondered whether she would have appreciated that; perhaps she would have preferred that I say she did not scare at all. At such moments, I resented the trickiness of working in such a political environment, where despite the best of intentions you were forced to compromise yourself.

Shirin's nervousness, and the urgency with which she spoke of Ganji and the importance of his strike, touched me. It struck me how fortunate Iranians were to have such people struggling on their behalf, and how regrettable it was that they could not pay more attention. I decided to write about Ganji, an opinion piece that would let me talk about all these feelings with as much un-objective emotion as I wished. An editor at the *Los Angeles Times,* my old employer, agreed enthusiastically to the proposal.

I phoned Mr. X and told him I would be writing about Iran's most important dissident. "Was this your own idea?" he asked. Mr. X was always curious to know whether my stories, especially the provocative ones, were written on my own initiative or at an editor's behest. I guessed the answers helped him decide what sort of journalist I was.

Did I work innocently and independently, or was I the type of reporter who functioned in coordination with powerful people—who was used to leak damaging information about Iran and encouraged to write stories that exaggerated its radical image? His paranoia in this regard had in the past made me reluctant to break news, because I knew I would be asked how I had come across my information. On occasion, I had passed scoops to colleagues in New York or Washington, preferring to save myself the hassle with Mr. X.

"Yes, it was entirely mine." I reminded him that I had reported on Ganji back in 2000, and that it was natural for journalists to follow the same subject over time.

"I see."

"I'll be noting that most people aren't following news of his hunger strike," I said. I figured this sad truth would comfort him: I wouldn't be writing a story about thousands of Iranians rallying to the support of a would-be martyr for democracy.

"Is that what you have found?" He was silent for a moment, as though writing something down.

After we hung up, I sat down to write what I hoped would be a moving tribute to Ganji. The image of his emaciated frame had begun to haunt me.

A few days later, in the first week of August 2005, Ahmadinejad officially became president of Iran. His first official act was to select a cabinet. Of the twenty-one nominees he presented to parliament, several lacked any experience in government whatsoever, others were personal friends from the university where he had taught, and two had been implicated by human rights groups in political killings.

The evening the president announced his nominees, I arrived at Shirin khanoum's office around dusk. We had dinner plans with her husband and Parastou Forouhar, the daughter of the slain dissidents Dariush and Parvaneh Forouhar. In the fall of 1998, assassins working for the Intelligence Ministry had broken into the couple's home and stabbed them to death. Parastou's brother had come home and found the bodies of his parents, brutally chopped into pieces. Shirin khanoum had legally represented the family in court, though the judge, as so often happened in her trials, presided with all the indifference and political bias that characterized the Iranian judiciary. That her parents' killers would never be brought to justice was a reality that Parastou had accepted in the painful years that followed. But she knew that the very process of seeking resolution through the legal system, of needling the system into accountability, was meaningful in its own right: the trial had effectively ended the political careers of the senior officials implicated. Ever since, they had lurked in the shadows of public life, where both Shirin and Parastou had hoped they would remain. But that was not to be the case: Ahmadinejad's nominee for minister of interior was the man suspected of ordering the killings and drawing up the list of other targets for assassination, which had included Shirin.

The evening was warm, and we smoked silently in Shirin's office. I didn't say anything about the day's news. All I could think about was how tremendously composed Parastou seemed, given that her parents had been murdered, and that the man considered responsible had just been appointed to head a key government ministry.

When I look back on the early months of the Ahmadinejad era, my recollections of this evening are more vivid than any other, mostly because it was so tinged with fear. For Shirin and Parastou, but for Shirin especially, these appointments were not simply a distressing shift toward radical governance but tantamount to a renewed death sentence. When a man you believe plotted and sought your death is put forth to head a crucial government ministry, it is difficult not to consider this a license for him to return to his fatal agenda.

The government had assigned Shirin two security guards, allegedly out of fear of an attack on her life. Recently the guards had told her that the police had received credible information of an imminent threat, and had instructed her to begin wearing a bulletproof vest outside.

"What do you think," she had asked me earlier that week, "should I wear it? Or perhaps they're just trying to intimidate me." She often asked my opinion on such matters with an intense, hushed air, as though hoping the scope of my contacts and work as a reporter might endow me with special insight into her situation. I always felt my responses were inadequate.

"It seems to me," I had replied, "that if they're that concerned you should first be driven in a bulletproof car, no?"

Our debate went around in circles, and we concluded that one cannot properly assess the security prescriptions of a government that itself previously conspired to kill you. The presence of the two guards, with their shadow of stubble and their collared shirts buttoned to the top, lent an unnatural air to the evening. They accompanied us to dinner, sitting on a nearby raised bed at the outdoor restaurant in Darband. We spoke in low tones so as not to be overheard. Parastou reminisced about the revolution, about the high esteem in which the Ayatollah Khomeini had held her father. Shirin's husband warned her about eating carbohydrates in the evening and teased me about avoiding the fresh onions everyone else munched along with their meal. As dinner came to an end, I realized I would have no chance that evening to speak to Shirin privately. I had wanted to tell her about the incident at the jeweler and ask her advice, but this would have to wait.

We filed out of the restaurant and into the crowd of families and young couples strolling through Darband. The warm night air was filled with the calls of vendors selling wheel-size, paper-thin rolls of dried-fruit roll-up, and children loudly begging their parents for ice cream. A couple recognized Shirin khanoum as we walked toward the car, and stopped to greet her excitedly. With her work appearing less frequently in newspapers (cautious editors were likely trying to avoid stories that would get their papers banned), and with the online news site she wrote for now censored by the authorities, Shirin khanoum's presence in Iranian life had grown muted in recent months. Watching the shining faces of the couple who were speaking to her, I realized just how successful the state campaign had been. Even I, her co-author, charged with noticing her role in Iranian society, was guilty of forgetting just how much she meant to people.

I ordered a pomegranate martini, leaned back into plump velvet cushions, and surveyed the latticework of the *mashrabiya* (a wooden shade) lining one end of the lounge. Through its ornate pattern I could see the glistening waters of the Persian Gulf. The sun was setting over a landscape of cheerful palm trees, and on all sides of the room stylishly dressed Iranians held light conversations, picking at stuffed olives and Mediterranean tapas, the ice of their cocktails tinkling. Arash and I were meeting his friends Homayoun and Gita, and of course we were not in Iran. Along with hundreds of thousands of other Iranians in search of a freer life and superior business opportunities, they had moved to Dubai, which had become a sort of Persian satellite in the United Arab Emirates. Just a hundred miles south of Iran's southernmost point, Iranians had created out of Dubai, effectively, an Iranian city; the distance lent itself to commuting, the government permitted unrestricted travel, inexpensive airlines made the short trip occasionally affordable for even middle-class Iranians, and a sprawling Iranian embassy facilitated all this coming and going, making the emirate accessible as a hub of capital and culture. Painters we knew now regularly held gallery exhibitions in Dubai, and Homayoun, the musician son of Iran's foremost vocalist, Mohammad-Reza Shajarian, had chosen to establish himself there.

Looking out at the gulf's placid waters, I was struck by the peculiar twists of the region's history. Today, all these Iranians had fled the repressive Islamic rule of their homeland for an Arab state, while in the seventh century, it was the Arab conquest of Persia that had delivered Islam to Iranians in the first place. Stripped of their ancient religion, their literature, and their history, the Persians sought to preserve vestiges of their old traditions over centuries, crafting poetry and myth around their epic kings and resisting the invaders by simultaneously adapting and Persianizing their faith and language. Fourteen centuries later, it was Dubai, an Arab outpost the size of Rhode Island, that was generously hosting Iranian painting and music, while homegrown Islamic theocrats labeled the fine arts "western garbage."

As our drinks arrived, we briefed Homayoun and Gita (both of whom drank iced tea) on the short space of time since Ahmadinejad had taken office.

"The only truly annoying thing actually happened to me this very morning on the way to the airport," I said. After I'd hoisted my suit-case onto the belt of the women's security check earlier, a female security guard in chador took me aside.

"Too short," she barked. "Sleeves, manteau, jeans. All too short."

That summer, the police had announced they would "deal in a serious manner" with women who flouted "proper" Islamic dress codes. They had made this pronouncement every summer for the past seven years, and not once had the rules actually been enforced in a "serious manner." Women continued wearing short coats and pushed-back veils, treating the announcement like the toothless paternalistic griping they had been subjected to as teenagers on the way out the door. That year, the judiciary and another branch of the police had even contradicted the police department's warnings in newspaper in-terviews, insisting the country's security forces were focused on finan-cial corruption and serious moral issues, such as prostitution.

"I'm accustomed to traveling in this manteau, and frankly, it's not that objectionable," I told the guard. Compared to what young women wore about the streets of Tehran, it was positively demure.

"Don't you read the newspaper?" she said.

"Yes, don't you? The head of the judiciary contradicted the police warning."

"Well, you're just going to have to take something long-sleeved out of your luggage and change."

"I'm going to miss my flight, and I don't have time for this," I said curtly. When I had first arrived in Iran, fresh and green from northern California, I had obeyed like a schoolgirl in such situations, naïvely deferential to authority, certain the worst could not happen to me, of all people. Only when the worst (arrest, near arrest, public humilia-tion, and so forth) befell me, repeatedly, as a result of my submissive-ness, did I learn to respond like the Iranian young people of my generation: with loud, shrill confrontation. This was the rather simple trick by which my friends—indeed, most young Iranians—managed to evade the bullying ways of the Islamic system: by shouting down its enforcers, daring them to engage in hostile, full-fledged confrontation. It sounds counterintuitive, but it was actually effective. Very often the authority figure in question was either too young, cowed, bored, or poorly paid to deal with an angry female whose shrieks typically gained her the solidarity of passers-by.

I described this kind of resistance in my first book as the culture of "as if," a mode that involved behaving "as if" most of the regime's rules did not exist. Although it was technically illegal to reveal locks of hair, listen to western music, read censored books, and consort with members of the opposite sex, Iranian young people rendered these restrictions meaningless by ignoring them. In pushing back this way, they had reasserted some control over their daily lives. If you had asked me at the time, I would have said that it meant the authorities would never again be able to impose their harshest codes, that the days of telling Iranians exactly what to wear, say, watch, and do were over. The mullahs could not, after all, do battle against an entire generation, I thought.

The rebelliousness of Iranian young people often led outside observers to conclude that they were willing to confront authority in more meaningful, or more overtly political, ways. But I never found this to be the case. Every few months an editor at *Time* would ask whether we could do an "Iranian youth at boiling point" story, and I would explain that Iranian youth weren't even heating up yet. That they were willing to shout down a police officer or flirt during a public Islamic ritual meant mostly that they were concerned with freedom in their immediate ten-foot radius. Beyond that, the risks involved in rebellion swiftly outgrew the rewards. Busy investing in the logistics of emigration—the English proficiency tests, visa applications, and language courses—many young people envisioned their futures abroad, and were unwilling to compromise those hopes for the sake of somehow changing Iran, a notion they considered chimerical, costly, and best left to a future generation.

The localized subversion they practiced was not unlike shooing away mosquitoes in high summer. The pests would buzz off momentarily, perhaps drawn to the neighbor's porch light. But they would always be back, until someone mustered the energy to seek a more enduring solution.

At the airport on my way to Dubai, the guard let me pass through to the gate, though she first made me sign a *ta'ahod* promising not to repeat my offense. Certain she would toss it out without a glance, I signed it Googoosh, the name of a famous Iranian pop diva, and headed out to find Arash. If the ease with which one entered or left the airport was any measure of whether the government was tightening or loosening its controls on women's dress, the incident was worrisome. It was unheard-of to be asked to sign a *ta'ahod* at Mehrabad, the capital's main airport, but we were flying out of the new Imam Khomeini airport (IKIA), located in the desolate stretch of desert between Tehran and the holy city of Qom. "What a difference a vowel makes," I'd said to Arash, pointing to the freeway signs directing us to IKIA. "Just imagine, if that second 'I' were an 'E,' what kind of country this would be." IKEA, after all, could supply Iranians with more of what they actually needed.

With its vaulted ceilings, its tunnels to the planes, and its smart café serving cappuccino and berry tart from Tehran's finest bakery, IKIA matched the standards of the developed world's airports. Unfortunately, it had been designed to meet the travel needs of Iran circa 1980, and the decades of delay in its construction made it rather useless. IKIA was far too small to function as the chief airport of a nation of seventy million, and on many mornings the outgoing flights quickly overwhelmed its capacity. The lines for the departure hall's handful of two-stall bathrooms, for example, were grounds enough to merit the commissioning of another two terminals.

Built largely in cooperation with the Revolutionary Guards, the airport had been embroiled since 2004 in the conflict between Iran and Europe over the country's nuclear program. The Guards were a military force distinct from the conventional army, and notorious as the trouble-making arm of the Islamic Republic; they oversaw the country's ties with Islamic militant groups and were accused by the United States of destabilizing the fledgling Iraqi government. Inside Iran, their economic clout had expanded in recent years, and now major infrastructural projects, instead of being sourced to firms with technical expertise, were granted directly to the Guards. European countries, irritated by Tehran's diplomatic antics, balked at letting their carriers fly in and out of IKIA, citing a runway problem that they privately admitted was manageable. The Europeans' ban on the new airport would almost certainly be dropped in the months to come, but in the meantime it reminded Iranians that their government had lost its credibility in the world.

As I recounted the airport run-in, I hastened to add what I considered an important detail. "Ahmadinejad himself doesn't support this kind of harassment," I said. "He said in a public speech that our country's problem is not the hejab, which I think made him look quite sensible."

At the time, I believed Ahmadinejad. I thought his practical approach to hejab (which in Iran refers to the practice of women covering their hair) was a cunning way to win over educated, urban Iranians who would be wary of his hard-line religious views.

Arash, Homayoun, and Gita looked at me skeptically, but I continued, arguing that the harassment at the new airport didn't represent a new wave of repression but only the heavy-handedness one should expect of establishments run by the Revolutionary Guards. Like so many people at the time, reluctant to brace for the worst, I looked everywhere for hopeful signs that under this new president perhaps our lives would not change so dramatically.

After three days in Dubai, Arash and I returned to Tehran. On the way back from the airport, we stopped to eat liver kabobs near the old slaughterhouse district of the city. As we pulled the succulent meat off the skewers, I gazed around at the plastic tables of the fluorescent-lit dive, at the photos of Ayatollahs Khomeni and Khamenei hanging on the wall, and felt a pang of intense doubt. Was this the life I really wanted? I wasn't uncertain about being with Arash, of course; traveling together had only underscored how well we fit and how close we had become. But did I truly want to live in Iran again, given how uncertain the country's prospects seemed? If Ahmadinejad turned out to be intolerant of criticism, the climate for journalists would likely deteriorate. And I couldn't imagine myself living in Iran and not working as a reporter. But since work and study tied Arash to Iran for at least the near future, I saw no choice for myself but to stay put and hope for the best.

One afternoon a couple of weeks later, Arash called me from his office. "Is everything all right? You haven't noticed anything out of the ordinary today, have you?" No, I replied. Why? Nothing special, he said. We'll talk when I get home.

We never discussed anything private or sensitive on the phone, for we were certain the lines were tapped. I knew that the authorities had tapped the phones I used back in 2000: Mr. X occasionally revealed information he could not have had without access to my private conversations. And since I had moved in to Arash's apartment, the quality of the phone line had deteriorated. The crackles and hums, which mysteriously afflicted only our line, not the others in the building, convinced me we were being listened to. That the authorities knew we were living together did not concern me particularly. If one day they decided they wanted to toss me into prison, a spotless record of celibacy would not deter them. Now I impatiently waited for Arash to come home.

"I was followed the whole day," he said, immediately upon opening the door. He had first noticed the man in the morning, lingering outside the door to the office building. Arash's alertness to detail was exquisite, bordering on preternatural. At a glance he would notice the faulty knot in a silk carpet, the minute flaw in an intricate piece of jewelry. But the man who followed him stood out so dramatically that he surely wanted to be noticed. He had worn a polished suit, a bright tie, and dark sunglasses, and he was closely shaven. You could walk the streets of Tehran for an entire day and not encounter a man with such appearance, for though shaving had become commonplace (strictly observant Muslim men wear either a beard or stubble), the tie, as a western accessory, was still unwelcome in public space. In addition to his striking attire, the man had a memorably hooked nose.

He was still standing across the street when Arash left the office; he surfaced again near the entrance to a building where Arash had a meeting, and indeed he appeared outside every place Arash went the rest of the day. "Are you sure it hasn't to do with you?" I suggested hopefully. "Some textile mischief?"

While I had been monitored by Mr. X since the moment I began working in Iran, I had never, to my knowledge, been followed. The incident at the jewelry stop was the first indication that my movements were being watched, and Arash's experience was the first time someone close to me had been followed. To be harassed for your own work, which you have chosen of your own free will knowing the consequences, is one thing; it is entirely another to feel the impact of that choice in the lives of those close to you. For the first time, living in Iran seemed truly dangerous. I felt miserable that I had inflicted this upon Arash, however indirectly. Though it was not my fault, I also felt somehow ashamed.

Two days later, we met for lunch at a kabob restaurant near Sayee Park, and the man appeared in the crowd, made brief eye contact with us, and disappeared. I couldn't swallow my food knowing he might be in the restaurant, and walked through both floors to ensure he was gone. Arash behaved gracefully, never once blaming me for the intrusion of the henchmen of the Islamic Republic into his life, but I could see that he was worried. The man with the colossal nose had followed him on a workday and his lurking outside the offices seemed to signal that the company itself, in addition to Arash, was in his sights.

"I'm a little nervous," I confided to Shirin khanoum the next day. "What if Arash thinks a relationship with me is too much of a liability? And if he doesn't think so, what if his parents find out and *they* think so?"

Working in the media carries a certain cachet in the West, but in Iran many considered it unseemly, for the output of the Iranian media, accustomed to a lapdog relationship to government, was either propaganda or just sloppy and unprofessional. The press's reputation did not improve in the Khatami era. Although real independent newspapers emerged alongside the reform movement, the independent press was linked so closely to the activists and writers who advocated political change that journalism came to be regarded as de facto political activity. And traditionally, Iranians looked down on politics, considering it a dangerous arena full of people of compromised character.

"Liability! Ridiculous! He'll think no such thing," Shirin khanoum said indignantly, sliding easily into the role of a Jane Austen mother, intent upon and confident of her daughter's marriageability. "There are a hundred reasons why you benefit him. He should think of those. In fact, why don't we all go out to dinner, and I can walk him through it. Yes, that's perfect. That's what we'll do." A while later she phoned her husband and asked him when he might be free to have dinner with "Azadeh and her *namzad*" (traditional Iranians do not recognize the category of boyfriends, who are elevated in discourse to fiancés).

Perhaps she was worried that Arash might genuinely harbor second thoughts; perhaps she feared we were settling into that infertile, indefinite cohabitation so common in the West (the previous month, when we adopted a beagle and a St. Bernard, she scolded me: "Azadeh, you need to get rid of those dogs and get yourself a baby!"). Either way, out of the purposeful warmth that was part of her nature, she sought to do me a good turn, directing her considerable talents to the task of protecting our courtship from the regime's nosy stalker.

One lonely weekday afternoon—since I worked from home, most afternoons seemed lonely to me—I nearly flung a mug of coffee at the computer screen in frustration. I was trying to check some facts for Shirin khanoum's book, and nearly half the websites I needed to access were blocked by the government filter. The inclusion of the word "women" in a Google search produced the maddening "Access Denied" screen; even the site of the U.N. Development Fund for Women was blocked. The censors' crude policing tools seemed to have become more aggressive, filtering the most innocuous sites.

I called Arash at work to complain. "How am I supposed to get any work done? The connection is dead slow, and I can't find the information I need."

He promised to bring home some filter-cracking software that would help, but warned that it would probably only work for a couple of days. The government updated its censorship software regularly, catching and filtering the proxy websites, tools used to help Iranians skirt the government barrier.

It occurred to me that I probably wasn't the only one suffering from the sealing off of the Internet; perhaps there was a story in the seemingly stepped-up censorship. I began making calls to bloggers, journalists, and women's rights activists, and discovered that, indeed, the government had launched a fresh onslaught.

Ever since perhaps 2001, when the Internet took off as an arena for Iranians to express themselves, criticize the government, and organize around such issues as women's rights, the government had sought to intervene. In 2004, it began arresting Web technicians and bloggers, and prosecuted at least twenty writers for posting "subversive" material online, handing them jail terms ranging from a few days to fourteen years. The recent campaign, which activists said had begun in June, targeted the websites and blogs themselves. Using keyword filters and censorship software pirated from U.S. firms, the government blocked thousands of websites containing news, political content, and satire.

The editor of the *Iranian Feminist Tribune,* who used to run a website devoted to women's issues, told me that at its busiest, the site had attracted seventy thousand visitors a day; it ran news articles the country's print press would never carry and spread the word about sit-ins and seminars. "The end result is a marginalization of women and women's issues," another activist told me. What she said seemed to confirm what I had observed myself, watching the government try to marginalize Shirin khanoum. Added together, all this amounted to a fresh, pernicious, and systematic campaign to repress the country's vibrant women's movement. Most Iranians, I knew, had no idea. Did I dare write the story? Of course not. I had no wish to jeopardize my press credentials, and clearly other journalists avoiding the story shared my caution. Instead, I chose to write about stepped-up Internet censorship in general. I could weave in the targeting of women's activists, and attentive readers could work out for themselves what was afoot. When I began reporting in the Middle East, I had considered journalists who approached stories in such a roundabout manner as cowardly. But I had quickly learned that all governments, from eastern dictatorships to western democracies, tend to blackball journalists who holler inconvenient truths too loudly. The real art was to convey as much of reality as possible while maintaining one's access. That did not feel pleasant to me, but I believed subtle reporting about a repressive regime accomplished more than no reporting at all.

Hearing Arash's key in the lock, I looked at my watch in surprise. He was home early, probably because I had been so eager for the anti-filter software. I had meant to call Mr. X and tell him about my story before Arash arrived, and now I would need to make the call in front of him. Arash disliked my contacts with Mr. X; he thought I was too accommodating and should deal with him more firmly. This made me miserable. I wanted Arash's sympathy rather than his judgment, and argued that being more assertive might make it impossible for me to do my work.

Arash smiled so sweetly upon opening the door, a box of my favorite cardamom cupcakes tucked under his arm, that I decided to postpone the call.

CHAPTER 7

A President Without Qualities

Winter gently settled into Tehran, and the Alborz Mountains loomed over the city, sentinel-like and imposing in their fine coat of snow. In the windless cold, the pollution condensed into a thick, sickly gray mist that hovered across the capital, obscuring rooftops just three blocks away. The question that had preoccupied us in the fall, of whether life would change under Ahmadinejad, had been replaced by a more breathless query: What had we done to deserve him? His transformation from poorly regarded ideologue to national hero took place swiftly, taking all but his own supporters (who believed Allah shepherded his presidency) by surprise. His personal advisers and religious conservative backers held doctrinaire views, among them the belief that Ahmadinejad's tenure was a proper "miracle." The most influential of these supporters was Ayatollah Mohammad Taqi Mesbah-Yazdi, a leading cleric in Qom who had issued an election-time fatwa in support of Ahmadinejad and who, after his victory, declared that Iran finally had a proper Islamic government and could henceforth dispense with elections. But debates about theocracy did not concern the Iranians who had actually voted for the president. They cared mainly about redressing inequality, improving their lives, and if this happened on the watch of a president who understood the resonance of Shia Islam in their lives, then so much the better.

Though Ahmadinejad had filled his administration with personal friends, colleagues from his days as mayor or from the university where he taught, he still lacked real clout within the regime. His main authority, it was becoming clear, was the backing of Supreme Leader Ayatollah Khamenei, who found it expedient to support the novice president. This reflected not so much the Supreme Leader's militant mood or beliefs, but the political nature of the Islamic Republic—an opaque system composed of plural, rival power centers. Though he occupied a position of vast, unchecked power, Ayatollah Khamenei faced opposition from senior clerics such as former president Rafsanjani, who held a different vision for Iran's future than the ayatollah and had enough influence to compete with him. During the presidency of the moderate Khatami, the Supreme Leader had been thrust into the awkward role of opposing broadly popular change. With Ahmadinejad in the presidency, he no longer figured in the country's imagination as a staid obstacle to progress, but as a wise balancer, the man keeping the brash new president in check.

But this dynamic also secured for Ahmadinejad all the potential that his administration would never have earned on its own merit, and it helped turn him into a leader of significance. First, the jokes ceased. Passed about by text message, repeated by taxi drivers, they had mocked the president's hygiene, likening him to the monkey cartoon on bags of Iranian Cheetos. In their place, I heard instead exclamations of mild admiration, which soon developed into expressions of actual regard. The extent of Ahmadinejad's sudden popularity became clear to me one sunny day at Shemshak, a ski resort just outside Tehran where we spent many weekends gliding down powdery slopes that rival any in the Rockies or the Alps.

Before the revolution, Shemshak would have been the last place where you could take the temperature of Iranian public opinion. Back then, it was exclusive to westernized, wealthy Iranians: the sort of exclusive, snobby place Arash would have refused to go, but in our generation, as in so many other ways, these distinctions were eroding. Arash's mountaineering friends, young men and women from south Tehran whose parents had only scaled these mountains on foot, now bought secondhand skis and could be found on the slopes alongside

their more privileged peers. At Shemshak nowadays, you might encounter a tour guide or a bazaar merchant, as well as a venture capi-
talist who lived between north Tehran and Palo Alto.

As we waited in line for the lifts, a young man in an orange parka
began chatting up a pretty engineering student from Yazd.

"He's brilliant, defends our rights like no one else has," the young
man said.

"Yeah, he stood behind his word like a man," the woman agreed.
"I used to have doubts, but now I couldn't be happier with him."

They were talking about Ahmadinejad. Throughout the day, we
heard many such expressions of nationalist ardor, as we glided down
the slopes, as we sipped hot chocolate in the shadow of the daz-
zling sun. Everyone, it seemed, from secular Iranians to the traditional
to the cosmopolitan wealthy, had concluded the president was doing
something right after all.

History is full of undistinguished men pushing their way onto the
world stage, leaving their grubby fingerprints on an era to which they
should have been irrelevant. This was such a time. Under different
circumstances, Ahmadinejad would have been remembered only by
Iranians, and then only for his amateurish economic policies. But in
the short months since he had taken office, he had begun using the
increasingly tense standoff over Iran's nuclear energy program to
broaden his appeal at home and extend it abroad. He framed the West
as an enemy bent on weakening Iran by denying it legitimate access to
technology, and pitched a slogan ("Nuclear energy is our absolute
right") that Iranians first mocked, then concluded was Truth. The
changing political climate in the Middle East since 2001 had left
Iranians feeling vulnerable, concerned with bolstering their place in
the region and receptive to the crass, assertive nationalism that Ahmadinejad peddled. With little evidence of American progress in re-
building either Afghanistan or Iraq, Iranians had grown increasingly
skeptical of U.S. power in the Middle East. Their fondness for the
United States, which had reached its height in 2001 when an opinion
poll found that 74 percent of Iranians supported restoring ties with
America, had largely evaporated.

Although the removal of Iran's most dangerous enemies, along with the rise of a sympathetic Shia government in Iraq, had realigned the Middle East in a manner that favored the country, this state of affairs did not yet dominate perceptions among Iranians. A scarce few months had passed since the Baghdad regime came to power, and it was not altogether clear that Iran's Shia friends would remain ascendant. The possibility that Iraq might fall apart altogether still loomed, with the accompanying refugee influx and border insecurity that would plague Iran. As for Afghanistan, vast stretches of it ran wild, outside the control of the central government, and Taliban groups hostile to Iran were reasserting themselves. The United States continued rattling the saber of regime change, and the mullahs were as convinced as ever that Washington was plotting their demise. The Arab states friendly with Washington—Jordan, Egypt, and Saudi Arabia—resented the reshuffling that had strengthened Iran's position, and they broadcast alarmist propaganda about a "Shia crescent" taking over the region. This created all manner of political trouble for Iran, which did not wish to alienate the region's Arabs. In short, Iran's influence had grown, but so had its problems and insecurities. Most people did not feel emboldened so much as embattled.

This mix of insecurity, ambivalence toward the United States, and an embarrassed sense of decline created fertile ground for stoking Iranians' nationalism over their nuclear program. Viewing themselves as inheritors of an ancient, sophisticated civilization stretching back thousands of years, they found Iran's present-day condition a source of shame. When they looked around the region, they saw a modern Turkey leaning toward Europe, they saw the sleek commercial prosperity of Dubai, and they felt pangs of humiliation. Their own failing economy and shabby capital skyline offered no similar source of pride. But in nuclear power, they could have something those other nations did not. Or so Ahmadinejad convinced them. And he did so in a manner that appealed to a broad spectrum of society. "Let America get mad," he once said. "Let it get mad and die of its anger!" These were the utterances of a petulant child, but Iranians, cornered by sanctions and by three decades of failed policies, found it easier to feel petulant than to take responsibility for the situation and take up the task of remedying it.

We were all taken in. I can't count the dinner parties I attended where otherwise sensible individuals breathlessly said things like "He says what is in my heart." Even Iranian businessmen, who should have been more wary, given the ten-billion-dollar drop in the Tehran Stock Exchange that accompanied the president's election, shared these sentiments. Arash was finishing up an MBA program run by a German university in Tehran, and his classmates were, as the director liked to say, "the future leaders of Iranian industry." The current leaders, their fathers, were seduced by Ahmadinejad's rhetoric.

Some, among them people like Arash's father, Mahmoud Agha, had specific and compelling reasons for giving the president the benefit of the doubt. In addition to his populist slogans, Ahmadinejad had emerged as a champion of Iranian industry, vowing in those early months to reshape the arthritic policies that hobbled domestic manufacturing. Before the revolution, Iranian industry, particularly in the textile sector, competed globally. Textile manufacturers provided the raw material for the uniforms of European police and delicate weaves that would be sewn into suits for Hugo Boss. But the economic chaos that accompanied the revolution undid Iranian manufacturing. A government indifferent to the economy looked away as smugglers flooded the country with imports, and exchange rates fluctuated wildly. Unable to compete with places like China, most Iranian industries ceased to turn profit and were veering toward extinction.

The textile business Mahmoud Agha founded in the late 1970s, called Laico, was one of the few exceptions. The creation of his company coincided with a fundamental shift in Iranian life, and its initial success lay in catering to the new needs that emerged. The migration of Iranians from the provinces to the cities, as well as the transformation of Tehran from a city of houses to one of apartment blocks, changed the way Iranians both lived and slept. As the population of Tehran grew beyond fourteen million, as traffic, long work hours, and the conventional rhythms of modern urban life took over the leisured pace of preindustrial Iran, extended families ceased to occupy physical space in each other's lives. Families no longer required heaps of floor mattresses to accommodate visiting relatives. Couples bore fewer children; in the space of just one generation, the urban Iranian family became a two-child, nuclear unit that slept in separate rooms on beds. Laico supplied the sheets, pillowcases, and assorted bedding the country needed for its evolving sleeping arrangements, with such dominance in the market that Iranians began using the word *laico* to mean a comforter.

Though Laico was competitive and managed to control the home textile market, the costs of domestic manufacturing ran high, and the company's profit margin was slim. Its potential suffered from the unregulated imports flooding the country, and the situation grew disastrous in 2003, when Mahmoud Agha acquired a government-run textile factory through the regime's much vaunted privatization scheme. After transferring ownership, the government disclosed the factory was millions of dollars in debt. Even apart from this, the firm was virtually inoperative. Its five hundred salaried employees spent their days playing soccer and volleyball around the factory yard, while million-dollar machinery languished in unopened containers. When Mahmoud Agha took over and asked the employees to actually work, many went on strike in Islamic shrouds, lying down before entrance doors with pious "Ya Hossein" bandannas tied about their heads. Their leaders, it turned out, were all related to the provincial bureaucracy, which did nothing to stop the protest, despite the fact that strikes are illegal under Iranian law. I was accustomed to reading about such travails in dense, business-oriented analyses of the Iranian economy, but for Arash's family they were vivid, living nightmares.

Ahmadinejad had promised to address all of this. His predecessor, Mohammad Khatami, for all his civilizing rhetoric about open and civil society, chose to overlook the economy altogether. The other major heavyweight in Iranian politics, Akbar Hashemi Rafsanjani, had made commercial trade his priority, enriching thousands of businessmen close to the regime through lucrative import and export deals that undermined local industry. For all his exaggerations and irresponsible fulminations, Ahmadinejad's focus on domestic industry seized the attention of manufacturers like Mahmoud Agha.

I hoped for his sake, for Arash's as well, that matters would improve. The factory was growing increasingly unmanageable, and each day they both came home gray and exhausted, tired of pouring their energies into an enterprise that, on its merits, should have been a success. The story of their company mirrored that of most Iranian private enterprise—a long, slogging struggle to stay competitive in an inhospitable, corrupt economy that sent foreign investors fleeing and that catered mainly to firms run by regime officials or linked to its military's engineering arms. An uncle of mine had helped found one of Iran's largest petrochemical firms back in the 1970s, and while it fared better than Laico (in technical fields, government firms needed to outsource their lucrative contracts to outfits with real professional expertise, while the decline of domestic manufacturing was mainly felt by ordinary Iranians forced to buy more expensive imported goods), it, too, suffered from the unfriendly economic climate.

When I first began reporting in Iran in 1999, I found stories about the economy, about the fate of such businesses, deadly boring, and preferred to report on flashier subjects, like reform-minded Islam and student politics. I thought the fate of the country would be determined in lofty struggles dominated by colorful clerics and rebellious students, rather than in gray realities of business competition. But in the intervening years, I discovered how utterly wrong I had been. The real story of modern Iran, what would drive the country's politics and future, was its failing economy and how it was sinking the prospects of millions of young people, who cared far more about finding jobs and raising their living standards than about whether Islam would become compatible with western-style democracy during their lifetime. In the years and months I spent in the offices of my uncle's firm, I watched teenage secretaries grow into young women on the verge of marriage, graphic designers struggle to manage their monthly rent, junior programmers drive taxis at night, burn out and then seek to emigrate.

That evening, after our day of skiing, we settled in to watch *Shabhaye Barareh* ("Barareh Nights"), a new comic soap opera that according to state television was being watched by 90 percent of the country. We adored it, as did all our friends and relatives, as did the whole neighborhood. Between eight and nine P.M., when it was broadcast, traffic actually dwindled and shopkeepers frowned when you distracted them from their televisions. The village of Barareh offered a microcosm of modern-day Iran, complete with rigged elections, a corrupt city council, a grouchy gendarme who censored the town newspaper, and a strident women's rights group. The village, like Tehran, was divided into "Upper" and "Lower" districts that reflected the social status of their residents. In Barareh, reporters were jailed for criticizing the government, the local poet was openly gay, and everyone supported the village's right to enrich nuclear peas, a thinly veiled subplot that took on the country's fracas with the West over nuclear power. Not only did the show offer clever writing and quality production; it also reflected Iranians' cynicism over the state of their country and its place in the world.

When I first watched *Barareh,* I found it refreshing and important that a government program so candidly voiced the country's ills. I thought it meant the state was growing aware of its weaknesses, admitting them before the public, and implying through the story line that it, too, might change. It hadn't occurred to me that *Barareh* might function as a pressure relief valve, until a family friend, an adviser to a very senior ayatollah, made the point. He believed the show encouraged Iranians' worst tendencies—an empty cynicism that pushed critique aside, a worldly sort of passivity. "This show, it's one of the savviest things this regime has ever done," he said. "It teaches people to think the worst, but not do anything about it. Daily life should be full of resistance, where people defend their rights. But people sit home at night laughing, and release all their frustration. The next day they're laughing in the street, not angry."

I called Mr. X one morning to inform him that I had begun reporting a new story, a chronicle of Ahmadinejad's transformation from marginal ideologue to national hero. I anticipated little resistance: Mr. X would surely appreciate such a narrative. But his reaction, to my mind, was a touch cool, and he quickly changed the subject.

"It is my responsibility to tell you that times are changing. The atmosphere no longer tolerates articles such as what you wrote last summer," he said, speaking in the vague, bureaucratic terms he reserved for uncomfortable matters.

Though he most likely had a reason for saying this, I saw no immediate cause for concern. That Ahmadinejad's new minister of culture had not replaced the director of the foreign press department signaled a willingness to treat journalists as Khatami's administration had. It was the first time Mr. X had mentioned my pre-election essay, and if all he meant was that I should desist from writing about the public consumption of cocktails, well, that was hardly worrisome. I filed away his warning, and proceeded with my story.

To better understand Ahmadinejad, Arash and I both turned for guidance to our acquaintance Mr. Tabibi, the president's close relative. He spent most evenings in Ahmadinejad's company, privy to closed-door conversations that when repeated sounded deceptively simple. "You shouldn't worry so much, he'll take care of all this," Mr. Tabibi assured us regularly, in reference to whatever catastrophe the president had recently unleashed. Whenever we were puzzled by the news, unable to make sense of Ahmadinejad or the direction in which he was taking the country, we relied on Mr. Tabibi as some sort of oracle.

He worked in the marketing department of a major rug exporter, and I had met him while reporting a story long ago, before his kinsman became president. He usually wore the oddly fitting green suits associated with bureaucratic Hezbollahis, religious Iranians who advertise their piety through lax grooming and purposefully unfashionable attire. But he seemed to spend most of the working day in pious flirtation with secretaries.

When Mr. Tabibi recounted to us the aims of the Ahmadinejad administration, he spoke of what "we" were trying to accomplish, and "our" challenges. Though he knew I was a journalist, he had never asked for which publication, and I never told him. This was perhaps unfair, because I knew he assumed I worked for an Iranian newspaper. But I worried that mention of *Time* would make him think I was a spy or an agent of imperialist powers, which inevitably would inhibit our discussions. I wasn't sure whether he conveyed Ahmadinejad's thoughts precisely, but his convictions mirrored the rhetoric of the president and his closest aides, and his mood rose and fell with the administration's successes and failures. He was a consummate insider, even if prone to adding his own interpretation.

The morning that the United States agreed to participate in European negotiations over Iran's nuclear program (it had refused for years, and Iranians considered the reversal a concession), his excitement was uncontainable. "This man is touched by God," he had said, thumping the newspapers on his desk. "He has brought the world to its knees!"

What I remember most about Mr. Tabibi's confidences was that they seemed at the same time sincere and lunatic. "Come on," I whispered to Arash one morning, when Mr. Tabibi had left his office to order tea. "Does he really think anyone besides college students is going to buy into this talk of ending corruption and helping the little person battle the bogeyman of globalization?"

"Of course he believes it," Arash said. "He thinks corruption is eroding the Islamic Republic's legitimacy. And he's right." The problem was that corruption, like a creeping vine, was intertwined in the innermost workings of the system, in its very structure.

When Mr. Tabibi returned with the office tea server, he looked dejected and uncharacteristically failed to look up as a young secretary in a peach headscarf lingered near his door.

"It's floundering," he said, shaking his head mournfully. Ahmadinejad's anticorruption drive, he continued, seemed doomed. The president had asked his aides to identify the most corrupt officials in key positions of urban management and had replaced them with inexperienced but in his view incorruptible individuals whose only credentials were war records and religious devotion.

"We placed a senior Basiji in the Saveh municipality. How long do you think it took for him to be bought out? In a month he was driving a Mercedes, as were his wife and sister."

As he spoke, Mr. Tabibi's face grew long and ashen, as though the story of the bribable Basiji wounded him personally. In his sensitive display of distress, I caught sight, just for a moment, of the appeal Ahmadinejad must have had in his pre-election television address. Corruption had indeed gutted Iran's economy, and it was indeed inhumane for a tiny clique of regime cronies to grow more conspicuously wealthy each day, while the tension and resentment of coping with runaway inflation stamped themselves on the faces of ordinary

Iranians. Ahmadinejad had offered curatives for these woes, and Mr. Tabibi, like so many millions, believed they would work. He believed God would help the president help the people, a sentiment that sounded naïve in the modern world of 2005 but that somehow still resonated with a minority of Iranians.

That winter, I flew to Beirut to pack up my apartment and have my things shipped to Tehran. It had been clear to both Arash and me when we moved in together that I would be relocating to Iran permanently. But my lease ran through the beginning of 2006, and I had lazily put off the physical act of rearranging myself. I spent scarcely a week in Beirut, just long enough to have movers put all my belongings into boxes, see my friends, and pick up leaflets for wedding caterers. Ever since visiting Lebanon together at the beginning of our relationship, Arash and I had lovingly nurtured plans for a Beirut wedding.

We had already picked out a faded, exquisite old palace in the cobblestoned Christian quarter, decided on the Lebanese wine that our guests would drink, and figured out how to make the garden overlooking the Mediterranean glow with the light of candles. Arash and I had explored the grounds together and found them perfectly suited to an Iranian ceremony. I was intent on Beirut because it was the only city in the world where the disparate strands of my life came together. The Mediterranean evoked the beaches of California where I had grown up; the Shia slums, adorned with pictures of Khomeini and loyal to Hezbollah, were like a pocket of the modern Iran that had become my home; and in the memories of my elderly Lebanese neighbors, with whom I would sit discussing the fashion sense of Farah Diba, the former empress of Iran, even Iran's past was alive.

My Lebanese friends loved the idea, and we spent my final dinner in the city immersed in girlish talk of wedding details. This warded off the pall of impending separation that usually hangs over farewell evenings, and supplied us with a pretext for drinking too much champagne (we needed to choose a variety for the as yet unscheduled reception). I returned to Iran in high spirits, eager to redecorate our apartment around all my soon-to-arrive belongings, and to subtly remind Arash that our Beirut wedding could not proceed unless he first proposed.

It was eight A.M., and we were already at nine thousand feet, eating date omelets at the small canteen of Shirpala, the first station in the ascent to Tochal peak. We had met Arash's mountaineering friends at Darband, the mountain's base, before dawn to begin our ascent. It would take most of the day to reach the summit—perhaps even longer, for the winter winds and waist-high snow would slow our climb. I uncomfortably twisted my veil to cover the North Face logo on my parka. Iranian mountaineers are familiar with such international brands of trekking gear, but most cannot afford them. Our group that day numbered only six, because the snow levels required hiking boots, and at least three of those present shared their boots with others, who would take their turn the following weekend. Arash and I were the only ones wearing crampons, because the machismo of the rest of the group did not permit them to use such a sissy accessory. Most of them lived in south Tehran, and subscribed to the virile conceptions of manhood that still held sway in that traditional, working-class quarter of the city. On the way up, a ten-year-old boy selling snacks in a village along the way had even taunted Arash for wearing them, "A mountaineer who's afraid of snow better stay off the mountain!"

For much of our group, climbing this mountain was a chief source of pleasure in life. It was the only soul-lifting pursuit available in this city that did not cost anything, at least no more than the gear it required. On the windy peaks, they could spend private time with their girlfriends, away from nosy families and the prying eyes of those who roamed the city's parks, to say nothing of policemen and sometimes Basij. Arash and I parted ways with the group halfway up the mountain, taking a detour to what was known as the fifth station. There we wrapped our hands around mugs of hot cocoa and reclined on chairs by the window, gazing out across the snowy peaks. I don't recall precisely how our conversation turned to religion—perhaps we were gossiping about one of the religious couples in the group—but I found myself describing to him for the first time how I felt about Islam.

It all started, I like to believe, in a dark auditorium in Oakland, California, in the early eighties. With the lights low, a small assembly of Iranians began chanting rhythmic lamentations and thumping their chests, creating an almost trancelike atmosphere in the warm room. Six years old, I was accompanying my veiled grandmother to an Ashoura commemoration, though I scarcely understood that at the time. I clutched my strawberry-shaped purse nervously. I don't recall the moment I actually fainted, just the fluorescent glare of the building's lobby where I was being revived, and the soothing voice of my grandmother, as she gently pressed a cup of lemonade to my lips. I hadn't been scared, exactly, just overwhelmed by the heat and the atmosphere of passionate flagellation. And once I finished my lemonade and ate a cookie, I remember being very impatient to go back inside.

That memory is how my lifelong fascination with Shia Islam began, and in many ways it is inseparable from my memories of my grandmother. It was only as I recounted this to Arash that I realized my grandmother is a construct for me, a way of avoiding my more messy adult relationship with Islam, which became complicated in earnest when I first moved to Tehran. Until then, I had associated the faith with the cozy, warm lap of my grandmother, who taught me the *fatiha,* the opening sura of the Koran, and let me crawl on her back when she was kneeling in prayer. She never chided me for stealing her prayer tablet (Shia Muslims touch their foreheads to a piece of clay during prayer), but scooped me a bowl of *yakh dar behesht* ("ice in heaven"), my favorite rice custard with rosewater and pistachios, and recounted the tale of Imam Hossein's martyrdom at Karbala, where the piece of clay had originated. My grandmother, whom we called Madara, was devout in the most appealing way. Though she prayed five times a day, wore a scarf over her hair outside, and never drank or smoked, she maintained a wry composure when her children drank whiskey and devoured sweet-and-sour pork in her presence. She even indulged in the occasional lotto ticket, though I was the only one who knew (she didn't speak English, so we negotiated the transaction together at 7-Eleven) and was bound to secrecy. In the fuzzy sunlight of her San Jose living room, where her nylon knee-highs rolled into doughnuts usually sat atop my grandfather's books of poetry, she taught me the principles of Islam as she saw them, and entertained my childish doubts.

"A true Muslim's heart must be pure, and free from hatred," she would say.

"But don't you hate the Ayatollah Khomeini? You must." If there was one lesson I had learned by the age of six, it was that we must all hate the ayatollah, the cause of our exile.

"No, not even him."

"But why not? He is a bad man."

"He has never done any harm to me *personally*," she would say. And I would lay my head on her chest, trying to feel her pacemaker, and fall asleep in the sun, contemplating what a noble spirit she must have. I adored my grandmother—her soapy smell, her serene doting, her impish humor. She died at our house one spring day when I was in junior high, and at the exact hour of her passing, I doubled over with stomach cramps in science class. She left me a knitted periwinkle purse that contained a handwritten version of the Ayat ol-Korsi, a verse of the Koran, and I felt thereafter that only the prayers she had taught me would keep me connected to her. That her legacy to me was Islam is not something I chose, or that I always liked. There were times when I lay awake in bed at night, refusing to recite the prayers, but sleep would elude me until I muttered them into the pillow, unsure whether I resented my grandmother or my own confusion.

While my attitude toward Islam grew out of my love for my grandmother and, later, out of my liberal American college education, Arash's, he told me as we finished our hot chocolate, was formed under more dramatic circumstances. He was nine in 1979, and the revolution had captured his preadolescent imagination. He fell in love with the dashing revolutionaries, especially the guerrillas. He built himself a wooden rifle out of popsicle sticks and marched around the backyard practicing maneuvers. On the occasion of Norouz, the Persian new year, which falls on the first day of spring, he collected in a brown envelope all the crisp new bills he had received as gifts, and took the money to the guerrilla headquarters to donate to the revolutionary cause. He lectured his sister, Solmaz, then five, about the importance of revolution, and convinced her to donate her Norouz cash as well.

When the revolution turned bloody, when the Islamic radicals began executing people in droves and terrorizing the populace, Arash felt betrayed to the depth of his boyish heart. Naturally, this history shaped his attitude more than it had mine, since at the time I was playing with Barbies and building sand castles in California.

I had grown enamored of Islam from afar, while he had grown skeptical from up close. Where I saw the potential for more democratic, modern interpretations in the work of Islamic reformists, he saw convoluted debates that whorled and led nowhere. In a way, our attitudes reflected the identities we had crafted for ourselves. I leaned toward Islam to anchor myself amid the distant culture of the West; he leaned away to anchor himself amid the chaotic culture of the Islamic Republic. With time, I hoped, each of us would feel enriched by the other's outlook. After all, I told myself, couples didn't need to feel the same way about everything.

That year, Ashoura, the holiday that commemorates the Imam Hossein's death, fell on a Friday in February. If you visit Iran, you will very quickly notice the imam everywhere. His name is planted in verdant letters on the banks of freeways; his portrait adorns kiosks, walls, and shopping centers. He plays a greater role in the Iranian and Shia consciousness than even the Prophet Mohammad himself, though to say so is considered heretical. The third in the line of Shia imams, the grandson of the prophet, Hossein died in 680 at the battle of Karbala, defending his family's claim to leadership of the Muslims. The battle is a defining moment in Islamic history, and each year Shias enact passion plays of Hossein and his seventy-two followers being slaughtered by their enemies. For the Shia, Hossein represents courage and resistance to injustice. For the pious, his martyrdom is an intimate event, as fresh a memory as last night's meal.

On the occasion of Ashoura, Shias hold mourning processions that wind through the streets of modern cities and tiny villages. Each year, I looked forward to the ritual, the remarkable transformation that it effected in Iranians, softening even the most jaded cynics into humbled weeping spectators. How glorious it must be, I had always thought, to be transported to such depths of emotion by local passion play reenactments, by the neighborhood dry cleaner dressed up as Hossein. Arash, for his part, preferred to stay home. "You know what it's going to be like," he said. "The streets are going to be full of thugs looking for a fight, and I don't feel like dealing with that."

Public space in Iran already bordered on violent. Traffic altercations often resulted in one party brandishing a pipe; walks through the park ended in confrontation, as angry young men ogled women visibly in the company of husbands or boyfriends, purposefully seeking out fights. This type of aggression, probably an outgrowth of the notion of manhood the state cultivated—Islamic, touchy, with "honor" easily offended—made even a trip to the bazaar a potential catastrophe. I had many girlfriends whose husbands refused to accompany them to such crowded places. Inevitably some sixteen-year-old with greasy hair would pinch the woman's behind, puffing his chest out eagerly, waiting for a reaction. To do nothing at all was humiliating, while to brawl with a sixteen-year-old who was probably carrying a knife was foolish. Avoiding the situation, which meant avoiding crowds altogether, was the best option of all.

"But I really want to go," I said, disappointed. "Wait, I have an idea!" I suggested we drive out to Lavasan to watch the *dasteh*s, the neighborhood mourning processions. The crowds in the suburb would be smaller than in Tehran, and less volatile. Arash agreed to go, and within a couple of hours we were walking toward the processions.

The mourners, all wearing black, filled the narrow streets, weeping, wailing, and self-flagellating. They hoisted *alam*s, towering metal structures adorned with Shia amulets that looked like giant ornate candelabras, high into the air. Their rhythmic chanting of "Hossein! Hossein! Hossein!" grew frenzied; the bodies pressed together with an almost sensual grief, soaked in the rosewater that was sprayed over the crowd.

At twilight, we walked to the village's main thoroughfare to buy groceries, and found the little shops busy, the weekend crowd preparing to hunker down in their villas for the holiday. Though they had spent the afternoon in the processions, it did not appear as though they planned to spend the evening in lamentation. They bought chips, creamy yogurt, pickles, and olives—traditional Iranian *mezze* (the term itself comes from Farsi, meaning "taste") typically accompanied with homemade vodka. Having spent the afternoon commemorating the martyrdom of Imam Hossein, they would now retire to their homes and, in the company of friends, indulge. Like so many Iranians, they had worked out a way to reconcile their faith with a secular lifestyle. Very devout Muslims would call this hypocrisy (and so did Arash), but it seemed more like Islam lite to me, an altogether modern form of devotion that reflected the way people around the world accommodated a secular, modern lifestyle to religious and cultural tradition. They partook of religion as they would of a culture, rather than a faith with tenets, if you will. In the same way, my Jewish friends in America kept only a flimsy form of kosher but unfailingly attended their parents' Passover seders.

Arash looked at the groceries people were buying. He turned to me with a disdainful expression, as if to say, "See what company you are in." My attraction to Ashoura incensed him no end. When we first met, perhaps assuming it was transient, or out of the magnanimity that characterizes the very beginning of relationships, he never mentioned his disdain for what he considered hypocrisy. But once we started living together, he would roll his eyes in bemusement whenever I spoke admiringly of Islam and call me a mullah. I tried to win him over. I spoke, in what I thought were moving terms, about how the beheading of the Prophet's grandson on the plains of Karbala (whose name means "Land of Sorrow") was a rich, multilayered legend that had animated Shia history for thirteen centuries.

Ashoura shaped the temperament of Shia Islam, imbuing the faith with a passion for lamentation, saints, and martyrs (not unlike strains of Roman Catholicism, as some scholars have noted). In the twentieth century, radical Shia politicians in the Middle East recast the tale of Ashoura to kindle support for their modern political aims. In their opportunistic retelling, the defeat of Hossein's small army became a lesson in political daring and rebellion. The new, combative spirit of Ashoura inspired a radical fervor that led to the Iranian revolution, as well as the militant movement in Lebanon that gave rise to today's Hezbollah.

I loved the folk mythology of the fallen Hossein as an erudite man who carried on the noble traditions of the Prophet's family, standing against the villainous Yazid, a man fond of power and drink, whose Umayyad clan had opposed the Prophet. In times and places where Shias were still in opposition or perceived themselves as persecuted—in the south of Lebanon, or in the Shah's Iran—Ashoura commemorations seethed with anger and resentment. They were political demonstrations shrouded in the history of Hossein, an expression of grievances given religious form.

Young Shias throughout the Arab and Islamic world identified intimately with Hossein's legend. Though many young middle-class Iranians still participated in Ashoura celebrations, they were less drawn to the ritual than their peers in other parts of the Shia world. Instead, they were attracted to the West and its traditions, which represented the freer lifestyle the clerical regime denied them. The government seemed to acknowledge this, and had developed a strategy in response.

Instead of dealing with young people's alienation from religious ritual only politically, by amplifying its Islamic propaganda in the media and the educational curriculum, it had recently begun to engage culturally as well. The religious murals throughout the city had been redesigned, staid Persian calligraphy replaced by edgy, modernist graphics that might have been done by a talented graffiti artist. And on the birthday of Fatemeh, the Prophet Mohammad's daughter, the authorities had launched a new commemoration campaign dubbed Fatemieh, or the Week of Remembering Fatemeh. The stylish posters and billboards across the city were clearly meant to appeal to a more savvy, less traditionally pious demographic.

In its own way, the campaign reflected a major evolution in the state's goal of entrenching Islamic piety. Back in 1988, a state radio program in Tehran had interviewed women on the street on Fatemeh's birthday. One young woman replied that she did not consider Fatemeh a role model at all, and that she identified far more with Oshin, the heroine of a popular Japanese drama series being broadcast by Iranian television at the time. The Ayatollah Khomeini was enraged, and by different versions sent the head of state radio to prison and ordered the young woman found and killed.

Compared to such times, the authorities today were handling Iranians' piety deficit altogether more moderately. A glossy ad campaign to promote Fatemeh seemed just the thing for a society in which people mourned Hossein by day and had cocktails by night.

I continued reporting and working on Shirin's book, Arash continued working, and we both waited for life to darken in our respective and shared spheres, but it did not. The hook-nosed stalker who had followed Arash never reappeared, and neither did Mr. X intrude more into my life. The harsher social restrictions everyone had feared simply never materialized. See, people murmured among themselves, the time for such repression has passed. They know they can no longer control these young people. They have learned, become wiser.

Even Shirin khanoum seemed more relaxed. Her bodyguards had disappeared, and on the clear, frosty night we finally went to dinner with her husband, her mood was almost effervescent. After dinner we took a walk along the road leading to Velenjak, in the foothills of the Alborz Mountains, discussing Iranian classical music in the moonlight and collectively agreeing that a holiday at the world's first hotel built entirely of ice should become an immediate priority. She intended the evening to help nudge my relationship with Arash toward permanence, because even for independent-minded Iranian women, marriage was viewed as fundamental to a successful life. With all the time one would eventually lose while having children, the only answer was to hurry hurry hurry (waiting only meant that your mother and mother-in-law would grow too old to help raise your kids, so that you would waste precious time dealing with babies during the prime of your career rather than at its outset).

Looking back, I view that evening with fondness but also a touch of amusement, for though none of us knew it, the question had already been sealed by a reality more immediate than career calculations or matrimonial ambitions. As I discovered later that week, I was pregnant. Had we lived in New York or Berlin or any of a number of other places, this would not have been cause for alarm. But in the Islamic Republic of Iran, one could not be unmarried and pregnant. That social category of individual simply did not exist. The crushing moral condemnation of a traditional culture aside, there were also practical considerations: if any matter arose requiring a hospital visit, my *shenasname,* or identification papers, would reflect my single status, at which point, depending on the whim of the hospital in question, this could either not be an issue, or it could be grounds for execution (or so I imagined at the time).

"I could be stoned!" I wailed, waving the test stick in the air, aware that I was being dramatic, but unable to collect myself. I told myself that the worst could not happen to me, that such cases were restricted to a handful a year, that they befell helpless girls in the provinces who found themselves at the mercy of vengeful fundamentalist judges. I reminded myself that life in Iran was premised on the culture of "as if," where everyone behaved as if the laws did not proscribe the behavior most Iranians considered natural. But all of this interior dialogue failed to soothe me, because wearing a short manteau "as if" the dress codes permitted individual choice was an entirely different matter from being pregnant, "as if" that reality did not qualify one for execution. And perhaps the crucial difference was that in matters of everyday concern, such as going to parties, dating, or dress, you still retained some measure of control, minimizing your vulnerability by carrying an extra scarf, skipping a party on an inauspicious evening, planning your dates for the middle of the week.

But as a pregnant woman, you had no such room for maneuver. You could not ensure that you would not experience spotting, as so many women do, and require a trip to the emergency room. You could not with certainty avoid a car accident, a slip on a sidewalk, or the myriad of other circumstances that might necessitate an encounter with the doctors and police, who might or might not choose to shield you from harm. As if the potential mishaps common to daily life were not enough to consider, there was also the distant worry of falling into the hands of the morality police, who had the mandate to punish men and women with lashings for drinking alcohol or attending mixed parties. While such invasions of private life had lessened dramatically during the Khatami years, there were always exceptions. One still heard of parties being raided, and the implications of this happening to a pregnant woman were altogether more grave.

My uncle worked as a doctor at one of Tehran's more prominent hospitals, and I had heard too many tales of the emergency room to take the potential for trouble lightly. In particular I recalled him telling us of a woman who had been admitted one night after being whipped by the morality police. She had told them she was pregnant, but "we'll beat the filth out of you," one of them had said. She proceeded to miscarry. I remember hearing the story vividly, for it was one of the darker episodes in my uncle's medical career. The night he returned from treating the young woman who had miscarried, he described her bloodied back, her anguished husband, in numb tones.

If the authorities were capable of such cruelty toward a pregnant woman who was married, how might they treat a pregnant woman who was not? The harsh Islamic criminal codes that governed the Iranian judiciary, the lawless, random cruelty of the morality police, ceased being abstract material that I described in news stories or spun into dramatic episodes highlighting Shirin's cases. And I ceased being an observer, a single, privileged, peripatetic social anthropologist who was protected from Iranian reality by her American passport and career. I suddenly glimpsed reality from the vantage of a nameless, faceless Iranian woman susceptible to the vagaries of her society, and my skin turned cold with anxiety. These were not the most romantic preludes to thoughts of marriage, but there were limits to living in Tehran as if it were Manhattan.

Circumstance had intervened, so I tore up the cards of the Lebanese florists and caterers, made myself a cup of Turkish coffee, and stared out in the dark night, trying to absorb how in just a matter of hours nearly everything in my life had changed. I turned the cup over and examined the grainy streaks and suggestive outlines that had appeared in the grounds, unable to decide whether they resembled foreboding clouds, or tulips.

CHAPTER 8

The Islamic Republic of Iran
Invites You to Chat About Sex

The next day, I was sitting on the floor, surrounded by books on Islam, researching the provisions of the Iranian penal code that governed premarital sex. I assumed the law unambiguously prescribed stoning, but wanted to know for sure. Arash walked into the room and surveyed the books curiously. I explained my mission.

"Of course you're not going to be stoned. Why on earth would you think that? Everyone knows only adulterers are stoned."

I wasn't so sure. But after I'd leafed through several more books, it seemed to me he was right. Only adultery was punishable by stoning, which fell under the category of punishment known as *hudud,* or mandated by God. Adultery was the only hudud punishment that didn't appear in the Koran, I discovered; it appears only in the hadith, the record of the Prophet Mohammad's life which supplies the source for much of Islamic practice as well as jurisprudence. Because the sources of hadith vary in reliability, and have been debated for centuries by Islamic scholars, this meant that the classification of stoning as hudud was an entirely open question. I also related to Arash a rather ghastly piece of information I had come across: the Iranian penal code laid out guidelines for such executions, including the types of stones that should be used. Article 104 states, "The stones should not be so large that the person dies upon being hit by one or two of them; neither should they be so small that they could not be defined as stones."

"You shouldn't spend your time on such morbid stuff," Arash said. "Why don't you look through a baby name book instead?" He began putting the books back on the shelf and told me his mother had just dropped off some rice pudding. The thick grape syrup drizzled across the top, *doshab*, tasted of molasses and wine. Together we ate it out of the bowl, leaning against the kitchen counter.

Arash's first reaction to my pregnancy had been a frustratingly detached confusion. I was thrilled and wanted him to share my excitement. But he seemed to feel responsible for my welfare, and the uncertainty of the situation made him anxious. He worried that a hospital might refuse to admit me should some complication arise. But that nervousness soon gave way to anticipation, and he began looking forward to all the fun baby decisions we had to make. Did we want to know whether it was a boy or a girl? Should we paint its room with fairies or dinosaurs? What name would we choose?

But now I was the one preoccupied with serious thoughts. No matter how much I tried, I couldn't stop thinking about the more dramatic legal dimensions of being pregnant. Although I would be in no danger of death by stoning—no stone too big, none too small—the punishment for unadulterous premarital sex still proclaimed its origins in the tribal customs of seventh-century Arabia: a hundred lashes, and possibly a year of banishment. That was the legal reality, though in practice millions of Iranian young people engaged in premarital sex with no worry more serious than whether it would be enjoyable. Although, every year or two, some judge ordered a lashing, under ordinary circumstances the law was not enforced in any meaningful way. This was just one of the many respects in which the Iranian government had grown pragmatic. It also distributed clean syringes to heroin addicts, and condoms to prostitutes and prison inmates. This was rather astonishing, given that it also punished drug use and homosexuality with anything from flogging to death.

I was not sure how concerned I needed to be for myself. Even if I ended up miscarrying or needing medical attention for some other reason, it was unlikely that the hospital staff would turn me over to the authorities. Most Iranians were not fundamentalist in that particular way; it was the government and the ayatollahs who claimed to be puritans. I had single girlfriends who had checked into the city's hospitals for abortions, which were of course legally forbidden. For the equivalent of a few hundred dollars, the doctors and nurses simply filled out paperwork for another procedure. I knew women who had undergone hymen repair on the eve of their marriage to men who thought them virgins. Gynecologists might treat you for years without asking whether you were married or single; even if they did, they would never mention that your anatomy did not match your marital status.

Of much more immediate concern than the mullahs' wrath was the disapproval of our families. Arash and I agreed that no one should know for the time being. Both our families were educated and well-traveled, the sort of people who should not be especially upset at such news. But in all likelihood, it *would* upset them. Westernized Iranians might have evolved to accommodate dating and don't-ask-don't-tell premarital sex, but pregnancy out of wedlock would almost always test the limits of their liberality. I even began to wonder whether I was not more bourgeois at heart than I had imagined. Something about my situation—well, it embarrassed me. I kept reminding myself that it was utterly normal. That if I still lived in New York it would never occur to me to feel shamefaced, and that I should not let myself be influenced by the censorious environment. Arash found my occasional bouts of mortification amusing, and reminded me of his German friends who had been nudged into marriage by unexpected pregnancies. This did not help much, though, because he was the man. If the news leaked, no one would spread hurtful rumors about him entrapping me.

There's never a good time to find yourself unmarried and pregnant in Tehran. But for me, the timing that spring was particularly rotten. The standoff between Iran and the West over the country's nuclear program dominated the world's attention, and the magazine constantly asked for reporting that explained Iran's position. Above all, the top editors wanted me to get an interview with President Ahmadinejad. They urged me to exploit my best connections, pester his press aides, and generally do everything possible to secure a meeting. Meanwhile, my mother was due to arrive from California for a month-long visit. She had timed her trip to coincide with Norouz, the Persian new year, which meant frequent lunches and dinners with relatives, just the sort of leisurely Iranian socializing that I wouldn't have time for.

The morning of her arrival, I was struggling to finish a briefing file about the nuclear issue for my *Time* colleagues, as well as a list of questions for the Ahmadinejad interview (it had not been granted yet, but often journalists were notified just hours in advance and we needed to be ready). Though I had done extensive reporting, I found it hard to explain the many contradictory and confusing aspects of Iran's quest for nuclear energy. If the Islamic system did not vest the president with real power, then how was Ahmadinejad managing to set the country's nuclear policy? What was he trying to achieve with threats of withdrawing Iran from the Nuclear Non-Proliferation Treaty? Didn't more sensible elements within the regime worry about the threat of sanctions, and if so, why weren't they intervening? Iranians seemed to support the country's right to nuclear power, but did they realize its costs? The answers lay in the convoluted reality of Iranian society and politics. While the constitution granted the president little actual power, Ahmadinejad had bypassed it by appealing to the street, fueling popular support for a crisis that the clerical establishment wished to avoid. As for his goals, my best sources told me the president was a fundamentalist on a mission, aiming to provoke a confrontation with the "enemy" that would re-instill in Iranian society the lost idealism of 1979. That was certainly plausible, but I had a hard time believing the man could harbor such dramatic ambitions. And such a project would pit him against the ruling establishment, which no longer held such revolutionary aspirations.

Most worrisome of all was how the regime shaped news coverage of the nuclear debate, denying Iranians the information they needed to judge its benefits for themselves. State television sometimes broadcast interviews with Iranians on the street, and in response to a question regarding nuclear power, a woman chirped: "Of course, every home should have it!"

"Most people don't know the difference between nuclear energy and a pizza," one of my sources told me. "If it's a question of simply having something, of course everyone will say yes, we should have it. Everyone wants to have something if they think it's free. But if they understood the costs, would they feel the same way? I doubt it."

I hurriedly put the last touches on my file, sent it off, and rushed to dress. My mother was staying with one of her relatives, who had invited half the family over for a pre-Norouz lunch. (New Year's Day itself was next week, but we were celebrating early, as many of our relatives would be leaving to spend the holiday at the Caspian Sea). It would be her first time meeting Arash, and I wanted everything to go smoothly. Truth be told, my mother is not always an easygoing person. She often fretted about me, concerned from afar about everything from my digestion to my persistent singleness. One might expect that my relationship with Arash would make her happy. He was from a good family, mature, and exceedingly bright. But my mother was prone to expressing love through worry. She would likely find some cause for anxiety. I prepared myself.

The lunch seemed to begin comfortably. My mother was thrilled to see me and was excited, as usual, about being back in Iran, which she had visited only a handful of times since immigrating to California in the 1970s. She greeted Arash warmly and ushered us to the table—we were late, and everyone had started. My male relatives asked Arash congenial questions about work, and the women fussed over him hospitably, passing him yogurt, fresh herbs, and pickles, the accompaniments to an Iranian meal. Although often reserved with new people, Arash engaged warmly with everyone, and I leaned back in relief. Shortly after lunch, having drunk tea and complimented the cook profusely, we rose to leave. We needed to visit Arash's relatives as well, and more work awaited me at home.

"They haven't been bothering you lately, have they?" my mother whispered, as she walked us to the door. She meant Mr. X and the authorities, whose presence in my life filled her with apprehension.

"No, everything has been okay lately. Maybe they're pleased I'm finally settling down." I patted Arash's arm. I wanted my mother to realize how much he grounded me, how his support helped me do my job in a difficult climate. We said goodbye and headed toward Arash's uncle's house. There we would eat the same crumbly Norouz chick-pea cookies, laugh at the same political jokes about Ahmadinejad's grooming, and endure the same questions about our matrimonial in-tentions. Norouz demanded relentless socializing from Iranians, and no one—not Mr. X or even President Ahmadinejad himself—would be spared.

The next afternoon, Arash called me into the living room to show me an ornate, leather-bound volume of Persian poetry I had never seen before. I saw that it was the *Quintet* of Nezami Ganjavi, a twelfth-century Persian poet whom we both adored. He suggested we look through it together. I was surprised, given how much we had to do that day, but was happy to procrastinate. He began to read aloud the love story of Khosrow, a seventh-century king of Persia's Sassanid em-pire, and Shirin, an Armenian Christian princess. In 1000 C.E., Fer-dowsi first told of their romance in the *Shahnameh,* the *Book of Kings,* the national epic that records in verse the history of Iran before the Islamic conquest in the seventh century. When the verses grew too intricate for my command of Farsi, Arash slowed and explained the story. He described how Khosrow, a cultured monarch with a deep appreciation for the arts, fell in love with Shirin after she appeared in one of his dreams. The story of their romance is beloved by Iranians for many reasons—the depth of the characters, the exciting intrigue that plagues them, the verses' lyrical eroticism, and the sumptuous descrip-tions of the ancient court. In Iran, everyone lives with such protago-nists of Persian literature and poetry as though they are neighbors. Even illiterate Iranians know of Khosrow and Shirin, their qualities and their struggles.

We talked about how fascinating this was, how richly Persian po-etry infused daily life. People would often explain themselves by recit-ing couplets, and even schoolchildren were intimate with the master poets of centuries past.

"Don't you think—"

"—that we should buy *Shahnameh* picture books for the baby? Definitely." Arash had an uncanny way of finishing my thoughts. Being understood so well sometimes made me squirm, but more often it reminded me of why I loved Arash so deeply. I had never thought it possible to share everything that was essential to me with one person. Like most people who live between two cultures, I had grown accustomed to constantly translating and explaining my feelings to someone who could not relate. The ability to communicate with just a few words how I felt—about anything from a line of Persian verse, a V. S. Naipaul novel, an Iranian politician, a vexing aunt, the mist over the Golden Gate Bridge, the cut of a Hezbollahi suit—was the greatest luxury I had ever known.

In the softening light of the late afternoon, Arash turned to the book's inleaf. I hadn't realized the book was a gift for me, until I bent to read the inscription. Written in elegantly composed Farsi, it ended with the proposal of marriage I had long been waiting for.

We had had informal conversations about marriage, but Arash had never formally asked me to marry him, and I had been dropping miffed hints for days. It had occurred to me that I could ask him, and I once suggested as much in a teasing text message. He responded warmly to the idea, but I never managed to gather the courage. After all, in the classic Persian wedding ceremony the bride must be asked *three times* before giving her consent; while I considered that an excessive display of coquettishness, I was not quite bold enough to ask myself.

I smoothed my fingers over the book's cool, illuminated pages, so immersed in Khosrow and Shirin's story and in my delight at what I considered the most original proposal ever, that I forgot to respond.

He cleared his throat. "So, are you going to say something?"

"Sorry. Of course, yes!"

Our first outing as an officially engaged couple was neither a romantic dinner nor an afternoon of ring shopping, as I would have hoped. Instead, Arash drove me past all the Danish pastry shops in Tehran, so I could inspect their signage. The previous month, a number of Middle Eastern governments, including Iran's, had organized protests against caricatures of the Prophet Mohammad published in a Danish newspaper. Danish pastries were extremely popular in Iran, and rumors swirled that the government (or the pastry bakers' union, depending on the version) had ordered them renamed "Roses of the Prophet Mohammad." *Time* was running a story on the cartoon controversy, and was calling for reporting from its correspondents around the world. I needed to find out whether the rumors were true.

Indeed, a black banner obscured the "Danish" in the name of the pastry shop nearest our house. I loved the pastries, the subtle layer of cream buried beneath the flaky folds, and stopped inside to buy some. I wanted to keep a box with the original Danish pastry logo, a navy blue baker with a poofy hat, as a memento of less fraught times. But the clerk who was dutifully blacking out the logo with a marker refused politely to leave my box unmarked. Most of the patrons inside seemed more amused by the renaming of the pastry than anything else. It reflected, I wrote later in my story, Iranians' remarkable reluctance to get angry about the cartoons. While many were certainly dismayed— Iranians, after all, do esteem their religion and its prophet—people were not upset enough to hold huge, violent demonstrations. The case was otherwise in many Muslim nations, where rage against the West seemed perpetually ready to combust.

Though Iranians continued to placidly eat what they continued to call Danish pastry, President Ahmadinejad seized upon the controversy to boost his image in the Arab and Islamic world. Having already called the Holocaust a "myth," his government had recently announced a conference that would "examine" historical evidence supporting it. And that month, a state newspaper run by the president's allies had called for a Holocaust cartoon competition. In response to criticism from within Iran and around the world, its publisher invoked the same freedom of expression the West did in defending the caricatures of the Prophet.

Most of the people around me reacted to all this with irritation. While many Iranians sympathized with the Palestinians and resented America's support for Israel, these sentiments were not felt as intimately as in other parts of the region. Being Persians, culturally, historically, and linguistically distinct from the Arabs of the Middle East, Iranians did not consider the Palestinian plight their own. They disapproved of their president outraging the world and sullying Iran's reputation for the sake of needling Israel and pandering to Arab public opinion. Beyond such political calculations, most Iranians found the president's anti-Semitic rhetoric distasteful. Jews had long enjoyed a more comfortable minority status in Iran than elsewhere in the Middle East; in fact, Iran still had the largest Jewish community in the region, outside Israel. Though it was both small and dwindling (Jewish leaders estimated around thirty thousand members), its presence kept Jewish Iranians involved in Iranian life. In Iran, I had never encountered the open, careless anti-Semitism that was rampant in Arab countries, where often people truly did conflate Jewishness with the most repressive aspects of Israeli Zionism.

That evening, I sat before my laptop wondering how to convince readers of this. Most people in the West probably believed Ahmadinejad's vitriolic remarks about Israel and the Holocaust reflected the opinion of a majority of Iranians. It didn't help matters that the media always mentioned Iran among the countries where people had protested the Danish cartoons. I had attended one of the so-called protests outside a European embassy. The demonstration had been small, and composed entirely of the Basiji and chadori types that journalists in Tehran referred to as "rent-a-crowd." Though the protest had been in a bustling part of the city, it never grew to include the ordinary people who worked and lived in the area. I had spoken with a few of the protesters, and had been able to tell immediately that their presence was orchestrated. The men had likely been sent by their Basij unit, and the women told to attend by either a local mosque or a state employer. One woman even whispered to me that she had voted for Rafsanjani, and that she was disappointed in Ahmadinejad's performance. Western diplomats believed the most radical factions within the regime dispatched such crowds to drive a wedge between Iran and the West, especially during critical junctures in the nuclear negotiations.

This was all far too complex to elucidate in a standard six-hundred-word news story, and I despaired of ever being able to convince Americans that Iran was not a country full of hysterical anti-Semites. Even my own best friend in California, who had read my stories for years and had a better sense of Iran than most, had asked in an e-mail that day whether it would be safe for her to come to my wedding. I had written back, "Of course it's safe! People love Americans here. You'll get marriage proposals in the street, probably." (Her problem would not be safety, but the difficulty Americans faced in securing Iranian visas. The United States granted Iranians visas so stingily, and Iran responded in kind, making the visa process for Americans enormously complicated. Most likely, my best friend would not be able to attend my wedding. I thought about this glumly as I sent off my story, reaching for what was probably my tenth Danish pastry of the day.)

Like most Islamic theocracies, the Iranian government preferred that women skip the life stage known in the West as single adulthood. Presumably this is why the legal marriage age was thirteen for girls (it was raised from nine under the Khatami presidency) and fifteen for boys. It explained the low-interest loans for wedding costs, and the use of compulsory marriage as one punishment for young couples caught dating on more than three occasions. These measures were designed to ensure that Iranian women conducted their lives in accordance with strict Islamic custom, by which a woman existed only as an appendage to a man—as a daughter, wife, or mother—and that any frivolous interval during which she occupied none of these roles should be hurried through with great haste. Given these attitudes and the laws that reflected them, I assumed that getting married in Iran would be about as complicated as buying a melon.

But when Arash contacted a local marriage notary—like many, this one was a cleric—to check what sort of paperwork we would need, he learned that, at least for us, a the process would be inordinately complicated. "But she's twenty-nine!" Arash protested.

I was eavesdropping on the speaker-phone. "I don't care if she's twenty or a hundred," the mullah snapped, "if she's a *dooshizeh* [a previously unmarried woman] then she needs either her father's permission or his death certificate." I had spent years reporting on women's inferior legal status in the Islamic Republic, and could repeat by rote the most egregious examples: their testimony as witnesses counted for only a third of a man's; their families were entitled to only half the compensation, or "blood money," that the families of male victims received; their custody rights over children were partial at best. But somehow I had missed this particular instance of discrimination.

My father, who lived in northern California, belonged to that category of émigré who considered a trip to Iran only slightly less distasteful than a vacation in North Korea. He was born in Mashad, but had studied engineering at U.C. Berkeley in the 1960s and took part in the Iranian student movement abroad that pushed for democratic reform of the Shah's government. Later he returned to Iran, believing his training as an industrial engineer could help modernize the country, and devoted himself to building construction equipment. Although he and my mother had already moved to California by 1979, they considered their relocation temporary. The revolution permanently canceled any hope of one day returning to Iran, and my father felt fiercely betrayed. He had dedicated years of his life to a practical discipline he did not enjoy, for the sole purpose of serving his country's most urgent needs. Believing that Iran needed democracy as badly as it needed modern freeways and bulldozers, he had invested years in student politics. What became the mullahs' revolution made a mockery of his life, with its return to Shia ideals, with Khomeini's pronouncement that the western-educated should simply go. My father's disappointment infused the rest of his personality; in the loneliness of his exile, he began despising Iran. He nurtured a keen hatred not only for its present regime, but also for its culture and its Islamic traditions. He taught me to revere the *Shahnameh* for its celebration of Persian ideals before the arrival of Islam (his car's vanity plate was RAKSH, for the epic's mythical steed). And he instilled in me a love for Persian gardens. But he always told me to be wary of Iran the actual existing nation, run by mullahs. At the time I considered this very normal, since nearly all educated male Iranians of the diaspora felt this way, just as they were all addicted to their monthly poker games and political debates.

Save for one trip in the early 1980s, he had stayed away for nearly three decades, declining to appear at his father's deathbed or to attend either parent's funeral. Convincing him to fly to Iran on such short notice would be virtually impossible. "Ask him if my mother's signature will do," I whispered to Arash, who shook his head. Mothers played little role in the legal lives of their children. Their names did not appear on children's identification forms and passports, and their permission was irrelevant in all the instances where a parent's consent is required (foreign travel, contracts for ownership of land or other property). Although my mother, the woman who raised me single-handedly for eighteen years, was actually in Tehran, her signature would be as meaningful to my marriage contract as a doodle.

The only option, the mullah explained, would be to secure a power of attorney from my father authorizing a male relative to sign on his behalf. Once he had such a document in hand, he assured us, he could marry us within a few hours. This solution seemed reasonable enough, until I investigated the website of the Islamic Republic's interests section in Washington, housed within the Pakistani embassy. (Because the United States and Iran had severed diplomatic ties in 1979, Iran lacked a formal presence of its own.) I found that my father was not eligible to sign a power of attorney. To be eligible, he would need to apply for a newly instituted national identity card. (This "national" card, introduced with much fanfare and at great expense, was, unfathomably, decorated with Arabic/Islamic graphics—a reminder that the Islamic Republic identified more with its Islamic character than with its distinct Iranianness.) As it happened, few official institutions accepted the card as identification, and the government was constantly admonishing its own bodies through state media to recognize it.

It had taken me eight months to receive my national ID; I could only imagine how long the process would take by mail in the United States. That step aside, the power-of-attorney paperwork itself involved a daunting number of procedures that surely could not be completed in under a month's time. The endless downloadable forms blurred before my eyes, and I put my head down on the laptop in frustration.

Arash twisted my ponytail about gently, pulling my shoulders back up from the keyboard, grimy from coffee spills and cigarette ash, and boiled water to make us tea. During such fretful times we consumed cup after cup, quiet except for the occasional sound of my front teeth biting off a corner of a small chunk of sugar cube. In the Iranian style, one sipped tea through the sugar, allowing the granules to dissolve on the tongue, their sweetness mingling with the slightly bitter brew.

"I have an idea," Arash said. "Let's get married somewhere abroad, and bring the documents back with us." That way we would have proof of marriage, its date still within the bounds of what might be a reasonable period of conception (I was only about six weeks pregnant). We could then take our time having it all officially translated in Tehran.

"That's brilliant!" I clapped my hands in excitement, relieved to have found a solution, and privately pleased, though I didn't say it, at the chance of restoring some allure to our forthcoming union, which had devolved into a drab, bureaucratic muddle. "I propose Monaco."

"Monaco?" Arash snorted. "Why not Liechtenstein? If we're going for miniature states, let's at least pick one that's German-speaking."

"Liechtenstein doesn't connote anything to me," I said. He left me to stay up late researching the regulations of evocative, cozy European nations, distracted only by the occasional wet-nosed nudging of our beagle London, signaling his need to relieve himself on the balcony. His friend and ally Geneva, the St. Bernard puppy, was not yet housebroken and frequently rose from a seated position to reveal a veritable lake of urine. At three months, she was already a very large puppy, and would soon need to join Inuk the husky, who lived most of the year in Lavasan, at Arash's family house. By around one A.M. it became clear that most western countries simply do not allow non-resident foreign nationals to traipse in and secure marriage licenses. The exceptions were Cyprus and Malta, both of which seemed unappealing to me for no particular reason. These prospects sent me shuffling to bed dejected, kicking the dogs' chew toys off the rug along the way.

Arash was brushing his teeth the next morning when I announced the results of my search. "I know we can't really be choosy. But isn't there something seedy about a Maltese marriage?" By this point it was becoming obvious that I was obsessing over the perfect destination as a way to avoid thinking about what might happen if something went wrong—if I ended up miscarrying, for example, or if someone discovered I was pregnant before I could produce proof of my married status. Both of us participated in this diversion. Before leaving for work, Arash darted back into the room: "Nepal. Nepal is perfect. Research."

I was weighing whether the current unrest in Kathmandu was severe enough to disrupt the authorities' usual marriage procedures when the phone rang. It was my father's brother, my uncle Shahrokh, calling to invite us to a dinner. I accepted quickly, then launched into a diatribe about how the regime's paternalism was forcing us to consider the most inconvenient, far-flung options for a simple legal procedure. Most of our relatives had tactfully declined to ask why we were in such a rush, why we couldn't simply wait for the months it would take to either persuade my father to come to Iran, or wade through the various bureaucratic requirements that would enable someone to sign in his stead.

"You know, now that you mention it, I think I actually *have* a power of attorney from your father," my uncle said on the phone. "Let me go to the office and see if it's still in my files." Shahrokh was the only sibling on my father's side to remain in Tehran after the revolution, and this had made him responsible for the thankless task of pursuing family assets appropriated after the revolution. This had required a properly notarized and processed power of attorney that, if still valid, might be the answer to our plight.

That evening Shahrokh stopped by our apartment with a copy of the document, pleased to be facilitating our matrimony and thus our happiness, but equally glad to be encouraging the production of more nieces and nephews (little did he know) to frolic about the vineyard in Sonoma he was planning to build when he retired. Perhaps out of discretion he refrained from asking the obvious question: why we were suffering through this maddening, woman-hostile bureaucracy, when we could have flown to San Francisco and gotten married at city hall. The whole procedure would have taken an afternoon, we wouldn't have needed anyone's permission, and I wouldn't have needed to anticipate polygamy clauses in the contract. In short, I would have the assurance of being married under a legal system that functioned as it was meant to, justly, and that safeguarded my basic rights. But the truth is, all justice systems, not just those of dictatorships such as Iran, are vulnerable to failure. Arash had experienced that firsthand in a California divorce court two years prior, and he was reluctant to expose himself once again to the vagaries of American justice.

He had told me when we first met how acrimoniously his four-year marriage to an Iranian-American—someone not unlike me—had ended. They had been married in California, and their major conflict in the divorce had centered on custody of their young daughter, but soon money emerged as an issue as well. As the stakes grew higher, the divorce devolved into a family feud, for Arash and his ex were cousins. The court ended up giving full custody to his ex-wife, a judgment I found both unfair and suspect once I read the court documents. Arash's experience jarred me deeply; I had, perhaps naïvely, assumed that an American court would never act so unjustly, at least not in personal matters like divorce. I understood why Arash was reluctant to enter into another American marriage, and I did not press the point.

Although being married in Iran made me uneasy, two factors helped me agree to the idea: We would eventually be able to register our marriage in Germany, which meant that we would have recourse to the laws of a modern European democracy. Also, in recent years the Iranian government had revised some of its most discriminatory child custody codes. In practice, Iranian women still encountered serious obstacles in the courtroom, but matters had improved considerably. These realities combined to keep us on our present course, despite its manifold irritations and absurdities. On one or two occasions, when the complications piled upon on each other, I felt momentarily disoriented, wondering how I had come to be in such a situation, in such a place. But I told myself that the future is always uncertain, that the best marriages in the most civilized places can devolve into mercenary duels, and that no justice system functions with impeccable fairness.

Since Shahrokh never asked why we had not considered the California option, the evening passed without any reference to this sad history. We drank tea and discussed relatives, and my uncle left for a dinner party. Assured that we now possessed all that was required to officiate our marriage, we ordered pizza and settled in to watch a DVD of *Desperate Housewives,* which although presumably banned was circulating around half the city with Farsi subtitles. Iranians, like people the world over, were titillated by mystery, and being prone culturally to uphold warm social manners even when with people they disliked, identified with the malaise of the suburban drama.

The next morning we arrived at the marriage health bureau, prepared to undergo tests to prove that we were not carriers of Mediterranean hemophilia (a blood disorder that afflicts some Iranians) or substance abusers. Cartoonish antidrug posters covered the walls, part of the government's growing effort to address the country's heroin problem, the world's largest according to the U.N. World Drug Report. The four other couples waiting comprised disparate social types, from clearly pious (chador/beard) to secular and middle-class (dyed blond fringe/body builder). An older, plump woman was there with a much younger, feckless-looking man—the sort of pair that would strike one as a green card match, were this a country where legal residency was in demand. Only those compelled by irregular circumstances, it seemed, would be getting married over the Norouz holiday.

After completing our tests, we were directed to wait for the mandatory premarital class. The term suggested something like couples counseling—instruction in communication skills, or perhaps on what to do when the romance faded. But I could not imagine why that would require couples to be separated by sex. I sat down in the women's classroom, where the instructor launched into a description of the anatomy of the female reproductive system, not unlike the weekly sex education class that I had giggled through in the fifth grade. She waved about a blue condom, explaining the various forms of birth control available to brides-to-be. From a drawer she removed a heap of birth control pills; "Pay special attention to these," she said, holding up a strip of tiny pills for what she called "urgent contraception." I realized she was referring to emergency contraceptive pills, sometimes called morning-after pills, which can prevent pregnancy after unprotected sex. All five of the women she addressed, including the chadori and a slim young woman wearing a nautical headscarf, took notes attentively. How impressive, I thought, that the Islamic Republic of Iran promoted the use of controversial up-to-date contraception.

For all the state's conservatism, it ran an extraordinary family planning program. Although in the early days of the revolution the Ayatollah Khomeini had encouraged Iranians to procreate with abandon in order to boost the numbers of soldiers available to fight in the war against Iraq, the regime had reversed the policy in the early 1990s as part of its postwar reconstruction drive. You could buy birth control pills over the counter for the price of a candy bar, and more than one of my Iranian-American girlfriends had me ship their yearly supplies to them in New York or California.

The instructor finished the birth control lecture with an admonition: "It's very important that you don't get pregnant too quickly. You should wait at least two or three years and see whether your marriage is going to work out. If you don't have a child, you can easily get divorced after a couple of years and reenter society with your prospects intact. That's not going to be the case for a divorced, single parent."

What she said was harsh, but true. Most single mothers faced tremendous challenges in Iran. From the lack of affordable day care to the impossibility of living on one meager salary, the difficulties were steep enough to keep the majority of women in bad marriages from seeking legal release. A divorced woman unburdened with a child, however, would fare well in comparison. With the stigma of divorce receding, she could easily remarry, provided she lowered her standards a shade.

The instructor sat down behind the wooden desk, adjusted her caramel-colored *maghnaeh,* a hoodlike headscarf, and proceeded to impart the most surprising lesson of all. "Ladies," she began, "you must also derive pleasure from sexual interactions. This is natural and nothing to feel ashamed of. Don't be embarrassed to ask your husband to be patient. If he does not know, you can tell him: women's bodies are different. They are built differently, and this matters. Why? Because for women, arousal takes longer."

Since when had the government concerned itself with women's sexual fulfillment? Since when had it, in fact, acknowledged that women had sexual desires at all? This seemed rather at odds with the authorities' general hostility toward pleasure and the flesh. Perhaps alarmed by the rising rates of divorce and of urban prostitution, the state had decided to shore up the institution of marriage rather than simply make it a yoke held in place by repressive divorce laws.

"Does anyone have any questions?" the instructor asked.

The woman in the nautical scarf raised her hand. "I've heard that you can pick up bacteria by giving a man a blow job. Is that true?" She spoke self-assuredly, with no hint of embarrassment.

"If both you and your partner have tested negative for STDs, then no. But if you haven't been tested, you should use a condom."

Two other women asked similar questions about sexual health. I found it striking how comfortable everyone seemed with the frank discussion, as though at a Planned Parenthood session in San Francisco. At the class's end, the instructor passed out bags filled with starter packs of several types of contraceptive pills. She then directed us to the nurse's office next door for the final check on our forms, a tetanus shot administered by a woman in a white coat. The other women pulled up their sleeves, but I fiddled with mine, stalling until they had all gotten their shots. When they had gone, I explained that I was pregnant and would prefer to skip the live vaccine. I was afraid any other objection would be waved aside, and something in the nurse's kindly manner as she administered the shots gave me confi-

dence. "That's fine," she said, smiling broadly. "Congratulations."
She initialed the box, and sent me on my way.

Once reunited with Arash, I discovered that his class had learned
about contraception by watching an instructional cartoon. After the
film, the instructor counseled the class to regard sex more holistically.
"He told us that for women, sex is an emotional experience. That we
shouldn't just roll over and go to sleep when it's over."

"Really!"

"There's more. He said that if we were more attentive afterward,
our marriage would improve outside the bedroom."

We drove through the overcast morning to the notary's office, to
announce that our paperwork was complete and to set a time for the
proceedings. The office was situated on the south side of Zardosht
Street, a thoroughfare in central Tehran dotted with medical clinics
and florists. We climbed up a narrow staircase, and Arash opened the
frosted glass door, only to have the handle inauspiciously come off in
his hand. We bent over trying to fix it, whispering, and I couldn't escape the feeling that we'd been cast in an absurdist comedy. The handle hastily affixed, we entered a long hallway lined with shoes and
slippers. That shoes were not permitted inside signaled a mosque atmosphere, natural enough given this was a mullah-notary, but a
minor crisis for me: I had not imagined needing to remove my boots,
and had paired a pink argyle sock with a plain black one. Hoping no
one would look below my knees, I stepped onto the machine-woven
Persian rugs, which smelled like two decades' worth of unwashed
feet. Inside, hanging fluorescent lights cast a sickly corporate glow on
white stucco walls covered with mirror mosaics of palm trees. The
place had the air of a kabob palace in Fallujah.

The notary, whom we would call Hajj Agha as is customary,
greeted us warmly and introduced us to his son Mohammad. A series
of photographs—prison mug shots of Hajj Agha—formed a column
beside the palm tree mosaic. In these, Hajj Agha's head was shaved,
his expression was scowling, and he looked about forty pounds thin-
ner than the avuncular and portly man before us. Wondering why our
marriage officiant had a prison record and especially why he used that

fact in his décor, I nudged Arash to look up at the photos. He nodded and turned his attention back to Mohammad, a young, wily mullah-notary in training who acted as his father's assistant.

"He was a political prisoner under the Shah," Arash said, under his breath. "Look at the books." The bookshelf behind the desk was lined with numerous copies of three books, all authored by Hajj Agha. "Thirty Years of Resistance, Imprisoned and Tortured on 25 Occasions" read a line of sticker-tape underneath the mug shot on one cover. I leafed through the index, learning that in his years as a young, radical mullah organizing against the Shah's unpopular regime, Hajj Agha had kept company with Iran's foremost revolutionaries, holding court at the legendary Hosseiniyeh Ershad, a religious center that was a platform for the famous ayatollahs of the day. "See, he's practically a celebrity," Arash said.

Hajj Agha riffled through our papers, scanning the faded power of attorney through a pair of thick-rimmed black glasses. "This power of attorney bestows the right of signature over matters of finance and property only," he said, the folds of his turban precise and creamy white, as if pressed from an icing tube. "There is a separate power of attorney for marriage, and that is what you need to bring me."

My hands began to flutter, tucking imaginary strands of hair under my headscarf. I wondered whether I would have been able to talk my way through this were I able to speak more refined, native Farsi, or whether the situation required a man-to-man resolution. I suspected the latter, as somehow Hajj Agha did not strike me as the sort of man accustomed to bargaining with women over their futures. Arash settled back into the loudly patterned sofa, arranging his limbs in the relaxed pose that I knew meant he was preparing to negotiate; he would unfurl long, ornate sentences of Farsi that bore little relevance to the matter at hand yet that indirectly conveyed both the urgency of our position, and how far we were prepared to go to remedy it. He excelled at handling these moments, which so frequently occurred in Tehran—situations that seemed intractable owing to a rigid regulation or someone's fixed position, but that he managed to maneuver around with flattery and creative problem solving. It was a matter of speaking their language, he always said, though he was German enough at heart that the hours involved, the tea drinking, and the sycophantism incensed him.

Hajj Agha listened patiently, but in the end it fell to his son, Mohammad, so thoroughly a child of the Islamic Republic, a shifty composite of piety and cunning, to suggest a solution. We would produce a faxed, handwritten letter from my father (they would provide the text) authorizing our marriage, and my uncle would be permitted to sign in his stead, on condition that within sixty days my father would present himself in Tehran and sign the official certificate himself. I inserted myself into the conversation, explaining that my mother was in Tehran and would be happy to attend and vouch for my father's permission. Given the irregularity of our situation, I felt it couldn't hurt to bring along physical proof of parental blessing, to ward off any sense that ours was an illicit love match made without their approval. I didn't imagine Hajj Agha needed to know that my parents were divorced. "That's a very good idea, my daughter, it would be helpful to have her here," he said.

The only problem was that for the next two days we couldn't find my father. I dimly recalled some mention of a backpacking trip, but couldn't be sure, and in my irritation imagined him reclining in a meadow high in the Sierra Nevada, smoking and reading a John le Carré novel. I phoned my mother to tell her we would be signing the *aghd* contract any day now.

"But it's Moharram!" she said. It is in the month of Moharram that Shias commemorate the martyrdom of Imam Hossein. My mother had rediscovered her devotion to Islam in recent years, a shift for which I credited geography. She lived in Carmel, far from any sizable Muslim population and from the reality of life in a theocracy. Thus removed, she could freely enjoy the faith's finer spiritual qualities without the unpleasant dogmatism of its mullahs and other stern adherents. The decades she had spent straying from the faith had distanced her from the fine points of observance, so now she tended to overdo her fidelity. Islam, its Shia and Sunni sects alike, permitted marriage on any day of the year. It could perhaps be considered *in-*

auspicious to marry during a period of mourning, but given that we were compelled by circumstances, and given that the idea didn't offend Hajj Agha, I felt she should relax her position.

"The mullah doesn't have a problem with it, why should you?" I demanded. "Do I need to start calling you Mesbah-Yazdi again?" In recent years, when my mother's piety bordered on the reactionary, I had begun teasingly calling her by the name of a famously fundamentalist ayatollah, Ahmadinejad's main clerical champion.

Unmoved, she wailed about how our timing disrespected her values, how no one who was *adam-hesabi,* good people, got married at the notary anyway, how there should be at least some pretense made of *khaste-gari.* This custom, by which the groom's parents formally visit the bride's family to ask for her hand in marriage, was no longer as widespread as in her youth. Many couples knew each other too well before marriage for such formalities, and our ages and independence made the idea quite preposterous.

I reminded her that it was also Norouz, a celebration of joy and rebirth, and that she could focus on this instead. I told her that a great deal had changed since the Iran of her era, and that her expectations were now passé. I recounted the case of my cousin Ghazal, who was married to the nephew of Jalal Al-e Ahmad, a famous social critic of the 1950s and 1960s who had devised the term "westoxification" to describe how Iranians had abandoned their traditions in their pursuit of modernity. You couldn't find a family more traditionally religious than the Al-e Ahmads, but Ghazal and Ahmad had not involved their parents in any *khaste-gari.*

It frustrated me that, in many ways, my mother remained more conservative than the parents of my friends and relatives in Tehran. The Iranian diaspora community in the West had remained frozen in the mind-set of the 1960s and 1970s, the era of its emigration. My mother, for example, and the mothers of many of my Iranian-American friends, had frowned on our having boyfriends in high school; they thought their daughters would be corrupted by such forward American ways. But most middle-class moms in Tehran, nudged by the country's changing social mores into revising their expectations of young people's behavior, accepted boyfriends as a fact of life. How ironic, I thought, that the Iranian women who immigrated to the West and benefited from its education and its freedoms clung to their paternalistic traditions, while those who'd stayed in Iran, under the thumb of the Islamic Republic, accommodated to the ways of the younger generation.

In today's Iran, the signing and reading of the *aghd,* the marriage contract, was a procedural matter and it often took place weeks or months ahead of the actual ceremony and celebration. Many couples needed the extra time to find and furnish an apartment; others were waiting for the groom to finish his military service.

Characteristically skeptical of all my pronouncements, claiming I reflected only the views of an alien, westernized fringe of Iranian society, my mother remained perturbed, opposing. In her politics, she was an American liberal, reflexively skeptical of what the U.S. media reported about Iran. Like many Iranian-Americans, she believed that reporters like me should not write openly about Iranian young people's liberal lifestyles, their openness to the West, and in particular, how their despair over the slow pace of change sometimes led them to hope for a U.S. intervention that would unseat the mullahs. Such coverage, they believed, would be used by hawks in the Bush administration who, in seeking a military confrontation with Iran, argued that in the event of a U.S. attack Iranians would rise up against the regime (this was a delusion of course, Iranians were staunch nationalists and would always side with their own rulers, however abhorrent). I understood this view, but disagreed with it entirely. You could not ignore the legitimate frustration of millions of young people for the sake of thwarting hawks in Washington who might seek to exploit it.

But beneath the leftist contours of my mother's personality, there also lurked an Iranian matron's bourgeois regard for propriety, and a Shia Muslim's enthusiasm for sacrificing sheep on religious occasions. Often it seemed to me that I couldn't locate my mother amid the swirl of her values; they were unworkable, too disparate to be contained in one person. The enmity between Iran and America saddened her; poverty in Africa saddened her; the class stratification wrought by first-world capitalism saddened her. The Germans have a term for the condition of perpetual sorrow over the state of the world: Welt-schmerz. My mother was the queen of Weltschmerz. And, once fixed in a particular position, she refused to budge.

I told her about all my middle-class friends who had married with-out *khaste-gari*. In exasperation I finally said that if Jalal Al-e Ah-mad's nephew didn't represent Iranian society sufficiently for her tastes, I didn't know who would. In the end, I abandoned my case, because it occurred to me we weren't really fighting about contemporary mari-tal mores or the etiquette of the religious calendar. My mother often resorted to battles over abstract values when she wished to avoid thinking about matters that upset her. Once I phoned her from the roof of my hotel in Baghdad, just weeks after the U.S. invasion, be-cause the cracking sound of sniper fire scared me. It likely scared her, too, but rather than console me she rebuked me for covering the war for *Time* instead of for *The Progressive*. What really concerned her now was my marriage itself, the marriage of her only child to a man who lived in Iran and thus posed a threat to any hope of my eventual return to northern California. I presumed that, like her opposition to my reporting and living in dangerous places, this, too, would pass.

CHAPTER 9

Honeymoon in Tehran

Finally, having cleared the many religio-bureaucratic obstacles in our way, we were ready to get married. My father had returned from the mountains and faxed us his permission. My mother still demanded we wait for a propitious date on Islam's calendar, but I assumed her dissent was mostly for show. Meanwhile, Hajj Agha had disappeared. I tried phoning him, but his mobile phone was either off or out of range. Eventually, sometime after nine in the evening, Arash got through, but the line crackled with so much static he could barely make out what Hajj Agha was saying.

"You're where? Khorramshahr?" Khorramshahr! What was our mullah doing hundreds of miles away, in a war-ravaged city on the border with Iraq? We called Mohammad for an explanation. He said his father was on his annual sermon tour of southern Iran. Why could he not be in Tehran like most proper mullahs, busy attending passion play reenactments with their families and enjoying the stew of lamb, split peas, and dried lime that was traditional Moharram fare? Hajj Agha perhaps still subscribed to the Ayatollah Khomeini's view that "every day is Karbala" and believed the holiday was a time to rekindle Iranians' Shia zeal. He would not return for at least a week.

"But I don't think Hajj Agha would have performed your *aghd* anyway," Mohammad said. "This is not really our line of work." It turned out Hajj Agha had been planning all along to refer us to another notary, one who was not above entering a slightly irregular marriage into his oversize book of contracts. By assisting us in this way, he was both doing us a good turn and securing for himself a sizable commission. Mohammad told us he knew a mullah in Khorasan Square, a grimy neighborhood in south Tehran, who would be pleased to perform our *aghd*. We phoned my uncle to apprise him of the change of plans, but he refused to venture anywhere south of central Tehran. "You will do yourselves no good starting your life together in such an area," he sniffed with a patrician finality.

This did not deter the resourceful Mohammad, who summoned the backup mullah uptown, reminding us that this would require more generous *shirini*, the literal term for sweets that was also a euphemism for a bribe. We arranged for everyone to assemble at the office of Hajj Agha's notary at four o'clock.

I phoned my mother two hours in advance to give her directions, assuming that her protests were mainly melodrama and that she would show up when she was supposed to. But she refused to come to the phone, conveying through auntie emissaries that she was napping. I knew she was not asleep. Probably she was taking revenge, in hopes that her absence would disrupt proceedings whose timing she considered a slight. I wanted to hide my exasperation from Arash, preferring him to believe that my mother's pleasure at our marriage was undiluted, but he could hear me exclaiming ("Napping? That's the most ridiculous thing I've ever heard. You should be ashamed to repeat it. Tell her to come to the phone *now*"), and later, as we drove through the eerily empty streets, I disclosed that my mother would not be joining us. He saw how upset I was, and patted my hand. "Don't worry about it. She'll come around eventually."

On the way we stopped in Qeytarieh to pick up Arash's best friend, Houshang, who would serve as his witness. He jumped into the backseat, observed our tense expressions, and quickly adjusted the iPod to a Manu Chao album. "Smile, please, you're both far too solemn." He offered us some of the *noghl* (sugar-coated almond slivers) he had brought along, and then recounted the details of his niece's job interview earlier that day with Iran Air, the state carrier. Many government-owned institutions still asked religious-ideological questions during interviews, as a way to screen out the impious or hypocrisy-averse. The interviewer asked Houshang's niece for the average length in meters of a *kafan,* the shroud used for Islamic burial. She told him that an airline should be asking questions about safety and first aid, not burial attire, and walked out.

At the age of forty-seven, Houshang devoted most of his affections to his nieces and nephews. He had vowed never to marry, squirmed out of any relationship that lasted longer than a month, and regarded us, on the brink of permanent entrapment, with affectionate sympathy. His *garçonnière* loft studio, embedded in a particularly conservative corner of Qeytarieh (a neighborhood near our own), could not accommodate a wife, and that was as he had designed it, along with the rest of his life. When I first met him and heard him hold forth on the incompatibility of marriage with a life devoted to Art, I assumed it was the sort of cocktail chatter one could expect from any artsy photographer-filmmaker wearing a lime-green Lacoste polo shirt and drinking mango-infused *aragh*. Freelance art photography was a favorite path of bored, affluent twenty- and thirtysomething socialites; once a year they held gallery parties to exhibit their work, and they affected "careers" that did not require them to rise before noon. But Houshang, though fond of grand pronouncements, was not a north Tehran dilettante. The males among that company had either been shipped off to the West during the war with Iraq, or managed to buy exemptions from military service. Houshang had enjoyed no such privilege; he was, in fact, a *shahid-e zendeh,* literally a living martyr, an appellation bestowed to war veterans who had survived the gravest dangers.

Sometimes when he told stories of the war—how soldiers harassed scorpions into biting them, for instance, because a scorpion bite earned two weeks' automatic furlough; how during long sieges he and his troop mates subsisted on the leaves of onions they had planted earlier—I could not quite believe such hardship had been endured by the urbane, Luis Buñuel–obsessed man before me. I wondered whether Houshang's time at the front had made him wary of emotional entanglements, but he never let on, even to his closest friends, always deflecting intimate questions with glib asides, claiming he could not be bothered to drink tea and make provincial small talk with a wife's relatives.

My uncle Shahrokh called to say he was just a few blocks away, and by the appointed hour we were all in place save my mother, whose absence no one remarked upon. The backup mullah arrived ten minutes late, dressed in a frayed, mustard-colored robe that cloaked his generous proportions. He addressed us in the nasal tones of a lifelong opium addict, and oozed into Hajj Agha's chair, listlessly playing with his prayer beads. His assistant, an energetic man with wiry black hair, took charge of our papers.

"You aren't related to Mr. Ali Moaveni, are you?" he asked my uncle.

"Yes, he was my father. He passed away three years ago."

"May God bless his soul, and what an honor this is indeed, this opportunity to be of service to his kin!" The assistant beamed, examining us all with new respect. Arash, Houshang, and I exchanged amused glances. We often said that in a Tehran of fourteen million, Iranians were linked by only two degrees of separation.

I took it as an auspicious omen that in this overflowing city someone who remembered my grandfather Pedar Joon would by chance preside over our marriage. In 2000, during his final days, when the pace of his daily walk down Villa Street had slowed and he grew forgetful, my elderly grandfather's dying wish had been to see me married. To advance that goal, he had pressed me to enroll in classes at the University of Tehran ("no place like college to find a husband"), and, when I showed no signs of progress, to list the qualities I required in a mate, so that he could more effectively take up the search on my behalf. At first I had taken the list as a joke, but during a summer trip to the Caspian he demanded it in earnest, pausing near the spot where I read Rohinton Mistry's novel *A Fine Balance* in the shade of a palm tree, shaking his wooden cane with a sly smile. "You are neither fat nor ugly, and both your family and career are distinguished," he often repeated, baffled by my spinsterhood.

The assistant briskly placed a marriage contract before us and asked which provisions he should amend. A generic contract leaves space for a husband to accord his wife certain privileges which the law enabled Iranian women to secure from their husbands: typically the right to divorce under particular terms, to travel out of the country alone, to acquire a passport. The basic contract, I noted, granted me the right to petition for divorce only under certain conditions, including "the husband's committing bigamy without his wife's consent, or unfair treatment of his wives"; "the husband's involvement in harmful addictions that would make life difficult for the wife"; and, curiously, "engaging in occupations found inconsistent with the wife's prestige." The juxtaposition of such abstruse language, alongside notations such as "the husband has no other wife," struck me as particularly Islamic Republic: at once prudish and indecent.

We spelled out that I would retain the right to a divorce based on any condition of my choosing, and to travel freely "without any preventions." Though these provisos should have been legally binding, they fell far short of actually guaranteeing what they implied. To renew my passport I would still need to acquire from Arash a separate, notarized document, and if I sought a divorce, I could easily be entangled in a court battle lasting years. Though I knew that by signing this contract I would be taking an immense risk—essentially gambling that Arash would never, in the throes of even the ugliest discord or divorce, choose to revoke the rights he had granted me—I felt no apprehension.

Female Iranian veterans of acrimonious divorce would likely consider my decision foolish; every family had instances of soured marriages in which the secular, civilized husband used the country's discriminatory laws to exact revenge or harass a wife. But for every such case, there was also an Iranian wife who had invoked the laws to her own advantage. My mother's cousin, married to a woman who had turned out to be a greedy mercenary, had been barred from leaving the country for five years. The wife had invoked her claim to her enormous *mehriyeh*, which is something between a prenup and alimony—a contractual pledge of money or property made by the groom to his bride; she can seek to collect on the pledge in the event of divorce. Men who can't pay can be punished with prison time or travel bans. My mother's cousin, unable to produce the thousands of gold coins foolishly pledged as *mehriyeh,* now suffered the consequences.

Meanwhile, Backup Mullah lazily turned his oversize head toward Houshang. "So what is it that you do?" he drawled.

"I'm a filmmaker," Houshang replied.

"I hope you don't make those sexy films . . . you know, the ones that people manage to get their hands on and watch." This question, which did little for the dignity of the proceeding, was the only thing I recall him saying, apart from the reading of the Koranic sura of marriage.

"No, no," Houshang said. "I produce documentary films about classical musicians."

Backup Mullah raised a doubtful eyebrow, as though this were scarcely better.

"And now," said the assistant, "we arrive at the question of *mehriyeh.*" The most contested line of any Iranian marriage contract, the *mehriyeh* has roots in something like a concept of back wages, for work performed while married. Today its legal role has become somewhat muddled, as civil law theoretically grants women the right to petition for assets accrued during the marriage. *Mehriyeh* is legally adjusted for inflation—a significant battle won by female legislators—and arguments over its size are the undoing of many affianced couples. For some *bazaari* families, the size of the *mehriyeh* reflects the status of the bride's family. A showily enormous *mehriyeh*—the bride's weight in gold, or gold coins in an amount equal to her birth year—is especially prized by nouveaux riches families, irrespective of whether the groom would ever actually be able to produce such sums. The engagement of two of our close friends was on the verge of collapse over *mehriyeh,* as she demanded "at least a house," and he insisted that the custom was vulgar and unfit for two modern, educated individuals.

In my mother's generation, when the binds of tradition began to loosen and urban middle-class women began working and choosing their own husbands, modern couples rejected the notion of *mehriyeh*

altogether. They would write something symbolic into the contract—
my mother chose a Koran and a string of sugar crystals—to signify
that their marriage was a love match, that they refused to measure the
bride's worth in grams of gold.

Those involved in preparing the contract hoped for a substantial
mehriyeh, as this would inevitably trickle down into a heftier *shirini.*
I had forgotten the symbolic number Arash and I had agreed upon,
and whispered for him to remind me. He held up seven fingers.

"Seven gold coins," I said. The equivalent of about a thousand
dollars.

The assistant was visibly disappointed. Perhaps he was concerned
that Arash hoped to marry Mr. Ali Moaveni's granddaughter on the
cheap. He looked to my uncle for approval. My uncle nodded, and
the assistant scribbled furiously. Backup Mullah was apparently
asleep, his eyes half closed. I crossed my arms over the slim hunter-
green dress I was wearing over dark jeans. I didn't consider this our
wedding, and had dressed casually to underscore the point.

The assistant opened the Koran to a particular page, placing it in
our laps. He nudged Backup Mullah awake to read the appropriate
sura. The mullah intoned the Arabic words with such a heavy Farsi
accent that I could scarcely understand them. When he was done we
were officially married. Mohammad passed around a bowl of chocolates, while my uncle opened his wallet, distributing *shirini* to those
assembled.

In the end, we paid three times more than the standard fee (about
five hundred dollars), to enable a man of God who indulged in opium
to overlook our flawed paperwork and marry us anyway. Though we
held a Koran on our knees and were wed by one of its prayers, the
shirini extracted lent the proceeding a dodgy air. We emerged feeling
as though we had just sold the title to a stolen car or hoodwinked
someone into buying a faulty apartment. If we had bribed ourselves
into wedlock anywhere besides Iran, I would have felt quite upset.
But here, bribery was a fact of daily life. Even everyday matters—
from a new passport to a postal address change—often required the
discreet exchange of a few notes; otherwise, your name was likely to

be misspelled, and the process would take months. Our ceremony, what I considered our actual wedding, would remain untouched by hypocrisy.

As we drove home, I turned my thoughts to my bridal bouquet, to whether our cake would be chocolate or marzipan, and to the candles that would line the garden. Outside, the sunset cast pink and lavender hues across the quiet city, bathing the unfinished minarets of the vast new prayer ground. To the north, luxury residential towers soared above Soviet-style apartment blocks in a shimmering light.

I jabbed at the remote control in frustration, searching for a channel, anything besides the Uzbek shopping network and the angry Saudi preacher station that was not jammed. Officially, satellite TV was banned in Iran, but for several years the authorities had not enforced the prohibition, and the majority of Iranians had dishes on their roofs. But in the past two years the authorities had found a more so-phisticated way to control what Iranians watched. They blocked the signals of particular stations they found objectionable, mainly Farsi-language networks that offered alternative sources of news and a plat-form for dissidents abroad. This way, they figured, they could permit housewives their pop psychology shows and teenagers their music video channels, while protecting everyone from seditious criticism of the regime. The technology by which they achieved this, however, did not function flawlessly, and sometimes most or all of our thousand channels were distorted. Such was the case that day, and when I gave up and turned off the TV, I heard singing from across the street.

They were either using a megaphone or nightclub-grade speakers, I couldn't be sure, but the nasal singing of the *rowzeh* blasted through our apartment. On days commemorating the deaths of Shia saints, pious Iranians invite *rowzeh-khan*s, or preachers of edifying stories, to their homes to recite from books with titles like *The Deluge of Weeping* and *The Mysteries of Martyrdom*.

The neighbors' house was *mosadereye*—that is, it had been confis-cated after its owners fled the revolution. The three families that had sectioned it off were typical of those who occupied the quarters of Iranians who had left the country. They were deeply religious, enough so that the women wrapped themselves in chador even when darting onto the balcony to hang laundry, and clearly affluent. They accrued their wealth by selling construction-grade stone in the Tehran bazaar, but nowhere was this prosperity apparent in their home's décor—machine-woven Persian rugs over cheap classroom carpet, and little furniture, for they mostly sat on the floor. Their affluence was displayed only in the ceremonies and parties they held on nearly all of the sixteen official religious holidays. I was familiar with some of these from my childhood, when I accompanied my grandmother to *sofreh*s, female religious rituals dedicated to various saints, where *rowzeh* was sung before a meal. The *sofreh*s I remember from my youth, though, only commemorated a handful of key saints. The neighbors across the street observed the death anniversaries of even minor religious figures, so they seemed to host a large party every few weeks.

On these occasions, they rented folding chairs, erected garden tents, and cooked food for half the neighborhood. I was envious of their expansive garden, especially its swimming pool, which they filled with fresh water each day of summer, indifferent to the country's chronic water shortage. The women rarely used the pool, but every so often, under cover of night, they would join their husbands in the water, flapping about amorously in wet black chador, coyly chirping "Hajj Agha, *nakon*!"—"Hajj Agha, don't!" Sometimes I watched them from our apartment, marveling to hear them address their husbands as if speaking to an older man or mullah.

Despite their conspicuous piety, they were mostly harmless as neighbors. They kept to themselves, never complaining about our alternative lifestyle. Between us, Arash's sister, Solmaz, and the eighteen-year-old son of the retired colonel upstairs, our building threw parties as often as they did, and they never reported us to the authorities, though it was not uncommon for neighbors to do so. Sometimes it was done out of genuine pious indignation, sometimes as revenge for neighborly quarrels. The neighbor of a friend reported him, he told me, for boycotting the building's plan to install an electric garage door opener.

The day our neighbors set up the powerful megaphones was
Norouz, the first day of the Persian new year (the holiday is celebrated
over thirteen days, and the term *Norouz* refers to both the period of
festivity and New Year's Day). Iranians had been celebrating this holiday on the spring equinox since around 1000 B.C.E., the era of the
prophet Zoroaster. This year, Norouz fell on the same day as Arbaeen, the fortieth day after Imam Hossein's death, another occasion
to mourn his martyrdom. The two holidays contrast rather dramatically. Norouz celebrates the spirit of joy and new life; children paint
eggs and everyone buys hyacinths. Arbaeen glorifies martyrdom and
resistance to political injustice; everyone wears black and keens in
lament.

Since Shia mourning and Norouz were of equal importance to Iranians, the only civilized response seemed to be for everyone to celebrate the holiday of their choice quietly, so as not to impose their
preference on others. The amplified wailing, however, signaled no
such forbearance. The neighbors chose Arbaeen, therefore so must
the block. For ten minutes I stood beside the window resenting the
way deeply religious Muslims imposed their beliefs on their surroundings. I believed there was a place for tolerance in Islam; in fact,
I was engrossed at the time in a book by that title. It argued that the
Koran enjoins Muslims to practice mercy, justice, and tolerance, to
accept diversity, and to pursue peace; that it was only the overly literal, ahistorical misreadings of radicals that distorted the faith's true
message. I was familiar with such reformist claims, and believed them
to be intellectually honest and historically accurate. The trouble was,
most pious Muslims either did not know there was a case for tolerance, or they disagreed with it. It occurred to me what a theoretical
space that was, confined to the elegantly spun discourse of a handful
of Muslim intellectuals adept at speaking to the West. I decided to do
something. I moved all four of our speakers directly in front of the
windows, and turned on a song by Haydeh, a beloved Persian singer,
at shattering volume.

Arash rushed to the window. "What are you doing?"

"I'm taking back the night!"

"You're mad."

"They're audio terrorists and I'm fighting back. They are sabotaging Norouz!"

"When are you ever going to understand this country? You don't have the right to voice that opinion. You're going to get us into trouble."

He was right, of course. I was being immature, my mood labile from the hormonal swings of early pregnancy. We did consider driving out to Lavasan, where we had spent Ashoura a month earlier, but decided to stay in Tehran. I wondered how often throughout history Norouz had coincided with Islamic holidays. Probably no more frequently than every few decades, given the difference between the Persian and Islamic calendars. Although Iran has struggled for centuries to reconcile the Islamic and Persian traditions, the inevitable friction between them still defines the culture today. In the seventh century C.E., when Arab nomads from the desert conquered what was then called Persia, Iranians practiced Zoroastrianism. This distinctly Iranian faith was the world's first monotheistic religion, and its belief in a future savior; its dualistic concept of good and evil, as embodied by the struggle between God and the devil—went on to influence Judaism, Christianity, and Islam. Zoroastrianism was the state religion of three great Persian empires, from 550 B.C.E. to 651 C.E. It shaped the identity, language, and culture of Persia for at least two millennia. When the Arabs invaded, they imposed Islam on the Persians, burning many of their books and seeking to erase their traditions. But although in other ancient lands they had conquered, such as Egypt and Iraq, they successfully imposed their culture, in Persia they failed. The Persians retained their language and identity. They developed a national epic poetry in which they preserved their myths. They began leaving their own indelible traces on the Arab religion, an influence of such profound importance that one historian calls it the "second advent of Islam itself."

In the twentieth century, Iran's political upheavals brought this past alive in the form of a modern culture war. The secular leaders charged with building the nation between the 1920s and the 1970s concluded that Islam was their chief obstacle. Since 1979, Iranians disappointed in the revolution's authoritarianism had blamed Islam.

Those who considered themselves secular, modern, and western began reconnecting with the Persian past and identifying with it. They believed that the Arab conquest had ended the golden age of Persian history, and they viewed Islam as a colonizing faith that had diluted Iranian civilization. These Iranians, my grandfather among them, named their children after the great kings of the pre-Islamic empires. Their heroes included the mythical figures of the *Shahnameh,* the national epic that recounts Persia's hostility to the Arab invaders. Ferdowsi, writing in the tenth century, captured a sentiment that many Iranians still feel today: "Damn this world, damn this time, damn this fate, / That uncivilized Arabs have come to make me Muslim."

Such Iranians tended to ignore facts that contradicted their bias: that Iran's most distinguished contribution to world civilization, Persian poetry, belonged to the post-Islamic era; that the *Shahnameh*'s author, Ferdowsi, was a pious believer; that in the early twentieth century it was the mullahs, not the king, who had rescued Iran from colonialists and promoted democratic rule. My family was full of such types and I found their pronouncements tedious and historically ignorant.

Growing up in California, I learned that Islam was fundamentalist and incapable of change. My grandfather had all sorts of unfair notions about devout Iranians—that only maids had names like Fatemeh, that the chador was backward, and that mullahs were hypocrites and seminaries hotbeds of homosexuality. As you can imagine, this left me with a rather distorted sense of Islam in Iran. I had no idea that a sizable percentage of Iranians obeyed the wisdom and decrees of grand ayatollahs, that they traveled to Islamic centers of learning and places of pilgrimage in Damascus, Karbala, and Najaf. I only discovered these realities as a foreign correspondent reporting in the Arab world, a rather circuitous route to learning about one's own homeland. I remember checking into a hotel in Najaf, Iraq, the city of the gold-domed shrine of Imam Ali, Shia Islam's holiest site, and being dumbfounded that the receptionist spoke Farsi. It was just weeks after the U.S. invasion, so there were no Iranian pilgrims in the city at the time, but before and after they traveled there in the tens of thousands. Everyone in a position to haggle—hotel clerks, street vendors, jewelers—spoke Farsi. While reporting in Lebanon on Hezbollah, I learned of the existence of a Shia clerical aristocracy; it was impossible to untangle whether its members were originally Iranian, Lebanese, or Iraqi, but many shaped the politics of all of these countries. I had known, before, that many Iranians were religious. But I hadn't known how deeply Shia and Persian culture were intertwined, hadn't known that I could not understand one without understanding the other.

Just as the pursuit of modernization biased many Iranians toward secularism, suspicions of both the West and modernity moved others in the opposite direction, to wage holy war against Iran's pre-Islamic traditions. The Islamic revolution brought men like Ayatollah Sadegh Khalkhali to power. Before 1979, the Shah's regime took seriously ahistorical attacks on the pre-Islamic Iranian dynasties. It imprisoned Khalkhali for authoring a tract called "Impostor Koorosh," which portrayed the great Persian king (known in English as Cyrus the Great) as a tyrant and a liar. After the revolution, Khalkhali dispatched bulldozers and militiamen around the country to raze everything Persian: the ancient ruins of Persepolis (the seat of Persia's great empires); the tomb of Ferdowsi; the Pahlavi family mausoleum, the resting place of Reza Shah, who could be credited with building modern Iran (Khalkhali built a public toilet in its place). Arash recalls how one day, state television began broadcasting dramas in which the heroes were named after Islamic figures while the villains bore Persian names. The regime banned hundreds of names that harked back to the era before Islam, and rewrote history books to reflect an Islamicized view of the past.

Often I would open the morning newspaper to stories about the regime's ongoing campaign to physically rid Iran of traces of its pre-Islamic past. It had blithely chosen a gorge near Pasargadae, the tomb of Koorosh, as the site for an immense dam. The tomb stood to crumble away entirely owing to its proximity. Few rulers in history are remembered with such reverence as Koorosh. In 539 B.C.E., his first year in Babylon, Koorosh issued a decree authorizing the Jews to return to their land and rebuild their temple at Jerusalem. Both the Bible and other Hebrew texts speak of him admiringly, and in her Nobel speech Shirin Ebadi referred to herself as a "descendant of Koorosh."

The evening of my loudspeaker showdown, I logged onto Shiachat, a forum where Shias from around the world discussed their sect. A number of Arabs on the forum were chiding the Iranian Shias for wishing each other a happy Norouz. One Iranian member, who identified himself by the blood-red emblem of the Shia Imam Hossein, responded angrily that "congratulating each other on the occasion of Norouz is not only a fine act, but Islamically advised." From across the street, I heard the long hiss and sudden pop of Norouz firecrackers. The neighbors' children, having concluded their Islamic lament, were sending brilliant purple sparklers into the air.

Not long after Norouz, in early April, I flew to the United States for the paperback release of my book *Lipstick Jihad*. Before I began the promotional tour, though, I spent a weekend in California buying a wedding dress. My friends in Tehran had encouraged me to have my dress made by a seamstress. But that would have involved multiple fittings over long weeks, and at some point I would have needed to explain my expanding proportions. I had no wish to be candid about my pregnancy with a perfect stranger in Iran. What if the seamstress turned out to be extremely devout, privately considered my situation immoral, and sabotaged my dress? While that was unlikely, I felt more comfortable all around dress shopping in California, where people considered it sweet to be an expecting bride. Because I was already beginning to lose my waist, the first sign of the baby weight to come, I discarded my dreams of a form-fitting Badgley Mischka wedding gown. A pregnant figure requires a simpler dress, and I found a lovely A-line at a bridal shop in a suburban strip mall in Sunnyvale.

The young Korean saleswoman had worked with pregnant brides before, and helped me estimate how much weight I would gain by June, at which time I would be five months pregnant.

"So where's your wedding?" she asked. Her dressing room was

covered with photos of brides posing at Napa wineries and on sandy beaches.

"Iran."

She looked rather concerned upon hearing this, but did not probe.

My dress was sent away to be hemmed and joined me two weeks later in New York, my last stop before I flew back to Tehran. I spent a morning seeing my editors, then called on Javad Zarif, then Iran's ambassador to the United Nations. He was one of the country's most skilled diplomats, and always at the center of its negotiations with the West. Not only was I seeking his sophisticated analysis of Iran's present bargaining position; I wanted to ask a favor.

"Could you help my best friend get a visa to Iran? I would usually never ask this, but it's for my wedding."

"That's lovely news; congratulations. I wish I could help, but the visa process for Americans is complicated." Visas were vetted by multiple state bodies, and the ambassador said he couldn't easily intervene.

I said I understood, and we continued our discussion. As we talked, I wondered what it must be like for such a pragmatic, erudite, and worldly man to represent a country whose president sought only confrontation. Unspeakably frustrating, I imagined.

The next day, as I was packing to leave for the airport, an editor called to ask for my help. Could I please write a one-paragraph profile of Ahmadinejad for the "*Time* 100"? This annual issue lists the world's most influential people, at least according to the *Time* editors, and the magazine had been unable to find someone just right to cover Ahmadinejad. Ordinarily I would have agreed instantly. The prestigious issue drew millions of readers, and profilers were invited to mingle with their subjects at a black-tie party in New York. I wouldn't be able to fly back for the event, but that didn't trouble me. How could I profile Ahmadinejad, whose Holocaust denial had encouraged most in the West to consider him a monster, without offending the Iranian authorities? I would need to choose my words carefully. In the end, I agreed, if only so I could explain why Iranians had voted for him, a nuance that would surely be lost if some Washington pundit were to write the piece.

Pressed for time, I wrote it during my layover in Paris, keeping a close eye on the garment bag that contained my dress. An Iranian woman in the departure lounge listened curiously as I dictated over the phone, seemingly fascinated by the paragraph I read: "Mahmoud Ahmadinejad is a president unlike any Iran has ever known: belligerent, naïve, at once a fundamentalist and nationalist and a dark genius at mobilizing Iranian public opinion. In the first year of his presidency, he has risen out of obscurity to become one of the most troublesome and noteworthy leaders in the world. His uncompromising stand on his country's right to enrich uranium has . . . brought the United States and Iran closer to a military confrontation than ever in recent times. His campaign slogan 'We Can and We Will' implied fighting corruption, not building the Bomb. . . ."

By the time my plane landed in Tehran, however, the short paragraph I had written along the way receded from my mind. I had briefly considered informing Mr. X about it, but decided this was unnecessary. It wasn't a news story, after all, and I wasn't obligated to let him know about every line that appeared under my name. If I kept in touch with him too assiduously, I reasoned, he would just expect more and more. Perhaps this was a useful occasion to assert some distance from Mr. X.

I made my way through the crowded terminal and found Arash waiting near the exit doors, a bouquet of irises in his hand. I was so excited to go home and show him my dress that I forgot about Mr. X entirely.

It was May, and the 2006 World Cup soccer tournament was quickly approaching. Although, as an American, I was not emotionally bound to soccer, I was aware of the imminent competition, which is of course the most widely watched sporting event in the world. That year, the Iranian director Jafar Panahi would release his controversial film *Offside* on the first day of the World Cup. The film told the story of Iranian women soccer fans who dressed as men to sneak into games at Tehran's Azadi stadium. *Time*'s European edition, which often covered Iranian films closely, was running a story about *Offside* and the fate of cinema under Ahmadinejad. I had been asked to interview an

Iranian director and find out whether the new administration had stepped up censorship.

Many years ago, when he returned to Iran for a stint before starting university in Germany, Arash had worked as a film editing assistant. He had kept in touch with a handful of people from his cinema days, and suggested we talk to one of his old friends, the director Saman Moghaddam. One afternoon that week, we went to visit him together.

Like so many Iranian artists, Saman had moved to Dubai, but traveled back and forth to work on his films. His latest work, *Maxx,* had screened to packed cinemas for five weeks before being abruptly banned. A musical comedy of errors, in which an Iranian pop musician living in Los Angeles is accidentally invited to Tehran by the government, *Maxx* abounded with political humor. Everyone I knew, including Shirin khanoum, said it was one of the funniest Iranian films ever.

Though it had been pulled from cinemas after just five weeks, that it had been shown at all was promising. Under the Khatami government, Saman had spent four years trying to produce and screen *Maxx,* four years during which he was constantly at war with the film authorities.

"They quibbled with one hundred and forty points in an eighty-page screenplay," he said, pausing to pour us coffee. "They faulted it for things that were entirely common in other films. I edited it and sent it back to them, and then they rejected it altogether without even explaining why."

The Ministry of Culture and Islamic Guidance approved the film only two days before the end of the Khatami era, effectively passing the problem along to the Ahmadinejad administration. Many film directors said conservative governments tended to be more permissive when it came to moviemaking, because, unlike moderate administrations like Khatami's, they had no one to answer to. Saman said he agreed.

"We had a very brief golden era under Khatami, but most of the time we faced endless restrictions. You'd expect that a conservative government like this one would restrict our work, but that hasn't really happened. The environment we're working under now is certainly no more closed than before," he said.

"That's really counterintuitive, but it makes sense."

"You see, when there's lots of internal conflict within the government, artists and filmmakers often get stuck in the middle. But that's less the case when conservatives are in power, because they all agree with one another."

While Saman and Arash caught up, I leaned back to reflect on what the director had said. How perplexing to think that film actually fared better under a conservative leader than a moderate. I wondered if this held true for other artists, whether censorship of music and literature, for example, was lighter under a hard-line president. It seemed unlikely. As we left Saman's apartment, I thought briefly about Mr. X. I had no intention of telling him about our meeting with Saman, and I hoped he would not notice or mind. After all, I could always make the case that I was only contributing my reporting to the story, which someone else would write. Surely he would understand.

All across Iran, at every hour of the day, I found people arguing about Islam. Our downstairs neighbors, an irreverent architect fond of nasty jokes about Islam and his pious wife, who nonetheless liked to show some cleavage, even had one of those routines married couples perform for company. "Islam is like a vast, imposing ocean . . ." he would intone gravely, spreading his arms wide, and pausing for effect. "An ocean that is . . . two centimeters deep!" She, who prayed five times a day and cooked saffron custards for the building on the death anniversaries of Shia saints, would swat at him. "But darling, Islam is not like this, not the real Islam. These mullahs have ruined it." This conviction was popular among the portion of the middle class that did not wish to renounce its devotion, but could not reconcile it with the intolerant, decaying country around them.

Before I moved to Iran, my relationship to Islam was private and a source of rich intellectual and creative inspiration. My experience of Islam, of Shiism in particular, was intertwined with my study of Arabic, of Arabic literature and classical Islamic sciences, in my early twenties. This scholarly curiosity in time gave way to a more meditative exploration. I found myself struggling to decipher not only the complex grammar and verses of the Koran but also the book's moral meaning. Tariq Ramadan, a preeminent scholar of Islam, has written that in nearness to the Koran, "a woman or a man who possesses a spark of faith knows the path to follow, knows her or his own inadequacies." For me, the path to follow was to further reading. I read the *Nahj ol-Balagha,* the sermons of the Imam Ali, which are dear to Shia Muslims, and found myself mesmerized by the cadence and power of the language. Was I responding only to the text's rich literary charms, or had it aroused deeper, more spiritual feelings? I could not say myself, although I began preferring the silent company of these books to most any other pursuit. If you pushed me on the finer points of faith, I would still have claimed to be agnostic. Occasionally, I fasted during Ramazan; each night before going to bed I still whispered the *fatiha* prayer my grandmother had taught me; and I loved nothing more than staying up late reading Sufi parables. I wouldn't think of sending off an important article to my editor without whispering "Besmellah rahman rahim" ("In the name of God, the Compassionate, the Merciful"), the preamble to every Koranic sura, which practicing Muslims utter many times a day during prayer and before initiating many tasks. I had a set of flash cards denoting the chronology of the Shia imams, and when I traveled as a reporter through the Shia cities of Iraq where the dramas I had so long read about had unfolded, I felt an indescribable thrill.

When I moved to Tehran, I hoped to study classical Islamic philosophy or history with mullahs and scholars. Instead, Islam became a slipper with which I was frequently rapped on the head. Arash and I had yet to develop a public routine on the subject, but our most passionate arguments were over Islam. A particularly ferocious row arose one Friday morning over a wooden key holder I had bought in Lebanon. It was adorned with a patinated calligraphy that read "In the Name of God." It had hung near my door in Beirut, and I did not think to ask whether I might install it in our apartment.

Arash examined the key holder coldly. "I do not want the Islamic Republic in my home."

"This is not the Islamic Republic," I said. "It's a key holder that happens to bear a Koranic inscription."

I wondered how my key holder differed from the antique *panjtan* he had given me as a gift, a metal amulet in the shape of a hand, each finger representing one of the five members of the Prophet Mohammad's family. Or the CD of Kurdish Sufi music he had bought me the previous week, for that matter. The difference, he explained to me later, was between cultural tradition (Sufi dervishes, the poetry of Rumi, Isfahan's mosque architecture) and Islam on its own. Islam as a watermark to Iran's artistic heritage was acceptable; explicit religious symbols were to be held at arm's length.

"It's openly pious, and I don't want anything like that in my secular home."

"Don't be such a philistine!" I couldn't imagine why he couldn't view my key holder as I did—a beautiful token that evoked a place where, among many other things, people believed in God.

"This has nothing to do with aesthetics," he said. "For you, this is just an exotic, Oriental ornament. But for me, it's a religious symbol, the kind I see painted on walls all over this country. I prefer to keep faith private, not something I advertise to guests as part of my décor."

"Well, I just think you should recognize that Islam, apart from all these battles, has redeeming qualities. What about its ethos of justice?"

In these fights, we soon played predictable roles. Arash was the scarred veteran of Islamic theocracy, uninterested in abstract explorations of Islam's core principles. He was convinced that the reality on the ground—a state that imposed Islamic penalties such as stoning and that sanctioned violence in the religion's name—was the only relevant discussion. In our debates, I played the role of the western liberal, the lenient outsider who, in Arash's eyes, judged Islam from the privileged, secure perch of the West.

"Justice?" he said. "You're such an apologist. You're infatuated with Oriental culture because you think it's exotic. You come here and swoon over supposedly liberal clerics, but the moment you can't unbutton your manteau on a hike, you fall apart."

"Touchée. So I find the restrictions oppressive," I said. "But I read

Arabic, I have read the Koran, I have read the hadith, I have talked to clerics from Qom to Najaf to Beirut, and I can tell you that *this,* this obscene dictatorship, does not reflect Islam at its essence."

"Its essence is irrelevant. These are discussions you should have in cafés with your friends in New York. Do you notice how no one talks about such things here? No one apart from foreigners and western Iranians like you."

Arash was right. No one in Iran talked seriously anymore about reconciling Islam with democracy, about whether Islam was even *compatible* with democracy. In the late 1990s, intellectuals and activists had talked about nothing else. But the rich debates about Islamic democracy withered away as their symbols—former president Khatami and his moderate allies in parliament—failed to bring about the broad changes Iranians expected.

That day, I vowed to avoid discussing Islam with Arash, and if I could help it, with anyone else in Iran. It occurred to me that I had come across as insufferably out of touch, like some champagne Marxist from New York in the 1950s lecturing a Russian victim of Stalin about the nobility of communism. Like Arash, most of my friends in Iran could not understand my preoccupation with Islamic learning. For them, politics and Islam, violence and Islam, were inseparable, and no amount of erudite reasoning could convince them otherwise.

≈

CHAPTER 10

The Persian Bride's Handbook

In planning a traditional wedding, Iranian women face the same daunting rituals as brides in the West: the nearly impossible search for the perfect long, white dress; the pushy caterers who charge per head, per table, and per canapé; and the pressure from event professionals to include skywriting, images projected on the surface of the pool, and anything else that will produce a reception unrivaled in spectacle and expense. In Iranian tradition, however, the bride undertakes this harrowing journey in the company of her mother-in-law. The bride's family covers the *jaheziyeh,* which is not unlike a dowry and involves outfitting an entire apartment, including flatware, light fixtures, appliances, and curtains. The cost of the wedding, including a set of jewelry for the bride, falls to the groom's parents.

These arrangements only aggravate everyone's anxieties about the impending union. Generally, a bride-to-be is already uneasy in her mother-in-law's company. Having to plan a wedding with her— a process that requires everyone to be frank in matters of taste and expense—only intensifies this anxiety. The groom's family, for its part, must judge whether the *jaheziyeh* being assembled is commensurate with its own expenditures. The whole dynamic is intentionally fraught, an early test to ensure that the two families can accept each other's class standing and social position. Over and over again, the question is asked: Are they good enough for *us*? Or, are they spending as much as we are?

The morning when Arash's mother and I headed down to the wedding district on Berlin Street, I faced a classic bout of Iranian daughter-in-law nerves. I had always wanted a traditional Iranian wedding, and was excited to begin making preparations. I was relieved that my pregnancy still did not show, but with the end of my first trimester I had begun suffering migraines. I knew three hours in congested central Tehran would trigger one. I privately wished we could delegate such errands to a wedding coordinator, but I worried that would come across as the bourgeois demand of an over-westernized Iranian, so instead I tucked ibuprofen in my purse and went along gamely.

Among Iranian mothers-in-law, Eshrat khanoum was a rarity. She never nagged us with requests to visit extended family, and tended to us devotedly without expecting anything in return. She looked especially beautiful that day, impeccably dressed in a black poncho-style manteau that suited her fair complexion and petite figure. As we shopped, she posed every last wedding detail as a question, so that I might express my true taste without needing to defer to hers. Our task that day on Berlin Street involved buying all the various accessories required for the *sofreh-ye aghd*, the traditional Iranian wedding array. During the ceremony, the bride and groom sit on a bench before an elaborate array of items laid out on white satin or chiffon. The components are meant to augur good fortune for the couple's marriage—walnuts for fertility, bread for prosperity, *esfand* (rue seeds) to ward away the evil eye, and candles and a mirror to represent the light and energy of the sun. The array has its roots in Zoroastrian tradition, and it accommodates Islam only in that it is situated facing the direction of Mecca.

Each of the *sofreh*'s numerous accoutrements must be decorated and served in its own unique vessel, and we ducked in and out of the stores buying yards of lacy ribbon, miniature blossoms, and sugar cones. As we shopped, I noticed the defensively folded arms and pursed lips of the other bride-to-be/mother-in-law pairs. One duo seemed especially at odds, exchanging snarky comments about each other's taste in ribbons. The modern notion of the wedding day—as a chance for a young woman to express her individual taste before friends and family—conflicted with the behavior expected from a proper daughter-in-law in Iran. The mother-in-law often expected deference to her own taste and sensibilities—submission to her authority, really—especially since she was paying. The daughter-in-law could certainly express a hatred for gilt or insist on the expensive imported tulle, but in doing so she risked being whispered about as pushy or tasteless for the next several years. Everywhere we shopped, male shopkeepers tried to lighten the women's tension with flattery and jovial bargaining.

Berlin Street abuts Lalezar Avenue, which before the revolution was synonymous with pleasure, teeming with cinemas and cabarets. Notably, it was in a Lalezar Avenue café that the legendary singer Mahvash captivated audiences with her seductive glances. We turned south onto the street, its many shops now selling light fixtures that reflected nothing of the boulevard's former glory.

Back when you could drink cocktails in the cabarets of Lalezar, Iranian weddings were intimate events held at home in the presence of about fifty guests. These days many weddings were elaborate productions, opportunities for families to display their financial status and exercise their class aspirations. This behavior—in Farsi, *cheshm ham chesmi*—is condemned by Iranians from Los Angeles to Tehran, even as they commission colossal ice palaces, lay on buffets with sushi chefs and authentic stone ovens, and send out invitations to five-hundred-person engagement parties. Although the Shah's Iran is remembered for decadent, wealthy Iranians flaunting their cash, the consumption habits of that era were Amish by comparison with the widespread materialism of Iran today. Forty years before, Eshrat khanoum had sewn her own wedding dress, and my mother had cooked dinner for her guests.

A few days before our shopping trip, Maria, the Armenian woman who waxed my legs, asked how many guests I was inviting. "Four hundred? Five? Since you didn't have an engagement party, I doubt the parents will let you dip below four hundred." Maria had married off her twenty-seven-year-old son the previous year, and recounted the details with peacockish enthusiasm. When we first met in 1999, she was waxing clients on her dining room table and sharing the apartment's single bedroom with her husband and two children. Since then they had managed to move to a two-bedroom flat; with the second bedroom as work space she could keep the wax and hair out of the eating area, but everyone still occupied one room. Her income, combined with her taxi driver husband's, could scarcely have been more than 350,000 tomans (around $300) a month. But when it came time for their son to marry, they planned his wedding with the liberality of a family several shades more affluent.

"Take these," she said, stuffing into my purse some DVDs bearing a picture of the slow-dancing couple on the cover. Her daughter-in-law's dress, inspired by a frothy, hooped affair in a French bridal magazine, had cost $400, Maria told me, her makeup at least half that. "Everyone talked about the wedding for months," Maria said, the girlish delight softening the lines around her eyes. "They would call me and ask, 'Maria, where did the bride get her dress? Give me the name of the tailor,' and I would just say, 'She had it designed out of a magazine.' "

It was entirely normal for the average Iranian bride to spend at least $300 on a dress, while upper-middle-class women frequented seamstresses who charged $1,200 for a basic sheath, each trim of lace, line of sequins, or other embellishment added à la carte, at considerable charge (bear in mind the average monthly salary in Tehran ranges from $300 to $450). Each night, as I regaled Arash with tales of the predatory Iranian bridal industry, I leafed through the bridal magazines spread out across the kitchen table. I carefully marked the pages with elements I wished to re-create: a chocolate mint fondant cake trimmed with satin ribbon, a patterned bouquet dense with spring foliage, and a tousled chignon threaded with orange blossoms. Before moving back to Iran, I had never aspired to such bridal fripperies. Apart from the slinky dress I could now not wear, I had never imagined a particular sort of cake or veil. But people's excitement about such details was infectious, and I too found myself pondering whether the cake knife required its own corsage.

Having fought our way home through traffic, we typically ended our days exhausted on the couch, too tired to contemplate cooking.

Often we phoned upstairs to see if Eshrat khanoum could send down some of whatever she had on her stove. This was a habit of Iranian couples who lived in the same buildings as their families, one that had at first struck me as another abrogation of adult independence but now just seemed convenient. We found no one at home that evening, and decided to walk instead to a tiny deli in Qeytarieh famous for its old-style sandwiches with parsley and onion chutney. Most people drove to the deli, which had no seating, and ate in their parked cars, permanently jamming traffic on the street. Inside the cramped shop, the staff and handful of customers all craned their heads to watch a tiny television screen hung above the soda refrigerator.

The broadcaster on the nine o'clock news was reading aloud the text of an eighteen-page letter Ahmadinejad had recently sent to George W. Bush. It was the first letter dispatched by an Iranian head of state to an American president in nearly three decades. Undermining its own historic significance, the letter rambled on in a curious manner about American hypocrisy. More a lecture than a genuine attempt to engage, it seemed designed to enhance Ahmadinejad's popularity in the Arab and Islamic world, and indeed in any part of the world where people had grievances about America and its policies. The newscaster intoned the letter with dramatic flourishes: " 'All prophets speak of peace and tranquillity—based on monotheism, justice, and respect for human dignity. Do you not think that if all of us abide by these principles, we can overcome the world's problems? Will you not accept this invitation?' "

Everyone in the sandwich shop shook their head in disbelief, from the customers to the cook poking a skewer into the roasting sausages to the elderly man taking orders, the deli's owner. "Who does he think he is?" muttered the cook.

Iranians, by and large, disliked George W. Bush, for all the same reasons as much of the rest of the world did: his administration's failures in Iraq and Afghanistan, its arrogant manner of addressing the world, and its inflexible rejection of Iran's right to nuclear power. Iranians disliked Bush as much as they had admired Bill Clinton, who had managed to charm them (he publicly called Iran "one of the most wonderful places in all of human history") without taking real steps to undo the two countries' long enmity. Clinton had presided over an America Iranians had wished to befriend; a poll taken in the middle of his presidency found the majority of the country supported reestablishing ties. That cozy regard had evaporated under President Bush, but even so no one appreciated Ahmadinejad's partly ridiculous, partly insulting letter. It was embarrassing to Iran, and Iranians, like most people, were averse to humiliating themselves before the world.

Whereas in the West, weddings are often planned a year in advance, Iranian brides typically coordinate their receptions the month before. Desirable venues and photographers might be booked further ahead, but most of the party details—the flowers, the catering, the cake, the waiters—are decided on the cusp of the event. Each industry has its own reason for this. The florist, for example, said he could inform me about what imported flowers he had available only in the very week of the wedding. The bakery said the cake staff might lose track of the order if it came in too early. This last-minute approach frustrated me greatly, as I was reporting an important story that month and needed to get my bridal tasks out of the way.

For months, I had been discussing with my editors a profile of Ayatollah Ali Khamenei, the country's Supreme Leader. We agreed it would be a great story, and I expected to take up the assignment after the wedding. But that spring, the United Nations Security Council was considering sanctions on Iran for its refusal to halt uranium enrichment, the contested aspect of its nuclear program. The escalating clash between Iran and the West made the story especially timely. If the president's powers were indeed constrained by the Islamic Republic's legal structure, so that Ayatollah Khamenei was the man setting Iran's course, then there was no better moment to profile his leadership. My editors had asked me to press ahead with my reporting, and I had agreed.

Khamenei was reclusive and notoriously difficult to write about. His office granted virtually no access to foreign journalists, and his closest advisers tended to shun the press as well, so I needed all my creativity and my best sources if I was to assemble original information. Khamenei hailed from Mashad, my father's hometown, so I sought out relatives who knew his family. I spent many evenings with a family friend who worked closely with one of the ayatollah's most senior, trusted advisers. In the end, what I learned confirmed the impression of Khamenei I had developed over the years. He had all the qualities of a political mullah—ascetic, suspicious of the West, and keen to preserve Iran's austere revolutionary traditions. At the same time, his sensibilities were more modern than most clerics'; he hiked in jeans, read poetry, and played an Iranian string instrument. Those who knew him well considered him conservative to a fault and said he wished neither to reconcile with the West nor to court full-fledged confrontation. This was borne out by Khamenei's record—he clearly believed in Iran's right to nuclear power, but also sought to avoid punishments that could cripple Iran and shake the state's hold on power.

I wove this thesis into my story, which slowly took shape in the hours between calls to the florist and visits to the seamstress. I felt a lingering unease over not having contacted Mr. X, to brief him on my reporting for such a significant story. But I could not have disclosed what he would naturally have wanted to know. Most of my sources were relatives, family friends, or officials who had expressly wished to remain anonymous—in short, people whose privacy I was obligated to protect. I had a long-standing policy of not informing Mr. X about such sources, so it seemed prudent to keep quiet about the story altogether. To contact him only to say I could disclose nothing about my reporting seemed unnecessarily provocative. He would likely be upset when he read the article in translation and discovered he had been kept unaware. But I saw no better way of handling the situation, and decided not to worry myself about it in the meantime. If the story was well received by Khamenei's associates, perhaps their approval would quell his irritation. I hoped for the best, and once I finished the story I turned my full attention to the wedding I had scarcely a month to plan.

Nothing about the invitation we received that month to a friend's wedding, not the elegant ecru box in which it was delivered, not the marbled parchment on which it was printed, and most certainly not the text itself, suggested the reception was to be a sex-segregated affair. All the gossip about the wedding centered around the eight-hundred-person guest list, which was only slightly more extravagant than the four-hundred-person engagement party we had not been invited to. We discovered that men and women would be separated only when one of Arash's friends phoned to give me the cell phone number of his wife, so that we could find each other among the four hundred women relegated to the female ballroom. We had been invited because Arash was friends with the groom, and the fact that I didn't know the couple well myself suddenly seemed like a reason to stay home. Among the many indignities posed by the sex-segregated wedding, not least is the plight of the couple only one of whose members is connected to the wedding party. The other person is forced to wander among hundreds of strangers without the social crutch of the spouse who actually knows the pair, while the other's enjoyment is marred by the certainty that his or her partner is on the other side of the wall seething with resentment.

"Why should I even go," I complained, "if I won't know a single woman there?"

"I don't know, it just feels strange to put on a suit and go to a big wedding by myself," Arash said. "And you won't be bored. You can check out the caterer and the flowers. It'll be like a research trip."

We were spared the trouble of resolving this when it turned out that a close female relative of mine had also been invited and that I could sit at her table. When the evening finally arrived, as I touched up the polish on my toes and inched into my chiffon gown, it occurred to me that the knowledge that I was dressing up to hang out with four hundred other women somehow took all the anticipatory fizz out of getting ready.

We pulled up outside the venue, the Farmanieh Social and Sporting Club, the Islamic Republic's answer to a country club, where wealthy ayatollahs took swimming lessons and reclined in saunas. Iranian officials were inordinately fond of saunas. Everyone knew this, but no one could quite put their finger on why. Perhaps it was because they considered sweating in the sauna a quick and painless means of weight loss. The luxury residential towers that were going up all across northern Tehran, catering to the regime's new rich, all included master bedroom suites with built-in saunas. Once I had a cleric rush late into an interview, still pink from his sauna session. The Sporting Club contained four oversize saunas; many crucial decisions must have been taken in their wooden, eucalyptus-scented depths. During my brief tenure as a member, I found that women were less fond of saunas than were men. The sauna ruined their hair, and they preferred to converse while ambling on the treadmill or sipping fresh carrot juice at the gym café.

Hundreds of fragile, magenta-colored orchids enveloped the wide staircase that wound up to the women's level. "Those orchids cost eight dollars a stem," I informed Arash. "These people are obscene." I never imagined that importing and exporting paint, the family's main enterprise, could be so lucrative. I waved goodbye to Arash as he headed for the men's ballroom; we would coordinate our escape by text message if the evening grew too unbearable.

Inside, the atmosphere was more like a colossal tea party than a wedding, with petits fours and tisanes circulating on trays, except that everyone was wearing floor-length evening gowns. For a good hour, the female guests gossiped listlessly and stared at one another's jewelry. Shortly before dinner, Arash messaged to inform me their side had a stand-up comic: unfair. Even the bride looked dejected, arms crossed tightly across her designer gown, diamond tiara slightly askew, giving off the air of a recently deposed monarch.

Since the clerical regime forbids unmarried men and women to consort with one another publicly, reception halls and hotels require that guests be separated. One less popular option is to hold a dinner rather than a reception, because men and women may eat in each other's company. But without music, the dinners end up being solemn affairs, and they don't include the traditional rites of an Iranian wedding party, such as the "knife dance," in which the bride must retrieve a blade from carousing guests in order to cut the cake.

As we headed for our table, my cousin and I discussed whether, if given the choice, this particular couple would have chosen a mixed party at home. She had attended the wedding ceremony as well—it had been held earlier that day at home—and described their elaborate *sofreh.*

Pious families have always held segregated parties. Even in private homes, guests are separated, or the men leave after dinner so that the women can take off their veils and dance among themselves. As liberal as this couple was, their parents were traditional, and we agreed they would have held a segregated reception anyway, even were they not legally compelled to do so. The women ululated to signal that the groom had entered (he is permitted a brief visit to the women's side; the converse does not extend to his bride). The conservative among the guests swiftly reached for their coverings, and now came the most memorable sight of the evening: a Pucci chador.

The groom's mother began ushering everyone to the dinner buffet, which included everything from Persian sour-cherry rice to prawn kabobs and Thai curry. After this sumptuous meal, which intended to compensate for the single-sex misery but did not, some teenage girls did a perfunctory dance to the Persian pop song of the year, "Khosh-gelha Bayad Berakhsan," "The Pretty People Must Dance," and everyone filed out to look for their males. Once in the integrated lobby, the guests grew animated, laughed, and displayed other signs of having a good time, and as a result the doormen swiftly herded everyone onto the street. There was whispered talk of an after party at the groom's parents' apartment, with a live DJ. But someone had spoken to the bride's sister, who reported that police had stopped the DJ's car en route and confiscated the equipment. From the window, we could see the groom on the staircase, his face taut and angry, in animated conversation with his father. Helplessness was written all over the older man's face. It was one of those moments in Iran that gives even wealthy parents pause, when they realize that their money is meaningless in the face of the state's decrees, because it cannot buy their son something rather simple, after all: a dance with his bride on the eve of their wedding reception, in the company of friends.

The next day my cousin called and asked whether I had admired the pastry and the floral arrangements at the reception. If so, she could find out who had been responsible. In Tehran, once word gets out that you are planning a wedding, the females on both sides of the couple's extended family make it their business to help. They draw on the collected knowledge of all their own female friends and acquaintances, so that they can offer you a definitive roster of the wedding coordinator, caterer, and photographer of the moment.

For a full week our phone rang each day with relatives calling to say, "Shahrooz. Shahrooz and no one else." Shahrooz was the most coveted, most talked about wedding planner of the year, or at least of that spring. He offered a full range of services, including the unpleasant one of security. Anyone wishing to hold a mixed wedding at a private locale requires some form of security, for without it the reception stands to be raided by police. In the rare worst cases, the guests are carted off to the police station, either lashed or charged à la carte for their transgressions (nail polish, ten thousand toman; makeup, twenty thousand; being in the company of the opposite sex, fifty thousand); more fortunate consequences would include the opportunity to pay a sizable bribe, either to be left alone altogether, or for the party to end but without harassment of the guests.

A thriving clandestine industry had emerged in recent years to protect private weddings from such invasions. Like every other trade in Iran designed to supply what the state forbids, it grew ever more sophisticated and expensive. The first wedding I attended in Iran, back in 2000, was held at a rented garden in Karaj, on the outskirts of Tehran. Men and unveiled women mingled freely late into the night, periodically slipping flasks out of their purses and jackets, and the police never showed up. No one knew exactly who owned and operated the rental gardens of Karaj, but it was clear they worked with the authorities' tacit permission. The rental fee—around $6,000 per evening, exorbitant by local standards—guaranteed that the party would be safe from the local police. The Karaj gardens peaked in popularity in the early Khatami era, when security forces generally limited their incursions into people's private lives. This loosening slowly led to the emergence of wedding planners offering security packages, so that Iranians could hold mixed weddings in private homes with similar assurance. The popularity of this option had grown in recent months, as young couples, nervous that the Ahmadinejad government would not tolerate the Karaj gardens, were choosing to hold receptions at home.

We had already picked the location for our wedding. The ceremony would be held at my uncle's house in Shahabad, what had once been a village at the footsteps of the Alborz Mountains, but was now entirely within the sprawling city's limits. The house had been the family seat for decades, and it was important to me that Arash and I exchange our vows in a place where I had roots. Soaring sycamore trees surrounded the old house, reflected in the shimmering surface of the pool, and trellises of pink bougainvillea leaned against the brick walls. I loved the sycamores' broad leaves, their mottled, flaky bark, and their quintessential Iranianness. Iran is dense with sycamores, and the ancient Persian king Xerxes found the tree so beautiful that he showered it with gifts and wore an amulet engraved with its image.

My aunt had known most of the neighbors for decades and was certain they would not call the police. But recently, a new glass apartment tower had gone up across the street, home to a number of religious families whose willingness to accommodate the older residents' style had not yet been tested. After some discreet inquiries, it was concluded they would not pose any problems.

We would hold the reception at the home of Arash's parents in Lavasan. The expansive garden there would accommodate all our guests, and because Arash's father was one of the oldest landowners in the district, we did not anticipate trouble from the local police.

Arash and I arrived at Shahrooz's office on a warm weekday morning, passing through two photography studios—one in Grecian style, including urns and a terra-cotta background, and another resembling a Versailles drawing room—on the way to the reception area, which was crowded by two oversize gilt thrones covered in red velvet. A plate of almond cookies sat on the upholstered coffee table, and we sipped tea quietly until the perfectly coiffed receptionist duo (everything at Shahrooz seemed double or triple what was required) with their identical upturned noses, granted us their attention. From there we were escorted to the photographer's office, where a middle-aged man in a silk shirt opened a leather-bound album featuring portraits of brides and grooms in various unlikely poses: prostrate on a field of autumn leaves, perched in a tree, on the verge of rolling into a pool. This was the "conventional portrait" album, which we viewed before one that appeared to comprise stills from some eighties heavy-metal video in which the bride dies during the guitar solo. In this album, there were grooms saving brides from falling off bridges, drowning in murky pools, being lost in wooded grottoes. The last few photos were atmospheric shots of brides in what looked like boudoir settings, and my personal favorite, a bride in the garb and pose of a flamenco dancer.

Since most brides want to appear unveiled in their wedding photos, nearly every Iranian wedding photographer has a private garden at his disposal, the public parks of Tehran being off limits for such purposes. The impulse to appear unveiled (or at least only with a bridal veil) in photos seemed natural enough to me, but I didn't quite grasp the point of the dramatized portraits until we were shown the optional "couple's video," a separate production from the standard wedding video that records moments like the cutting of the cake. The "couple's video" was a fifteen-minute clip set to pounding club music that followed the given couple as they coyly searched for each other amid sandy ruins, galloped into the desert side by side on horses, rolled around on a sandy beach, and encountered each other on the candelit terrace of a palatial estate. Such heady romance being unavailable to the average Iranian couple, the video and the portraits seemed to re-create in images the carefree adventures and wealth that young people yearned for.

"Fortunately, both our family homes have gardens, so perhaps we could just take care of the pictures there," I ventured.

"The price of the garden is included in the fees," the photographer said condescendingly. He apparently thought we were being cheap.

Special effects, or the sorts of touches meant to provide the unsurpassed "Wow" moment when your jaded guests are finally impressed, occupied their own stop in the world of Shahrooz. You could be transported to the reception in an antique Mercedes-Benz; you could have plasma television screens mounted around the property, playing videos of the couple, or even a fireworks display.

By the time we finally reached the private sanctum of Shahrooz himself, we both wanted to bolt. But I had promised my uncle I would at least check out the security package, just in case. The planner of all planners sat behind a large oak desk, wearing a stylish suit with a striped orange tie; he had the attractive but vacant expression of a cologne model. He snapped open a latest-model laptop and began clicking through photos of other people's weddings, pointing out the chair backs and flowers we could select. In the waiting room, I had scanned their set dinner menus, the most basic of which included twelve choices of entrée, and asked whether we could have just five or six.

Shahrooz looked affronted.

"Don't worry," I said hastily, "we're happy to pay for twelve entrées, but because we think that's a trifle overblown, we would want you to serve just five."

"I am not willing to sacrifice the reputation of my institution," he said. "People expect a certain degree of quality from a Shahrooz wedding, and I must match that on every occasion."

"But this has nothing to do with quality. We just want *less*."

Shahrooz was nonplussed. If he had had a button underneath his desk that whisked away undesirable clients, he would surely have pressed it now. I could not imagine him walking into a local police station in his western banker's suit, but his operation necessitated some form of cooperation with the authorities. He, or someone less conspicuous in his employ, either bribed them directly or somehow made it worth their while to refrain from raiding his receptions. When families coordinated their own weddings, it usually fell to the bride's father or brother to deal with police who inevitably came knocking. I could see the appeal in delegating this repulsive task, but—even though he promised to bring ten security guards camouflaged as guests in suit and tie and equipped with earpiece walkie-talkies, and to set up a roadblock at the head of my uncle's street—Arash and I agreed that Shahrooz was not for us. We walked out of his office.

Next, we went to see the city's top wedding photographer. Photographs occupy an inconceivable degree of importance in the average couple's wedding. Between the studio portraits, the outdoor photography, and the time allotted to the videographer, most couples spend several hours of the day amassing an elaborate visual record of their union. It was not considered nearly enough to have focused and well-composed shots of one's guests and the key moments of the ceremony and party. Rather, the wedding day offered an opportunity for couples to create a glamour portfolio that reflected, in its lavish excess, the financial portfolio of their families.

This impulse seemed peculiar to me, as most people had an approximate sense of the financial position of their extended acquaintances and could guess that a middle-class family had gone into debt or burned through savings to pay for an extravagant wedding. Arash said I was being overliteral and underestimating the extent to which Iranian culture was preoccupied with family dignity. Iranians are notorious, at least among themselves, for their tendency to savage weddings the day after. By noon the next day, the women in attendance will have taken to the phones, excoriating the inadequacy of the dinner, the modesty of the fruit display, the way you needed a magnifying glass to see the gems in the bride's jewelry. A family would spend well above its means just to preclude this sort of gossip, especially from the bride's family. The groom's parents were aware that an event that did not meet the bride's family's expectations would entail a lifetime of in-law sniping and patronizing for their son. A wedding that did suffice could be viewed, in the context of such relations, as an investment in a son's future peace of mind.

Arash and I had no intention of devoting long hours of our wedding day to photography. Besides the fact that the idea was traumatic, it would take all my energy to make it through an afternoon ceremony and an evening reception. Regardless of what appears on the invitation, Iranians refuse to arrive at a private wedding party before nine or ten P.M., and inevitably our reception would last well past the middle of the night. We hoped the photographer we were on our way to see would understand our more circumscribed needs.

His name was Babak, and he came recommended by at least five friends, including one photojournalist who should have known better. In his mid-thirties, with thinning hair tied back in a ponytail, Babak greeted us, or I should say he greeted me, with a leering warmth.

"Don't worry, I'll make sure you look divine," he assured, inspecting me with an overlong glance.

Though I was nearly four months pregnant, thankfully this was not at all apparent. I had agonized over setting the date for the reception, anxious not to show in my wedding dress. Nearly everyone knew we were already officially married, and it was common for couples to hold their reception sometimes months or a year later. But I hadn't heard of any cases where the wife-bride was pregnant. Tehran was not ready for that kind of reception, and I did not want my wedding pictures to record a stomach bump for posterity. Some who knew me well noticed I looked slightly fuller than usual, but my weight often fluctuated according to how much time I spent at the gym, and my extra four or five pounds went mostly unremarked. I planned to wear four-inch heels to offset this thickening, and Arash's mother, who knew I was pregnant, had introduced me to her discreet seamstress, who monitored my dress's fit.

Babak's cell phone rang; he twisted his chair slightly away from us to hold a loud, five-minute conversation with a woman he kept referring to as "baby." Once finished with his phone call, he ordered his staff to serve us watermelon, while he sipped a Diet Coke and recounted a recent weekend spent at the Burj al-Arab in Dubai with Kamran and Houman, the Tehrangeles pop duo. I explained to him that we wanted very natural photography, nothing posed or stagey, just black-and-white shots of the ceremony and our guests at the reception. "That's me, that's exactly my kind of work!" he insisted, though the albums on the table before us contained photos entirely in the manner of Shahrooz's in-house photographer. He began pointing to certain photographs. "Do you see this smile? I *want* this smile. Do you see this shadow? I *want* this shadow."

At this point Arash interrupted him to ask about prices, and whether he took the photographs himself or sent assistants. "It all depends on whether you can afford me," he said. His assistant flipped through a calendar marked up with bookings, and informed us that he had no weekends free for the next six months. Competition was fierce, it seemed, to have Babak capture one's perfect day. Once the assistant handed us his price list, I whispered to Arash that we should leave. Babak charged the equivalent of several thousand dollars, which seemed excessive in a country where a loaf of bread cost ten cents.

That evening, I poured myself a glass of sour cherry soda and settled in to read the newspaper, eager to reconnect with a world that was not preoccupied with weddings. But the front page offered no respite. The government, it seemed, was equally concerned with matrimony. Troubled by the rise in large *mehriyeh*s and the growing demand for elaborate weddings that most young people could not afford but sought to hold anyway, it had thrown a major party to promote moderation, advertising the event in newspapers and on state media. A cartoon ran alongside the article I was reading, showing a bride and groom besieged by chattering flies that criticized everything from the groom's shoes to the bride's jewelry. Only young couples recently wed with *mehriyeh*s valued at less than fourteen gold coins (around $2,400) had been admitted to the government party. Once inside, guests were automatically enrolled in a lottery to win gold coins.

I laughed aloud and began reading the piece to Arash. It captured precisely why Shahrooz, and the entire Iranian wedding industry for that matter, was ascendant, despite the financial strain faced by most of the nation. The regime had chosen as the venue for the party an auditorium adorned with posters of Ali Akbar, the son of Imam Hossein, martyred in the seventh century alongside his father. A mullah had presided over this festive atmosphere, reading for ten minutes from the Koran. He had then introduced a special "celebrity" guest, an actor famous for his appearances in films about the Iran-Iraq War, who quipped, "I've been martyred twenty-three times . . . *on film*!" A smoke-and-light show followed, which, what with all the posters of Ali Akbar, must have lent the auditorium the strange feeling of an Islamic disco. The party favors included Ti-Top, a sponge cake popular as a snack for schoolchildren, and a book of advice for married couples penned by the Ayatollah Khamenei. In this teeming metropolis of at least six million young people of marriageable age, only three hundred had attended. The rest were, presumably, sitting at home with calculators trying to figure out how they could afford Shahrooz.

CHAPTER 11

Even the Therapist Wants Out

I suggested we start seeing a couples therapist over dinner one evening. We were at a restaurant Arash disliked, Bix, one of several new Tehran restaurants that sought, through the generous use of white pillows and curtains, dim lighting, and lounge music, to create the ambience of a French Caribbean nightclub. Arash was irritated by the pretentiousness of such places, filled with affected Iranians and arrogant waiters who preferred to speake English even when discussing an order of tea. But Bix was the only restaurant in the city that served salmon, and I was determined to eat a fish high in omega-3 at least once a month (the pregnancy books warned that otherwise one's baby would end up a dunce). Suddenly all the lights flooded on, the music went silent, and the waiters bustled nervously. The manager came over to apologize, in English: "The police are here, so we'll need to keep the music off for a while. Can I get you guys starters?"

The idea of seeing a therapist occurred to me when I found myself, for the third night in a row, eating ice cream out of the tub at three A.M. In retrospect, the issues we faced seem manageable, but at the time they were beginning to oppress me. The chief source of much of this stress was my mother. She was now insisting that I invite all of her extended family and friends in Tehran to the reception. She herself would not be able to attend, since she had just spent a month in the country and could not ask for more vacation time so soon. Such wedding stress had begun to affect how Arash and I were communicating.

My mother aside, even small reception details were proving tricky to resolve. For example, we could not decide whether to serve alcohol, and if so, in what manner. Most Iranians don't openly serve cocktails, or indeed alcohol in any form, at weddings, both because it makes the party more vulnerable to a police raid, and because it increases the likelihood of drunken brawling. At a friend's wedding recently, the bride's brothers had pummeled the tipsy groom for calling another sister *nan-e zireh kabob*, "the bread under the kabob," a playful but lubricious Persian term for sister-in-law (the bread under a plate of kabob is juicy and especially delicious). Often guests bring their own alcohol in flasks, or they disappear in groups to visit the trunk of a nearby car. While I understood why this happened, it seemed like the behavior of high school delinquents, which I suppose was how the mullahs viewed their citizens. I had chosen alcohol as my battle, and was prepared to sacrifice almost anything else—a buttercream cake over marzipan; a procession of flower girls—for the sake of a real bar with the best bartenders in Tehran, two Afghan brothers who were in high demand.

To complicate matters, our caterer, an Iranian woman married to the grandson of a former Lebanese president, was a fretful mess over the menu selections. She usually catered parties for European diplomats; would the Iranian guests appreciate her minimalist décor and cuisine? Her father and Arash's dad were professionally acquainted, and she had developed acute performance anxiety. We assured her that our guests were not terribly traditional and would not complain about insufficient portions or peculiar dishes. This did not calm her, and she often phoned to suggest adjustments, like replacing the Mediterranean salads on the menu with some Iranian lamb stew. One Saturday evening she called to breathlessly inform us that she was adding an "impressive lamb on a spit" and hung up.

Arash agreed to my suggestion of a therapist, so the following week we drove down to central Tehran for our first appointment with Dr. Majidi, a psychologist who came recommended by a family friend. We selected him from a handful of references, as Iranians had embraced therapy in recent years and the city was brimming with analysts, psychiatrists, and counselors of various specialties. The taboos associated with mental health had eroded over the last decade, partly because of Iranians' need to cope with their transforming society: its rising rates of divorce, the prevalence of premarital sex, and shifting gender roles. Behaviors considered normal in the context of collectivist Iranian culture—marrying the man selected by one's parents, devoting time to the care of family members who were not near relatives, following one's father into the family business—often seemed oppressive to a younger generation of Iranians who had been exposed to the individualist ethos of global culture. These strains were likely felt by young people across the world, but in Iran they were compounded by the social dynamics created by the revolution.

Several of my friends were in therapy sorting out how to reconcile their family's expectations with their own desires and sense of self— whether to emigrate despite the frailty of the parents living upstairs, whether to cancel the standing afternoon commitment to babysit the nephew downstairs. The impulse to seek out a therapist's advice was so widespread that one of the country's most prominent filmmakers, Tahmineh Milani, satirized it in her film *Ceasefire*, which became one of the highest-grossing Iranian films of all time.

Dr. Majidi's office functioned with considerable strictness. You were expected to pay in full for sessions canceled even well in advance, and if you showed up late more than twice, you were stricken from his client list altogether. (This severity did not preclude him from canceling appointments himself the day of the World Cup finals.) He shared his office suite with a psychiatrist, to whom he dispatched his incurable patients for prescriptions of Prozac, and the joint waiting room was usually so full that some clients had to sit in the stairwell. Often we waited an hour or more before being ushered into his office, which was painted in cheery buttercup yellow and decorated with photos of Persepolis. During our first few sessions, Dr. Majidi did more than his share of talking. We learned that he was divorced, had a teenage son with his second wife, and was torn over whether to move his family to Laguna Beach. This decision seemed to weigh so heavily on his consciousness that it, rather than our wedding dilemmas, dominated our sessions.

"On the one hand, I think, here we're surrounded by family. My son has an exceptional network of support. And to be honest with you, I don't look forward to the idea of transplanting myself professionally at this stage in my life. But then I think, I have brought a child into this world, and I'm responsible for his education. I just don't know if I could live with myself, putting him through Iranian schools. And Ahmadinejad. Who saw that coming?"

"We moved to Germany when I was fourteen," Arash ventured. "It was really difficult, but we managed. I went to university, everyone adjusted."

"Really? Interesting!" Dr. Majidi paused to sip tea, then began again. "You know what I think? I think, as a first step, my wife and I need to stop talking about our plans at dinner parties. You know how Iranians are—everyone needs to air their opinion and interfere in your decision. And of course it has nothing to do with what you are actually contemplating, but their own issues. If *they* can't leave, then you're a fool to consider it; if they can, then you're already a decade too late. . . . Well, time's up! See you next week."

"What do you think it means that our therapist only talks about himself?" I wondered, as we bought fresh *barbari* across the street. It was past eight when we emerged from Dr. Majidi's, and we sat on the street tearing off chunks of bread and discussing our session. "Maybe it's because he thinks we're really healthy and can work out all our problems on our own. Did you get a look at that mother and daughter in the waiting room?"

The pair had embodied the most extreme generational clash, the mother in über-chador, the kind with attachable sleevelets (used to keep the wrists and forearms covered, in case the chador and the manteau beneath it slipped back a couple inches), the daughter in a tight tunic, patterned tights, and sexy lace-up boots. Compared to such patients, perhaps our wedding stress struck Dr. Majidi as prosaic and undeserving of clinical attention. He would need to correct that attitude if he wanted to practice in Laguna Beach.

We decided to give him another chance, because it seemed unfair to judge him on our very first meeting. By our third session, Dr. Majidi seemed to have resolved his personal travails. He actually listened when I told him about my mother's opposition to the timing of our marriage, and volunteered some insight about how emigration adds strain to the natural tensions between parents and children. He warned us of the pitfalls of intercultural marriages, suggesting that just because we had a love of baklava and Rumi in common, we should not assume our attitudes about everything else were the same. We had already understood this and didn't particularly need such counsel, but Dr. Majidi seemed to mean well and we listened politely. As our very next visit drew to a close, he rubbed a hand against his broad stomach and cleared his throat. "It has been a real privilege working with the two of you, but sadly I won't be available after the end of the month. I'm flying to Los Angeles to enroll my son in school, and the family will join me shortly after. It kills me to leave, really it does. I know I'll never have a more comfortable life anywhere. But this country is sinking, and I owe it to my son to offer him something better."

"Is it really sinking?" I asked. "I mean, more than usual?" It was the early summer of 2006, and President Ahmadinejad's performance in office, though worrisome at moments, did not strike most people as dramatically worse than the typical clerical rule they were used to. Three times he had called for Israel to be wiped off the map, but to most Iranians, accustomed to hearing exaggerated rhetoric from their leaders and seeing its equivalent on murals around the city, this did not seem especially noteworthy. The most controversial aspect of his rule, his rash economic policy, was just starting to attract attention. Keen to bolster his popularity in the provinces, the president was constantly commissioning major infrastructure projects around Iran that injected vast amounts of cash into the economy. Economists warned of an inevitable spike in inflation. The Tehran stock exchange had seen a 26 percent decrease in its index, and fifty prominent economists had just published an open letter accusing the president of unsettling the investment climate and squandering oil revenue. But with parliament opposed to many of these policies, especially the raiding of the country's oil funds, it seemed plausible that Ahmadinejad would be forced to reconsider his positions. "It's all a matter of perspective," Dr. Majidi replied blandly, perhaps regretting his blunt word choice— after all, he was advising two people who were just beginning to build a life in the "sinking" country.

On the way home, we decided it was impossible to know Dr. Majidi's real motivations for leaving. In truth, we couldn't help feeling a twinge of unease at this departure. When your therapist, someone who is trained in identifying what is destructive in life, concludes that the society you live in is best left behind, it gives you particular pause. We concluded that Dr. Majidi was better off leaving, as he had become determined to see only gloom in his surroundings, and with that attitude he would inevitably create only a gloomy reality for himself. Had he been privy to our conversation, he would likely have pointed out that we were rationalizing. And perhaps we were. But we were not the only ones in Iran choosing to focus on what seemed promising. In fairness, much was happening to encourage such optimism. Most Iranians admired Ahmadinejad's firm position on the country's right to peaceful nuclear power, and believed he was serving Iran well by guaranteeing its future access to an alternative source of energy. The government argued that by building nuclear reactors, Iran could free up oil and its byproducts for export and thus bring significant income into the lumbering economy. If the president managed to negotiate a solution by which Iran retained this right without alienating the world, everyone stood to gain.

Two nights after our last meeting with Dr. Majidi, our families gathered at a middle-of-the-week dinner party at my uncle's house. He and my aunt had invited Arash's parents over so we could discuss the final details of the wedding, just a couple of weeks away. The air was gentle and warm, and we ate outside on the terrace, a casual summer meal of *kotlet*—patties of lamb and potato—and garlicky homemade pickles. Our families seemed to truly enjoy each other's company, laughing easily and considering a vacation together. The women talked about music, the men traded thoughts on business, and we all conferred excitedly about the day's news: President Ahmadinejad had waived the ban on women's attendance at soccer games. It was a truly astonishing act for an avowedly fundamentalist president who had until then scarcely acknowledged that women have rights.

The ban dated back to the revolution, when doctrinaire mullahs deemed the raucous atmosphere of a football stadium polluting to women. The episode during Khatami's presidency when women fans had successfully stormed a stadium one day had failed to change the authorities' position. Their precise reasoning was difficult to deduce. The regime objected to women watching the male players in their shorts, but since the games were broadcast live on national television, it hardly made sense to ban women from watching in public what they could view in their living rooms. The immense crowds at football matches also made gender segregation virtually impossible. For a regime that took coed mingling very seriously (lawmakers were now insisting that classes for girls and boys should be held not only in separate buildings, but in buildings a certain number of meters distant) it was easier to forbid women from attending altogether. But, as an activist I had spoken with earlier that day had pointed out, "unmarried men and women sit together in dark cinemas, which if you think about it is a lot worse."

"He's clearly trying to extend his popularity to the educated middle class," I said. Since state radio announced the news early that day, I had been talking to analysts and women's rights activists, and everyone agreed that the president's intentions were purely political. He would reap popularity points by positioning himself as a leader who risked a fight with the ayatollahs of Qom, the country's holy city, to win women their right to watch football.

For the most part, Ahmadinejad still drew the core of his support from a tiny fraction of diehard ideologues and from among the employed poor—minor civil servants and the lower ranks of the Basij and the military, people who found themselves benefiting from his expansionist economic policies. There was no reason to think the base of his support had grown significantly since the first round of the 2005 elections, when he received only 5.7 million votes, just 12 percent of the electorate (most Iranian analysts judged the number of his core supporters on the basis of the first round, before the Basij mobilized voters in the second). Compared with the nearly 22 million votes Khatami won in 2001, Ahmadinejad's constituency amounted to a small minority. But with a radical gamble like this, he could attract women and the educated urban class, the millions who had voted for Khatami and either boycotted the most recent election or supported Rafsanjani. Neither of those two presidents, far more moderate than Ahmadinejad, had dared such a bold policy reversal.

"Isn't it always the most conservative leaders who can take these kinds of decisions?" said Arash. "Because they're accepted by the hard-line establishment, they have room to maneuver in ways the liberals never do." Everyone offered their favorite examples of this phenomenon: the Israeli leader Ariel Sharon pulling out of Gaza; Prince Abdullah of Saudi Arabia and his peace initiative for ending the Israel-Palestine conflict.

"The timing is very clever," mused Mahmoud Agha, Arash's father. He reached for his glass, his bearing dignified as usual, an intrigued expression in his gold-specked brown eyes. Earlier that month, the nuclear crisis between Iran and the West had escalated considerably. The regime was digging in its heels over the right to enrich uranium, and Ahmadinejad was the defiant articulator of this tough line. The policy risked further international isolation, something Iranians had experienced quite enough of, and thus it demanded public support as never before. By taking today's bold step, the president could harness both secular ambitions and soccer patriotism to his own brand of religious nationalism. It seemed some critics were won over.

"I don't know exactly why he did this," my uncle Shahrokh said, "but perhaps we have another Reza Shah on our hands." Might Ahmadinejad be such a ferociously ambitious leader, willing to provoke the religious establishment for the sake of improving the nation? To me, the extent of his ambition seemed clear, but its true character still impossible to judge.

An important realignment was taking place in Iran's domestic politics and in the country's place in the world. Feeling newly emboldened in its confrontation with the West, a conservative administration was astutely reaching out to the vast, moderate spectrum of Iranian society to build support for its antagonistic foreign policy. This meant the depressing, dead-end dynamic of Iranian politics during the last decade—moderates attempting reform, only to be blocked by hard-liners—was finally being recast. Not since the earliest days of the Khatami tenure, back in 2000, had significant change seemed even remotely possible. The outcome was still very far from certain, and domestic openness for the sake of a belligerent posture in the world hardly constituted a desirable way forward. But if you looked at this from the point of view of an Iranian—accustomed to domestic repression as well as a government that misbehaved around the world—it was still progress. For the first time in as long as I could remember, the somber sense of living in an irretrievably failed society lifted, and the future seemed specked with, of all things, opportunity.

One weekday evening, just days after Ahmadinejad's astounding announcement, Arash prodded me into joining him and Houshang for an evening with a classical musician. Since I didn't know very much about Iranian classical music, its history, or its place in Iranian culture, I realized only much later the importance of the man we were going to meet: Ostad Mohammad Reza Lotfi, Iran's most accomplished classical musician and *tar* master. Arash played two classical instruments, the *tar* and the *setar,* and had been enamored of Iranian music since his adolescence. My appreciation for the music had grown since we met, and I was especially interested in how it intersected with Sufism and the poetry of Rumi.

"Isn't it a rather oddly timed return?" I asked, as we crawled through traffic. Lotfi had spent long years in exile in the West, and had just returned to re-found the school of music the authorities shut down after the 1979 revolution. Houshang had visited the school the previous day, and reported that hordes of eager young musicians had stood in interminable lines under the hot Tehran sun, instrument cases tucked under their arms, waiting to take the entrance exam. Enough women showed up for an all-women's orchestra. Arash explained that Iranian classical music is an oral tradition, and that with most of the great masters in exile, this young generation had entirely missed the opportunity for formal training.

"So what you're telling me is that after all these years, the government is relaxing its controls on music?" I asked. "Are you sure? Why haven't I read anything about this in the newspaper?" It occurred to me that this would make a very fine news story, another instance of the regime opening up when least expected to do so.

We finally reached downtown Tehran, and Ostad Lotfi climbed into the car. He was nearly six feet tall, with flowing white hair and an aquiline nose, and he wore loose Kurdish pants and elegant loafers. He lit a cigarette and began to talk. His conversation was stunning—witty, erudite, whirling between centuries and hemispheres. We spent the evening on the carpeted terrace of the country house in Lavasan. The air was laced with the perfume of fresh roses and oleaster trees, the nightingales twittered, the frogs chirped. We ate apricots and golden plums and looked out across the dark pool that irrigated the orchards, the moonlight in the willows.

While I knew the religious authorities who came to power during the revolution had dealt harshly with pop and western music, I was not aware that they had also been intolerant of Iranian classical music. They had declared classical musical instruments, as well as a woman's singing voice, to be *haram* (forbidden), thus extinguishing the classical tradition almost entirely. Museum-quality instruments were burned in bonfires, and instruments could not be shown on television, in films, in stores, or even in classrooms. Iranians born after the revolution couldn't tell a *tar* (a large, double-bowled string instrument) from a *setar* (a delicate, single-bowled lute). This was as if a western child were unable to tell a cello from a guitar.

The irony was that song—the revolutionary *sorood*s (anthems) that Lotfi and others composed—had energized the mass protests that brought down the Shah's regime. Ayatollah Khomeini, who was known to love Iranian classical music, issued a subtle fatwa just before his death in 1989 distinguishing between *haram* and *halal* (acceptable) forms of music. This fatwa is credited with resurrecting Iranian classical music, for it created small openings through which music crept back into public life. Arash's *tar* instructor recounts tales from this period, when it was no longer illegal to possess an instrument, but a permit was required, as though a string instrument might pose a real danger in the wrong hands. Musicians could apply to perform in public, although only the most committed could deal with the difficulties of renting suitable auditoriums, the censorship of lyrics, and the presence of mullahs dispatched to preach before the concert.

What I realized that evening, listening to Lotfi reminisce, was how these struggles over music reflected a long divide in Iranian history over Islam's interaction with art. Like most Iranians my age, or with few or wispy memories of pre-1979 Iran, I had assumed that censorship and disapproval of the fine arts began with the Islamic revolution. When I first walked through the sixteenth-century Safavid palaces in Isfahan, the capital of the Shia dynasty, I saw music rooms with ceiling carvings of instruments, and imagined those rulers must have approved of music, despite their piety. The Shah's government had supported musical broadcasting—a reflection of Iranian sensibilities, I imagined. But none of this was actually the case. The Safavid rulers never brought music out of the private realm—the intimate garden of a house or a palace, the *andaruni* quarters that were off-limits to the public; in the long tradition of cultured monarchs reigning over less refined subjects, they indulged their tastes in seclusion. And while the Shah believed that Iran should have grand European-style orchestras, the average Iranian considered music impure. At that time, even many educated Iranians considered music a low form of entertainment, and would have been embarrassed if their sons played an instrument.

This was as true in 1979 as it had been in 1949, when Jalal Al-e Ahmad wrote his short story "Setar," which castigates the narrow, puritanical style of Islam practiced by uneducated Iranians. The story follows a musician who has saved for three years to buy a *setar* only to have it smashed to pieces by an enraged perfume seller who catches him entering a mosque with it under his arm ("Atheist! With this instrument of infidels inside a mosque?!"). The tale ends with the musician creeping away, devastated. "The cup of his hope, just like the body of his new *setar,* had shattered into three pieces, and the pieces seemed to be cutting into his heart." When you considered this history, the revolution did not create so much as reflect a cultural climate hostile to music.

Today, that hostility was gone. Despite the clerical regime's restrictions, the views of the vast majority of Iranians had evolved and most people considered music both harmless and central to human existence. Even many conservative and religious Iranians now enjoyed music, and only a doctrinaire fringe considered all music sinful. Though it was frustrating that the government refused to fully recognize this transformation and was only slowly softening its restrictions, what seemed most important was that Iranian society had shed its resistance to musical expression. If all the years I had spent reporting around the Middle East had taught me one thing, it was the crucial importance of a society developing secular or modern values from the bottom up. The region was full of conservative countries led by secular leaders, and these countries were inevitably unstable.

"People seem to think that one person can somehow solve things," Lotfi said, leaning back against the cushions on the rug. "They think, 'If Lotfi stays, he'll fix it so that women can sing again, so that there will be concerts again.' Somehow it has fallen to me to create some solution, for the religious pressure to ease, to open the doors again." He looked very tired as he said this, as though the burden of rescuing an entire tradition weighed on his shoulders. Which in a way, it did.

The evening grew late, and as our conversation dwindled, Lofti pulled his *tar* into his lap. He looked up as though seeking inspiration from the heavens, and began playing "Navai," a song from the province of Khorasan, my father's family's home. It is one of the most exquisite folk melodies I have ever heard, and hearing it played in the warm dark of the garden, by a master who had returned from exile to rescue Iranian music from extinction, I felt more certain than ever that the country was mending and that we could live here forever.

Our wedding took place on an unseasonably warm day in June 2006, so warm I feared my slick coats of makeup would melt before the ceremony began. I had pleaded for Jilla, Tehran's top makeup artist, to dip lightly into her case of paints. "Usually, I'm a complete frump. I consider lip balm dressing up," I told her, exaggerating in hopes of not being lacquered beyond recognition.

Jilla, a plump, middle-aged woman from Tabriz, ran a beauty empire catering to the city's idle female rich. Her salon occupied half the second floor of a towering high-rise in the affluent district of Elahieh, the value of the real estate alone underscoring her accomplishment. Opening a beauty salon was among the most conventional ways for Iranian women to attain financial independence. Oftentimes they turned the basement of a building, or an extra room in the house, into a salon, a form of entrepreneurism that met with the approval of even the most controlling husbands since it kept the wives indoors, close to home, in the company of other women. These in-house salons earned a modest income, but Jilla had created something far more ambitious, an urban retreat that turned serious profit, making her one of the city's most successful female entrepreneurs.

She did not appreciate being admonished. "Do you think I approve of how our young brides want to be painted like vulgar Arab women?" she chided, pushing a button to release the back of the white leather chair.

Many salons advertised *arayesh-e khaliji*, or the "Gulf makeover," meaning the very particular, stylized makeup worn by Arab pop singers in music videos. Despite Jilla's xenophobic dismissal of the Arab-vixen look, I emerged from the salon with overarched eyebrows extending over lids dusted in about ten different shades of pearl. My only consolation was that I had paid just $100 for the application; the cost would have been five times higher had I admitted to being the bride, rather than the bride's cousin. "Look what they've done to me," I wailed to my father, who had arrived just four days ago and was waiting below to drive me to my uncle's house. "I look like an insane newscaster." Apart from a terse assurance that I did not, he remained mostly silent during the drive.

My father had been preoccupied from the moment of his arrival. He considered it bizarre and unwelcome that I was getting married in Iran. He regarded himself as a democrat, in contrast to the authoritarian ayatollahs, and would thus never dream of openly criticizing my decision. But his eloquent silence almost spoke for itself. Why, it said, have you returned to this country everyone sensible flees? Why are you embracing a life under the rule of odious mullahs, when I built for you a charmed existence in the sunny land of the world's greatest democracy? His bitterness toward Iran would never let him understand my need to reconcile with the country, despite its rulers and obscene flaws. My father now saw home in the orderliness of America's traffic, the convenience of its grocery stores, the hush of its well-stocked libraries. He had never understood my longing to live in more ancient places, places whose past bore a connection to my present.

So much had changed in the nearly twenty-five years since his last visit that he spent much of his time gazing at and remarking on the physical transformation of Tehran. "Have you seen what they've done with Tajrish Sqaure? With the hiking trail behind Shahabad?" he would exclaim after solitary forays into the city and the mountains, almost boyish in his astonishment. He would never admit that he was enjoying himself, but I hadn't seen him so animated in years, and I teased him for sounding like a tourist. But these bouts of excitement were punctuated by moody silences, when he seemed lost in thought and vaguely disappointed by what he saw around him. On one occasion he was rudely rebuked by a taxi driver for calling Vali Asr Boulevard by its pre-1979 name, Pahlavi. The driver hadn't believed that my father couldn't recall the new name, and their exchange had grown unpleasant. The incident had embodied for him the touchy hostility that characterized the new Iran around him.

"Are you sure it wasn't like this before, and you just don't remember?" I had asked him.

"No, it wasn't. It might have been many other things, but it wasn't like this."

Upon arrival at my uncle's house, I retired to the second-floor balcony, cooled by the breeze through the sycamore trees, to repair my face. That's how Arash found me, surrounded by piles of tissue, dabbing furiously at my eyes. "It's not so bad," he said, reassuringly. "Just keep wiping." He set at my feet a rose and a tin of Salad Olivier, my favorite potato salad, dense with mayonnaise and peas, and went to change.

My uncle's living room had been cleared of furniture, and our *sofreh* lay in the corner near the window. The spread was in the traditional style, the walnuts still in their shiny green skins instead of spray-painted with gold, the candlesticks and trays all antique silver, rather than the now customary gilt. The guests mingled on the terrace drinking champagne, and nibbling on *loz,* almond and saffron pastries delivered fresh from Tabriz. At some undetermined hour in the late afternoon, when most of the guests had arrived, we gathered everyone around the *sofreh,* and the ceremony began.

Arash had asked a family friend to officiate, preparing a few short paragraphs for him to read based on an old Zoroastrian wedding text. Most ceremonies are presided over by mullahs, who bore the guests by droning on in Arabic, which they do not understand. Intrigued at being addressed in Farsi, all our relatives and friends huddled in close to listen to the poetic and intimate text, their expressions rapt. After Arash and I repeated our vows, my female relatives lifted a tulle canopy over our heads and ground together two cones of sugar into its folds, symbolizing a life of sweetness. As is customary, we dipped our pinky fingers into a bowl of honey, and licked the syrup off each other's fingers. At that moment, as the women wiped away the smudges of mascara beneath their eyes, the *motreb*s slid into the crowd.

Motreb literally means "one who makes joy," and the term refers to the musician-entertainers who were long ago a beloved feature of the city's café culture. Our *motreb*s looked like relics themselves, in ill-fitting pants pulled high at the waist, their hair greased back, as if they were character actors in a Hollywood Mafia movie. To the music of accordion and violin, they began to sing their sly, rhyming verses, playfully slipping to the verge of crudeness and easing right back, and soon the whole room was alive with laughter, the guests chanting back their part in the music, creating a joyous, campy, poetic repartee. Then they played "Hava Nagila"—traditionally, most *motreb*s are Jewish—and everyone moved onto the terrace to twirl under the trees. Our pious relatives in dressy chadors of patterned black silk did not dance, but they smiled happily, sipping fresh watermelon juice and watching the *motreb*s thread through the crowd.

Although I had painstakingly carried my wedding dress by hand to Tehran from California, Arash's attire eclipsed mine. He had originally wanted to wear something authentically Iranian, a knee-length, stand-up-collar Qajar-era coat, but we hadn't managed to find a seamstress who knew what one should look like. Iranians, in their rush to westernize, had discarded indigenous wedding garb generations ago, and now no one could remember what precisely had been worn before the suit and tie and the poofy white dress. The closest thing we found to a Qajar coat was an Indian *sherwani,* which we ordered online—one-week express delivery—from New Delhi. Unlike Iranians, Indians had both retained their traditions and expertly marketed them to the world. Everyone surrounded Arash, playing with the tassels of his scarf, admiring the delicate fabric of his coat, fawning over him as if he were a visiting maharaja. I was only mildly piqued.

The reception later that evening was exquisite for many reasons— for the abundant, fragrant roses that crowded each corner of the garden, the glowing candles that lit the landscape pathways, the jewel-like pastries circulating on trays; but most of all for how it evoked, on a rather grand scale, an Iran that no longer existed. Men and women danced together inside the house, and in the lower garden, the alcohol flowed freely from a bar in the dining room, where a DJ tended to the young people, while the *motreb*s played classics outside. Receptions of this sort were usually only held in the rented gardens of Karaj, so couples were forced to choose between the coziness of home, and the security requirements of a proper party. In the Lavasan garden we could have such a party, and be at home at the same time. We were exceptionally fortunate in having such a special place to hold our wedding.

As we walked with our final guests down the petal-strewn path to the gates, passing the remnants of the lamb on a spit, I gazed around with a tender sense of satisfaction. Though I was not certain that our future in Iran would be blessed with the magic and security of this one evening, I was glad we had reminded people that you didn't need skywriting and fireworks to have a good time, and that the city's own rites and its *motreb*s offered the best entertainment anyone could hope for. That six main courses were just as good as twenty, and that there was something to be said for inviting only a hundred guests,

even if your family's social obligations might have merited a thousand. Though it had scarcely been our intention, the very next morning the phone began to ring with requests for information. Who had
written our vows? Would we share the text with others? Who had produced the invitation? In the months that followed, it became popular
to use Zoroastrian ceremonial texts and invitations, to have *motrebs*
play alongside DJs. Even friends of ours from observant Muslim families asked to use our text, so delighted were they with its Iranian sensibility and the idea of using Farsi rather than Arabic. Iranian young
people, lost between the domineering Islamic culture of the government
and the mindless embrace of western traditions that were equally foreign, lacked an authentic identity to call their own. Before long, Arash
and I became known in our social circle as the couple with the Zoroastrian wedding, the originators of what appeared more meaningful
than just another trend.

For our honeymoon, we spent a weekend in Shiraz, a city in south-
western Iran known for its orange blossom–scented gardens and the
shrines of great Persian poets. We spent a day exploring Persepolis,
the 2,500-year-old ruins of ancient Persia's capital. Thousands of Iranians strolled through the magnificent complex of temples, drawing
rooms, and palaces, gazing reverently at the towering columns. In 330
B.C.E., Alexander burned the imperial city to the ground, but what remained of the pre-Islamic kings' throne drew Iranians in vast numbers, more than any other attraction across the country. Families laid
out picnics in the shade; children played hide-and-seek around the
columns; and loudspeakers intoned warnings that demonstrated the
authorities' nonchalance about preservation. Instead of installing
guards every few meters to protect what remained of one of the most
sophisticated civilizations on earth, the government simply reminded
Iranians: "Please do not stub out your cigarette on Persepolis. . . .
Please do not write or carve on the ruins. . . ." We posed with the
winged creatures carved out of stone, and headed back to central Shiraz to eat rose sorbet laced with fragile rice noodles in the shade of an
eighteenth-century citadel. We walked backed to our hotel, and I
pressed Arash's hand in mine, enchanted with the city, with my new
husband, and the prospect of everything our future held in store.

CHAPTER 12

The Not So Reluctant
Fundamentalist

As odd as this might sound, most women in Iran consider marriage greatly liberating. The adjectives they use to describe their married lives—"independent," "unbound," "carefree"—are similar to those western women would apply to being single. Perhaps this is because the phenomena of single life—dating, premarital sex, parties—are still not openly acknowledged by many, however commonplace they have become. The single woman has to concoct excuses to spend long hours with a boyfriend, must connive with friends to secure places to be alone. Her parents call her cell phone constantly, demanding to know where she is and when she will return home. A single woman, in short, requires considerable subterfuge if she is to maintain the delicate pretense of being a respectable daughter living at home with her parents. Marriage ends the tiresome years of charade and releases the fetters of parental and societal oversight. The married woman is mistress of her time and space, accountable to no one but her husband. Provided, of course, the husband is not some jealous, controlling disaster of a spouse, as is sometimes the case, but often not. She can take bonsai classes, meet friends for coffee, disappear for an afternoon at the cinema, and dress as she pleases.

It had never occurred to me to view marriage in this way. Raised in the West, I conceived of the institution as unnecessary and potentially stultifying. I had viewed marriage as a distant, somewhat distressing fleck on the horizon, anxious that it would render my life banal. I became aware of the radically different Iranian view one fall afternoon some years ago, while I was waiting for my tape recorder to be checked by security at the presidential palace. A young member of the security staff, a woman in black chador, kept me company, and as we chatted she asked my age. She looked horrified upon discovering that at twenty-five I was not yet married. "Twenty-five! What on earth are you waiting for? Don't you want to be *free*?"

"Free?" I had repeated, confused. I didn't see any connection between marriage and freedom.

"Yes, free. You can finally leave your parents' house, no one telling you what to do." Adding in a mimic of a maternal whine, " 'Wake up, eat, sleep, come, go!' "

When the only escape from suffocating parental love was marriage, it was entirely reasonable, even if unrealistic, to imbue that institution with the charm of long-awaited autonomy. The eternal compromises of marriage, the need to continually adapt oneself to the demands of life with another human being, occupied no corner of this idealized picture.

Though I never expected marriage to bestow on me a new independence, I did believe that it would, in one important respect, secure my freedom: it would be my rescue from Mr. X. This conviction dated back to my earliest conversations with Shirin khanoum, when I inquired about how she managed the invasive presence of the state's security agents in her life. If they pestered me, an ordinary journalist, with such dogged zeal, then surely they must have terrorized the country's outspoken Nobel laureate. I had been deeply surprised to learn this had not been the case.

"I explained to them that as a proper, married woman, I could obviously not be seen having coffee with strange men in the lobbies of hotels," she told me. Since it was Islamically improper to meet them alone, on one occasion Shirin khanoum had even brought her husband along to the meeting. The agents had been mortified—something to do with one Iranian man respecting another man's territory—and afterward they had ceased to demand she meet with them.

Arash resented the presence of Mr. X in my life, though not out of any sense of encroachment on his *namoos,* the Islamic term for the honor and sanctity of a man's family. Arash simply considered my minder scum and wished I were not obliged to maintain contact with someone who bullied and intimidated people on behalf of a despotic state. When I told him that I could, in the manner of Shirin khanoum, use Islamic propriety and his purported displeasure as a pretext to end, or at least modify, the relationship, Arash readily agreed. Thus prepared to finally disrupt the years of menace and intrusion, I awaited Mr. X's inevitable phone call with much excitement.

The morning the numbers "1111111" appeared on my phone's caller ID—Mr. X phoned from the Ministry of Intelligence, I assume, with a blocked number—I picked up eagerly.

"May you not be tired. Are you well?" I said. We exchanged robotic pleasantries for a minute, before Mr. X asked when I might be free.

"There is something I must tell you," I said. "My husband does not consider it appropriate for me to meet men alone in an empty hotel room." I would wait to bring out the real ammunition, the word *namahram,* the term for someone who is not an immediate family member. Strict Muslims believe that men and women who are *namahram* should not be alone in each other's company. Any pedestrian mullah could tell you this; it was an edict as direct as the one about pork being *haram.* "He would be more comfortable if we met in an official government office, or at the very least in a public place, such as a hotel lobby. Alternatively, he would be happy to accompany me, if you preferred to continue to meet in seclusion."

"What right does your husband have to interfere in our work?" he asked. "Our work is *amneeat,* security." He emphasized this as if talking to a small child. "Do you think we can conduct sensitive intelligence work related to the nation's security in the lobbies of hotels?"

I felt like asking him whether the sorts of things he liked to know and that I refused to tell him—what the Irish third secretary had said at the Maldivian ambassador's tea party—truly protected Iran from grave and insidious threats. Instead, I remained civil. "That is for you to determine. But my husband's sensitivities must be respected."

"Has your husband not been in the West? How can it be that he has such a closed mind?"

I wished I were recording this. A henchman of the Islamic Republic was lecturing me on liberality. "My husband, regardless of his time abroad, is an Iranian man. And that means he has firm beliefs regarding the propriety of his wife's meetings with other men. As an Iranian man yourself, working for an Islamic government, I would presume you could appreciate that."

"I regret to hear that you're just not serious about work anymore." Mr. X sighed. "Maybe now that you're married you would just like to retire?"

Mr. X held veto power over my press credentials, as he often reminded me. I was on the verge of tears. Nothing was going as I had expected. Why had it worked for Shirin khanoum?

"You know that I'm very serious about work," I said, softening my tone. "Haven't I shown that by staying in regular contact? And the last time I was at the foreign press office, everyone was very pleased with my stories."

"Forget the foreign press office. They do not have security responsibilities." Apparently my file was on a par with negotiating rights over nuclear enrichment at the United Nations. Mr. X was very sensitive about the ministry's reputation, and puffed up regularly when discussing its myriad "responsibilities."

"What I'm asking is not so unreasonable," I pleaded. "Surely we can come to an agreement. There must be a room somewhere at the ministry, anywhere official, that we can use? Or perhaps you would like to meet my husband, and get to know him? He is very discreet."

But Mr. X was not interested in meeting Arash. "You should think again about these silly excuses you are making. I will make discussions on my end," he said, hanging up.

Perhaps it had been too much to hope that I could extricate myself from dealing with Mr. X altogether, but I had imagined I could at least negotiate a more balanced relationship. Meeting in public, or at least in a government building, would deny Mr. X the psychological weapon of creepy seclusion. Reducing my vulnerability in these meetings had been my central aim, and it had failed.

I wanted to call Shirin khanoum and tell her that her approach had not worked, but obviously I couldn't say such things over the phone. Mr. X had said in stark terms that security concerns, whatever that meant, took precedence over Islamic correctness. That pretty well summarized the ethos of the regime: security over everything—over development, over the ethical values of Islam, over the rights of its people. Although the state ruled in the name of Islam, had taken power through a revolution that was termed "Islamic," in its behavior it had everything in common with a dictatorship. When a government derived its authority from Islam, one had no other language with which to defend oneself. Mr. X defended his right to interrogate me in seclusion like the agent of a secular state, but I could not call upon any universal, secular values to challenge him. Neither, apparently, could I call upon Islamic ones.

"You won't need to meet Mr. X after all," I told Arash that evening, as we walked London and Geneva to the neighborhood vet to be dewormed. They stopped every two minutes, sniffing the leaves and candy wrappers floating down the sidewalk canal, best friends despite their ill-matched sizes—an elephant and a teacup, as the Farsi expression went.

I resolved to speak to someone, perhaps at the foreign press office Mr. X had dismissed, about my minder's wanton disregard for Islamic morality. There had to be someone in this Islamic state who would care.

Less than three weeks after our wedding I was in a taxi on the way to my monthly doctor's appointment, and for one disorienting moment thought I was back in Beirut. Not central Beirut, mind you, but the southern suburbs, where every intersection and thoroughfare is bedecked with the canary yellow flags of Hezbollah. The same government-supplied flags were now decorating the Tehran freeway. Banners depicting the militia's leader, Hassan Nasrallah, hoisting a rifle into the air flew from hundreds of lampposts.

Earlier that week, the group had kidnapped two Israeli soldiers on the Israeli-Lebanese border, provoking a ferocious Israeli response that had quickly erupted into the worst Arab-Israeli border conflict in over two decades. The Iranian government was cheering for Hezbollah.

Iran helped found Hezbollah in the early eighties, when the Ayatollah Khomeini was seeking to export Islamic revolution to places like Lebanon. Today radicals in both Tehran and Beirut had largely abandoned the ayatollah's fantasy; they acknowledged that the Lebanese, Christian and Muslim alike, had no desire for an Islamic state in Iran's image, and that one could not be imposed on them by force. Iran's modern relationship with Hezbollah reflected different ideological and political realities. Iran continued to serve as the group's primary patron. But through its military, financial, and political support for Hezbollah, Iran now sought influence in the Levant more obliquely: by ensuring that Lebanese Shia, who had no wish to become a western ally friendly with Israel, dominated the country's politics. For its part, Hezbollah used its Iranian patronage to supply much-needed social services to Lebanon's neglected Shia population. With Iranian aid and Hezbollah's leadership, Lebanese Shia began for the first time in decades to exert political influence commensurate with their numbers. Both sides benefited, to the West's chagrin.

How much control Iran exerted over Hezbollah was a vexed question. Israel and the West charged that Iran directed the militia as if by remote control, while Iran and Hezbollah allies like Syria insisted it was entirely independent. The truth lay somewhere in between. While Iran certainly had some sway, Hezbollah tended to conduct its own affairs, mainly consulting with Tehran ahead of major operations that it knew would reverberate around the region.

Whatever the nature of this relationship, however, most ordinary Iranians resented it. Each and every one of my friends and relatives— the pious and the secular, the anti-American and the westernized— perceived Iran's support for Hezbollah as a colossal waste. A couple

of my acquaintances voiced ambivalence rather than outright disapproval, but they were equally concerned about how aiding Hezbollah compromised Iran. The secular-minded, like my friend Neda,
objected to the state's nurturance of Islamic ideology beyond its borders. Many people, like my cousin at Tehran University and her classmates, lumped aid to Hezbollah with Iran's habit of building schools
in Arab countries and sending forces to "help" the Palestinians. They
disapproved of all these practices, arguing that as long as Iranians at
home were in dire need, not a toman should be spent abroad. One of
my relatives worried that if democratic forces in Iran ever gained
power through an election, the hard-liners would call on Lebanon's
Hezbollah to stomp them down. Yet another argued that Hezbollah
was a paper ally, that its fighters would sit back and watch in the
event Iran was attacked. For all these various reasons, consensus held
that the Iranian government should attend to its duties at home, and
abandon its nosy, fundamentalist meddling elsewhere.

   None of this is to say, of course, that Iranians did not sympathize
with Hezbollah and the Palestinians, on whose behalf the militant
group partly fought. Many of my friends, and indeed most Iranians,
considered Israel an unjust state, one that kept the Palestinians confined to hellish settlements while its own citizens luxuriated in the
trappings of an ultra-modern society. These sentiments meant that
many Iranians, from secular leftists to the deeply religious, commiser-
ated with Hezbollah's anti-Israel stance and thrilled to the group's
vigorous response to the far better equipped Israeli army. For the
majority of Iranians, though, such feelings were tempered by a cool
practicality—however just the militia's fight, it was not Iran's. A small
number of people, those whose devout faith included a strong measure of political militancy, felt otherwise. But these Iranians, ideological enough to sacrifice their immediate quality of life for a distant
cause, remained a distinct minority.

   The mood in Tehran was swinging between indifference—the
fighting hadn't made newspaper headlines a single day that week—
and irritation over the regime's ideological links to distant Arab
causes. Even my taxi driver that day, who judging from the hefty
Koran on his dashboard was a faithful Muslim, turned off his radio

impatiently when the announcer started in on the latest "Zionist atrocity."

"Don't you think it's our duty as Muslims to help Lebanon?" I asked. I would be writing a story later that evening, and no journalist is above asking the opinion of his or her taxi driver.

"What's happening is horrible. I saw charred bodies of children on the news last night. But did they consider it their Islamic duty to help us when we were fighting our war with Iraq?"

"No," I admitted. "That was an Arab fight against the Persians, and they picked their own side."

He nodded. "Well maybe, technically, it is our Islamic duty. But there are also realities."

"Like what?"

"I have to work a second shift every evening to make an extra five thousand toman," he said. This was the equivalent of $5. "It's just not right for us to be helping other people when our own are suffering."

I understood how he felt. But I knew some Iranians saw things differently and wanted to be sure that I was adequately portraying those who felt proud of Iran's support for Hezbollah. I used to volunteer at a Palestinian refugee school in Beirut, where the four-year-olds clamored around me in happy excitement because I was Iranian. In their eyes, Iran was the only country in the region to stand up to Israel, and a living, breathing Iranian deserved their most breathless thanks. I thought of the pride I witnessed all around me on that cloudless day in central Beirut in 2000, when the Israelis withdrew after twenty-two years of occupation. On that day, all of Lebanon—Christians and Muslims alike—considered Hezbollah heroes and rejoiced in their national victory. It was the first time I had seen anyone take pride in something that modern Iran, or perhaps I should say Islamic Iran, had accomplished. But now, in Tehran, I realized what an outsider's perspective that was: the reaction of someone who did not have to live with the consequences of the nation's foreign policy.

"So you're absolutely sure that you don't feel any pride that Iran helped the Lebanese push out the Israelis?" I asked. It was one of those moments when I felt I had to triple check, to make sure that Iranians truly were sensible and moderate on such questions. As a west-

ernized, secular Iranian, I was surrounded by people who were predictably critical of the government's radical policies; because of this, I
often tried to be exhaustively certain that my background didn't influence my work. This meant I generally did two or three times the
amount of reporting that was necessary, crisscrossing Tehran and
talking with the widest range of people I could find. I did this so I
could later defend my stories, which were often criticized by those
who had a stake in Iran's anti-American, anti-Israel image (a range of
people who included many politically conservative Americans, as well
as liberal Iranian Americans who enjoyed the defiant rhetoric the mullahs dished out to the Bush administration).

The driver inspected me in the mirror, as though noticing for the
first time that I was a bit alien, despite my familiar manners. "I'm not
proud at all. Do you know what would make me proud? If we could
solve our own problems. Like unemployment. That would be the
greatest help of all."

Soon we approached the immense floral clock the government had
created on the western bank of the Modarres freeway. It proudly proclaimed itself the largest clock in the world, as though this might invite tourism, enhance the appearance of the capital, or serve any other
useful function. While it was indeed the largest *flower* clock in the
world, it contended with two other giant clocks (one in New Jersey,
the other in Istanbul) for the title of biggest all around.

"I think you're quite right," I said, shamefaced.

"Remember," he said, quoting a Persian proverb, "If the lantern is
needed at home, it is *haram* to donate it to the mosque."

In the days that followed, the government continued to proclaim
its support for Hezbollah, dispatching honking cars full of young men
waving yellow flags. One evening, Arash and I were out eating ice
cream across the street from Mellat Park when one of these cars drove
past. In Beirut such a sight was common, but it simply did not register here, the fanfare of this distant group, embroiled in its distant conflict. The families picnicking on the lawn, pouring each other tea and
passing around mortadella sandwiches, failed to even look up. Later
that evening, state television broadcast an infomercial urging Iranians
to boycott what it called "Zionist products," including Pepsi, Nestlé,

and Calvin Klein. It warned that profits from these products "are converted into bullets piercing the chests of Lebanese and Palestinian children." As evidence, the voiceover intoned: "Pepsi stands for 'Pay Each Penny to Save Israel.' "

As was their way, Iranians ignored all this, being accustomed to the government's raving rhetoric, in which anger with Israel often blurred into a crude anti-Semitism. To me, and to many Iranians, such statements resounded with self-serving bias; while Palestinian children doubtless suffered in the crossfire of the conflict with Israel, the Iranian government had lost the legitimacy it needed to advocate on their behalf.

As the conflict in Lebanon wore on and Iran's reputation in the world as a backer of terrorism spread, many Iranians grew angry. One morning I walked to the square near our house to buy fresh bread for breakfast, but arrived to find the bakery doors locked and the stone oven cold. The early risers in my neighborhood milled about for a while and then began speculating about why the bakery should mysteriously be shut. Before long, they had settled on an explanation: the Iranian government had sent all the country's flour to Lebanon. After congregating briefly to vent their irritation ("What will they give them next, plasma TVs?"), everyone ambled back home.

That morning, though it had involved nothing more than griping with the neighbors over the country's politics, marked a turning point for me. When I first began reporting in Iran, I had assumed that my background as an upper-middle-class Iranian raised in the West was an obstacle to understanding the country properly. I imagined that, since my views were shaped by people of a similar class background, they were unrepresentative of Iran as a whole. Surely it was only a small minority of society, the affluent denizens of north Tehran, who held secular opinions about government, were open to the West, believed in democracy, and held the regime in contempt. To remedy what I considered a dangerous myopia, I began embracing all that stood in opposition to such a worldview. In 2000, during my first stint living in the country, I started hanging out with religious fundamentalists, convinced they represented the "real" Iran.

I spent those days sitting in a sparsely furnished living room, on couches whose pattern I would have described as tacky except that, trying to conquer my distaste, I made myself call it bright. The walls were bare save for a few Koranic inscriptions, and the table was covered with lace-patterned plastic. This was the home of my Arabic teacher in Tehran, who was the second wife of a Lebanese-Iranian political figure. Her husband was a revolutionary who had worked to start Hezbollah in Lebanon and now, although he spoke Farsi with an Arabic accent, held various positions of influence in the Tehran government. I had happily agreed to his suggestion that his wife tutor me—he did not mention at the time that she was one of two—and found myself snugly admitted into a world quite unlike any I had known. Here, in the company of radicals and their chador-wearing wives, I thought I had finally discovered the authentic soul of the country, the people who I assumed were steering the country's politics.

Most people called the second wife Um Hassan, or the mother of Hassan, but this form of appellation sounds peculiar in Farsi, so I simply called her Mrs. Khalil. In time I discovered that Mr. Khalil was a polygamist not by intention but by circumstance. His brother had died, or been martyred, during some clandestine military operation in the 1980s, and Mr. Khalil married Mrs. Khalil to rescue her from widowhood. I never mentioned Mrs. Khalil I to Mrs. Khalil II; and we kept our conversation focused on political and social issues of the day, reading aloud from Arabic magazines so I could hone my pronunciation. After my lesson we would chat over tea and baklava, and I would discover her sentiments about the day's news ("I'm really with bin Laden!"), which sounded especially chilling coming from a kind, roly-poly woman who made delicious salads.

Her views reflected, to my mind, her Arab background. Even among Iran's most highly religious, you would hear no such support for Osama bin Laden; to put it most bluntly, the malignant strain of anti-Americanism that produced support for Al Qaeda in the Arab and Muslim world did not exist in Iran. Iran's authoritarian regime was not aligned with the United States, whereas in places like Jordan, Pakistan, and Saudi Arabia, people resented America for propping up their local dictator, and that made bin Laden popular.

In time, I learned that Mrs. Khalil considered fighting jihad the moral duty of all Muslims, interpreted the Koran in ways that justified political violence, and considered the death of innocent victims, American, Israeli, or otherwise, an unavoidable consequence of the just war. My Arabic faltered during discussions involving abstract conceptions like justice and morality, and so I did not press her on these views.

Mr. Khalil was never present at our sessions, for which I was grateful, particularly since he had once phoned me at seven A.M. and proposed that we take a trip together. Through a sleepy fog, I worked up severe indignation, informing him that I was not accustomed to taking trips with male acquaintances. To be propositioned at such an ungodly hour by a married man would have been offensive enough, but coming from a polygamist it was especially infuriating. The nerve! As though two wives did not suffice. Since then, ill at ease with Mrs. Khalil, I had been wishing to extricate myself from her kindness, but I thought my access to her clique of devout friends was worth the discomfort. As the months passed, however, I began reconsidering this conviction; perhaps this corner of Iran was not the aid to a deeper understanding of the country, as I had originally believed.

In their militant politics, rigid devotion, and narrow worldview (they interpreted the world through the prism of Al Jazeera and Iranian state television) they were a minority, a small bubble of radical conservatism in a country teeming with worldly, sophisticated, and open young people. To the Khalil family, abstract values mattered more than anything. They would have Iran back their radical ideals— support for Islamic militant groups who resorted to terror tactics— at any price, from international isolation to the failing economy and joblessness that such policies created. Even the most pious, politically conservative Iranians I knew did not feel this way. They sympathized with the suffering of the Palestinians, with the Iraqis who were dying each day in the aftermath of the botched U.S. invasion, but they would not sacrifice their own quality of life for the sake of these remote Arabs. Perhaps the difference was that the Khalil families, both households, were subsidized by the Iranian state. It was a government body, after all, that provided Mr. Khalil's income. They didn't feel the costs of their politics the way ordinary Iranians did, so their militant opinions existed in a vacuum: the government had bought their radicalism.

Out of habit, I had continued seeing Mrs. Khalil occasionally, but that morning, standing outside the closed bakery, I decided it was time to stop courting the militant minority. I was now a married woman with years of experience in Iran to my credit, and I could finally stop trying to make up for my social background. Yes, I lived in north Tehran, and yes, I was far more privileged than most Iranians. But most of my friends, the people who composed my Iranian world and shaped my perceptions, belonged to the middle class, who in scope and significance were the core of the nation.

My friends in the western press corps, accustomed to reporting in nations like Afghanistan and Saudi Arabia, where the capital stood in stark contrast to the rest of the country, often asked me, "But what about the rest of Iran?" The divide that matters in Iran, I would tell them, is not between city and town, or wealthy and working-class. In any Iranian city, be it Isfahan, Yazd, or Shiraz, the relevant divide was between a minority of religious militants, many of whom had political and financial ties to the government, and the majority of moderate Iranians, who longed for stability and prosperity. The latter included many devout believers, who revered Islam and lived according to its edicts. But they had grown to consider their faith a private matter, altogether separate from the sort of accountable, democratic, secular government they had hoped for.

That I had begun reporting in Iran, and had published my first book about the country, at a young age had left me especially vulnerable to criticism about my work and perspective. Iranians living in America, many of whom had not spent significant amounts of time in Iran for decades, often accused me of conflating affluent north Tehran with the rest of the country. Reviewers of my book sometimes made a similar case. They were wrong. Secular Iranians—those who fasted during Ramazan but who during the rest of the year also enjoyed an occasional drink; those who believed that the mullahs should get out of politics—composed a sizable part of the population. This was a simple fact of Iranian society, as real as its more conservative, traditional spectrum. I knew it well. But I felt I needed to prove my perspective valid.

The doubts I had entertained along the way had been instructive. Apart from what it revealed about the inner lives of doctrinaire militants, my time with Mrs. Khalil had taught me how she and her family differed from my own devout friends and relatives. The latter might love to visit Mecca and fast during Ramazan, but they considered Osama bin Laden a murderous monster and believed Iran should repair its ties with the United States. This difference, between religious militants and ordinary believers with moderate politics, was the real key to understanding Iran, in my view.

Every country includes a radical minority. Although this is imperative to recognize, it is not through that minority that one can grasp the aspirations and reality of the country as a whole. Life, in the end, is not lived at the extremes. It is the wide, yawning middle that contains the real multitudes. That was a truth I had gleaned long ago from the novels of the Czech writer Milan Kundera, who wrote that "extremes mean borders beyond which life ends, and a passion for extremism, in art and politics, is a veiled longing for death." Perhaps Mr. and Mrs. Khalil did not long for death, but they certainly did not view it with the same trepidation and dread as ordinary people.

I sat at my computer that night, composing an e-mail to my editor in New York. I wanted to write a story that illustrated these experiences and the conclusions to which they had led. I tried to imagine my editor's response to my proposed article. Would the average American reader care? I wasn't altogether sure, but of course that's where the challenge always lay—to beguile those who might not ordinarily care into understanding the nuances of a distant, vaguely suspect nation.

CHAPTER 13

What to Expect When
You're Expecting in Iran

In July, two stories vied for prominence in the national headlines. The first concerned the imminent stoning of a thirty-seven-year-old woman convicted of adultery, a case taken up by a prominent women's rights lawyer. The condemned woman, a mother of four, had petitioned for a divorce years earlier; a local judge had denied it, insisting she must endure the marriage for her children's sake. She had also retracted the confession she had made under police interrogation. Sharia (classic Islamic law) held that stoning verdicts could not be implemented in cases where the accused retracted his or her confession. But a cruel judge might overlook the finer points of Sharia in the rush to mete out such harsh punishments. Feminist lawyers argued that, given this tendency, sentences such as stoning needed to be abolished. Back in 2000, progressive lawyers and other moderates had advocated a more liberal interpretation of Sharia. But in the intervening years, many had abandoned this position in favor of a wholesale adoption of secular civil and criminal law. They had realized that only responsible judges overseen by an accountable political system could be relied on to implement humane readings of Sharia. As they saw it, it was easier to rewrite problematic laws than refashion the structure of Iran's government.

The other story dominating the month's news was the country's

first women's polo tournament in more than a century. Polo originated in Iran about twenty-five hundred years ago as the sport of
kings and queens. The royal polo ground in Isfahan, a city in central-
north Iran, where the queen and her ladies-in-waiting competed
against the king and his court, provided the original dimensions for
polo fields across the world. After the 1979 revolution, the authorities
barred women from playing polo in public, but eased the ban in 2005.
The polo federation sought to recast the game as a national sport
rather than the pastime of aristocrats, and the regime had begun to
make concessions. Female players were still barred from competing
against men, and women had to wear manteaus and headscarves on
the field. I had ridden horses in Iran in 2003, overheating while wearing a veil under a helmet. But I imagined that in their excitement at finally being able to compete publicly, the women's team did not dwell
on such discomforts.

Each morning in the week after our wedding, I drank coffee and
read these news stories, pondering how it was possible for a nation to
stride forward and back at the same time. What I cared about most,
though, was usually buried somewhere in the back section: the pollution barometer, advising whether pregnant women could safely go
outside.

Newspapers often report that Tehranis breathe in seven and a half
times the amount of carbon monoxide considered safe. If you lived in
Tehran, your nose was constantly filled with black gunk and you
awoke from eight hours of sleep exhausted. You developed a head-
ache if you spent more than a couple of hours in central Tehran,
which is especially congested and where it is not uncommon to see
people wearing masks. During winter, a typically windless season,
polluted air is trapped over the city; in one recent winter, at least
eighteen hundred people died each month from pollution-related
ailments. One official likened living in the capital to "mass suicide."
The Alborz Mountains unhelpfully impeded the winds that blew over
the city during the spring, summer, and fall. But the chief source of the
pollution—fumes from old Peykans and spluttering buses—lent itself
to easy remedy. Each year, a host of strident environmental groups
challenged the government more and more. In 2007, the authorities

began offering free air filters to Peykan drivers, but the capital's toxic blanket had never seemed so thick.

The city's pollution even comes in second, after the Iran-Iraq War, in somber subjects that inspire the work of young artists. In 2000, three artists I knew produced a collection of paintings, statues, and installation videos called "The Children of Dark City," illustrating the pollution's impact on children. In one video segment, young girls filed down hazy school stairs, while in the background a little boy held a tissue against his mouth and slowly blurred into oblivion.

For three days that July, the city had been suffocating in especially dense muck-colored smog. The physically vulnerable—old people, babies, and the pregnant—were being warned to stay indoors. The pollution entirely obscured the Alborz Mountains, which on clear days perched with postcard vividness before our living room windows. After three days of being trapped indoors with a 1970s Lamaze DVD and annoyingly censored Internet, I was restive and ill-tempered. I was accustomed to running aground on the government's Internet filters, which blocked a vast array of content—numerous Farsi blogs, pro-reform websites, social networking sites, political opposition groups, Farsi news portals, and many American think tanks were all filtered. Arash had recently found he could not access the site for the typesetting software he was using to format his MBA thesis; the software was called LaTeX, which no doubt was a filtering term used to block pornography.

Sometimes I could guess why a term triggered the filter, but sometimes the censorship seemed entirely random. I often found myself cut off from medical information about pregnancy. Could I eat a certain type of cheese? Was it safe to take cough syrup? The answers were to be found on sites which, as the pop-up page informed me, "In accordance with the laws of the Islamic Republic of Iran and at the decree of judiciary officials" were not permitted. I began jotting down terms and sites that were blocked, hoping to find a rationale behind the censorship, but my list did not illuminate matters: "Lufthansa" + "pregnant travelers," "Bloomingdale's," "circumcision," "adult" + any noun/adjective, "women" + any noun/adjective/verb, *The New York Times* Style section, "varicose veins," "Pablo Neruda sonnets."

These distractions occupied my time, and it was with some dismay that I realized I was five months pregnant and had yet to settle on an obstetrician. I had already met five doctors, but had been forced to cancel two recent appointments with prospective candidates because of the pollution.

"You can't keep interviewing doctors forever," Arash said, practically, before leaving for work. He thought my pursuit of the ideal doctor was becoming obsessive and that I should just settle on someone reasonably experienced and personable.

"I know that." I frowned, envious of his ability to leave the house. "I just want to find someone I'm comfortable with."

The first doctor I interviewed, an elderly woman with thick glasses and a tasteful watch, seemed very capable, but her severe manner put me off. Her great advantage was that she opposed elective cesarean sections, which had become tremendously popular in Iran.

As my pregnancy progressed, the question relatives and total strangers asked most frequently was not whether I was having a girl or a boy, but whether I was having a c-section. Vaginal childbirth was very out these days in Tehran. The c-section had quickly edged out the nose job as the dominant medical trend among Iranians, a people very fond of surgery. No longer the provenance of last-minute complications, cesarean delivery was now viewed in Tehran as the modern woman's choice. My friends had all lined up to convince me to get sliced open. They cheerfully tugged up their shirts and flashed me their discreet little c-section scars, always pointing out how these fell under the bikini line. One, a slightly more intellectual type, advocated the procedure in nationalist and literary terms.

"The c-section is actually an Iranian procedure, referred to in the *Shahnameh* as 'Rostamzad,' " she said. The *Shahnameh*'s hero, Rostam, is born by cesarean. The labor of his mother, Rudabeh, the wife of the warrior Zal, has stalled because of Rostam's extraordinary size. Fearing that his wife will perish, Zal summons the Simorgh, a mythical bird embodying the purity and wisdom of the ages, who performs a cesarean section, or rather a *Rostamzad*.

"I think you're just pain averse," I told her. "And, if you don't mind my saying so, anxious to retain vaginal tone."

"Tone!" she gasped. "Azadeh!"

The subject had arisen two nights ago, when a relative visiting from the provincial town of Maragheh praised me for planning a natural delivery. Apparently vaginal labor had fallen out of favor even in that remote quarter of the country. "Good for you. Most women these days just aren't willing," he said wistfully. I enjoyed the encouragement, but felt rather discomfited by having this conversation with so many people. Though they were squeamish about our having lived together before marriage, even distant relatives demanded to know in the first minutes of a conversation whether I would be delivering the baby from between my legs.

The cachet of cesareans was a natural outgrowth of the surgery-obsessed culture that had emerged since the revolution. Forced to cover their bodies in Islamic dress, women focused on beautifying what remained visible: their faces. That turned Iran into the nose job capital of the world and made a generation receptive to elective surgery, particularly procedures that broke with tradition, be it the classically hooked Iranian nose or vaginal childbirth. Once having one's nose carved became as routine as a dental cleaning, Iranians grew more comfortable with other unnecessary types of surgery.

The appeal of c-sections was enhanced by the fact that they were widely available and affordable, and many Iranians wrongly believed only celebrities had access to them in the West. Given how little there was in the world uniquely available to both the average Iranian woman and Angelina Jolie, you could imagine the draw. "All women in the West would have cesareans if they could," a friend informed me. "It's just that insurance companies won't cover them." Nearly everyone seemed to believe this, and it made women who didn't face an overabundance of choice in their lives feel, in just this one instance, privileged. Many of the country's doctors were the first in their families to join this large and growing professional class, and they encouraged the surgery with particular zeal. Not only was it lucrative, but it also made them feel more modern as well, practicing cesareans rather than presiding over vaginal delivery, which humans had managed to do even when they lived in caves.

Since c-sections cost only a fraction more, about $200, than vaginal deliveries, their popularity extended throughout the middle class. Most Iranians received health care through their employers, and insurance plans accommodated their choice of delivery. Judging from the conversations I had eavesdropped on in the waiting rooms of my prospective obstetricians, traditional, chador-clad women were at least as likely, if not more so, as their westernized counterparts to choose c-sections. They were often heavier and unfit—a function of the richer foods they ate, the long hours they spent indoors, and the lingering traditional preference for the plump female figure—and doctors told them their bodies were too out of shape to deliver naturally. A handful of doctors sought to counter the c-section trend by popularizing the use of epidurals, which were neither well-known nor widely available in Iran. But rather than educating women about pain relief choices, they marketed what they termed "painless labor" as though it were a type of spa experience. Naturally, most women found the idea of painless vaginal labor altogether suspicious, and the epidural failed to catch on. Alarmed by the rising rate of cesareans, the government launched radio and television campaigns informing women of the risks the surgery carried for both infant and mother. But as far as I could see, so far women were not listening. They were easily duped by unethical doctors who told them they were too overweight/out of shape/angular/melancholy for a conventional birth.

The demand for c-sections was so widespread that it had actually altered the obstetrician landscape, making it a challenge to find a doctor willing to deliver naturally. Cesareans were quicker than vaginal delivery, and many doctors found it profitable to perform them exclusively, fitting in several per day. My friend's obstetrician unabashedly told her: "If I deliver you by c-section, we can plan the procedure in advance. I can show up freshly showered, my tie knotted properly, relaxed. Wouldn't you prefer that?" When my friends recommended a doctor, I had to first ask if he or she was "c-section only." That's why the stern, elderly female doctor came so enthusiastically recommended. She frowned on the c-section craze and would never have interrupted a vaginal delivery, to falsely advise the parents that the baby's heartbeat had slowed and that a cesarean was necessary. Arash, who worried that a doctor reluctant to facilitate vaginal birth would sabotage our choice during labor, promoted her as our choice.

We met the second candidate when we sought out a clinic that specialized in advanced, three-dimensional ultrasounds. She seemed a bit skittish as she guided the probe around my stomach, and began most of her sentences with the unreassuring phrase "Well, the textbook says . . ." Fresh out of residency, she was up on all the latest prenatal tests (half of which were not available in Iran, anyway), but she didn't inspire my confidence. She was also expensive. She charged the equivalent of $35 for an ultrasound, in a city where the usual rate was $7.

An elder, respected relative, himself a doctor, recommended a colleague who had been practicing for four decades at a prominent Tehran hospital. Half of the city, it seemed, wanted to be delivered by him, and his waiting room was packed with women in black chador. He barely spoke, and when words did emerge, they were few and barely audible. He clearly belonged to the women-have-been-birthing-in-Iran-for-centuries school of ob-gyns, and did not consider new-fangled notions like prenatal testing, heartrate monitors, and omega-3 supplements relevant to the age-old process of popping out a baby. As I ran down my list of questions, he and his midwife-assistant exchanged smiling glances, not bothering to conceal their amusement. Clearly they thought I was a neurotic, westernized Iranian who was taking childbirth far too seriously. They also immediately dismissed my request that Arash be permitted in the delivery room.

That Iranian hospitals prohibited men from being present as their wives gave birth was the only thing that had given me pause when we discussed whether to have the baby in Iran. The country's medical services were usually decent, in certain fields superb. A generation of doctors had trained during the bloody eight-year war with Iraq, quickly acquiring experience that surgeons in peaceful societies would gain only in a lifetime. Iranian medicine suffered from the limited availability of drugs for complicated cancer and HIV regimens and of instruments used for recently developed procedures. When our friend Neda's uncle, for example, was diagnosed with prostate cancer, she spent two full days a week tracking down and waiting in line for his chemotherapy medication. But for more commonplace matters—childbirth, cosmetic surgery, a fractured knee—Iran was one of the best places you could hope to find yourself.

Many affluent Iranians chose to go abroad for their deliveries, but this seemed to involve much expense and inconvenience for the sake of being able to remark "My Amir-Ali was born in Paris." I discovered the no-husbands policy only incidentally, when my friend Nazila recommended her doctor, adding at the end of her glowing endorsement, "And she even lets your husband stay in the room!"

"What do you mean, 'lets'? Where else would he be?" I had several pregnancy guides, and they all devoted at least three pages to the tasks delegated to the husband during delivery: the wiping of the brow, the proffering of snacks, the administration of massage, the cutting of the umbilical cord, not to mention the coaching in Lamaze breathing.

The policy, like so many of the regime's, lacked any agreed-upon or express rationale. Nazila suggested it was because some hospital delivery rooms included more than one bed, and it would be considered inappropriate for men to be among bareheaded, splay-legged women who were not their wives. The midwife of the reticent doctor offered another explanation.

"Men in Iran don't attend pregnancy and labor classes like men in the West," she said. "They aren't prepared for the visceral reality of childbirth, and they are liable to lose control. They might suddenly become furious with the doctor for touching their wife's private parts. Or they might somehow think the doctor is hurting her. If they freak out, they could compromise the labor."

It was as though she were describing a race of Neanderthals who communicated with grunts and clubs, rather than Iranian men in the twenty-first century.

"Lots of men in the West don't take any special classes," I said, unconvinced. "And they seem to do just fine."

"Then there is the situation our country is in," she said. As in Iraq, the word "situation" was colloquial shorthand for the complicated, painful political realities that invaded every aspect of daily life. I was not surprised, particularly, by the no-husbands regulation. It was in keeping with the wide range of human behavior the state's codes precluded—parties, dating, dancing. But it rankled more than those other restrictions, because it could not be ignored in private. You felt the sting of such limits only as the relevant circumstances arose and you realized yet one more thing you had never expected to be a problem was banned. The no-husbands rule was on par with the laws that meant a mother could never take her son swimming once he reached a certain age. I discovered this when a friend of mine, the divorced mother of a ten-year-old, called one day to ask whether Arash would take her son swimming. Pools and beaches are both separated by sex, and my friend's ex-husband was never around to take the boy. Witnessing the miracle of a child's birth, swimming together as a family— these were probably not basic human rights, I supposed. But they were small, modest joys that infused life with meaning.

I was lying on an examination table when the midwife entered, complaining about the husband of a patient in the next room. "What century are we living in? Who does this man think he is! Not even a doctor. Telling his wife an annual pap smear is 'unnecessary.' Silly man. I'll tell him what is unnecessary." The midwife, flushed and indignant, straightened her navy smock, and flounced back into the other room to challenge the unfortunate man who had deemed the routine monitoring of his wife's cervix superfluous.

Finally, I had found the perfect doctor. Dr. Laleh Amini: under forty, French-trained, confident, and attentive. The impeccably chic boots and shifts she wore under her white coat, I realize, should not have made a difference to me, but they added to my impression that we inhabited the same world—one in which husbands were meant to be in the delivery room ("Of *course* we'll smuggle him in, don't worry for a second") and expectant mothers' questions were answered respectfully. It was a well-known fact that Dr. Laleh was married to a prominent juice tycoon, which meant she worked out of passion for her job and would not market c-sections to maximize her profits. She cautioned her patients to resist the traditional Iranian ministrations to the pregnant woman: "They will try to turn you into a veal. They will keep you inside and make you eat twice or three times as much as you really need. Don't listen."

Given her European qualifications, Dr. Laleh could easily have charged exorbitant fees and catered to exclusively wealthy Iranians. But she asked no more than the most ordinary Tehran doctor. As a result her waiting room overflowed most days with everyone from Afghan immigrants to diplomatic wives. Other doctors constantly rang her cell phone for advice, and most of her responses involved her saying, "Well, the proper treatment for X disease is Y therapy or Z machine, but since we don't have either in Iran . . ."

Unlike the reticent doctor, she was hypervigilant, ordering a battery of blood tests that had the local laboratory blinking in confusion, and she checked her pregnant patients monthly for bladder infections. Her indignant midwife, a French-speaking Zoroastrian, shared her blunt way of handling men who accompanied their wives and interfered in their medical treatment. Neither of them wore a veil in the office, even when husbands were present. A brass *fravahar*, the age-old symbol of Zoroastrianism, hung near pictures of Dr. Laleh's children in the treatment room. I loved the bustle and cleanliness of the office, and most of all Dr. Laleh's uncompromising way of pushing everyone—the laboratories, the hospital maternity unit, the local pharmacies—to pay attention to detail, to aim higher. In this, of course, she was working against the current of the Islamic Republic, which permitted a culture of sloth and laxness in such places. People like her tended to burn out midcareer, exhausted from constantly taking on a culture that dwarfed their solitary purpose. But for now, she was here, zealous and chic, and I was thrilled to have found her.

One afternoon she told us we were having a boy, showing us his cycling legs and arms bobbing up and down on the ultrasound screen. Arash beamed with delight and pointed out how active he was, claiming this heralded a mischievous and jaunty personality. On our way out of the office, he paused by the elevator and asked me, "Do you realize the baby boy inside you will be considered legally more valu-able than you?" I ran a hand over my bump, and pondered this in a whole new way.

Troubled by an encounter earlier that day at the gym, I absentmind-edly stirred too much salt into the curry I was making for the evening's dinner party. I had arrived wearing one of the standard uni-forms of young women in the capital: a veil, a manteau, and jeans. As the receptionist handed me a locker key, she told me they had been visited earlier by the local authorities, who warned that unless their patrons started dressing more conservatively, the gym would be shut down during its morning hours, those reserved for women. She tugged uncomfortably at a strand of hair as she relayed the message. It had been a long, long while since the government had launched a widespread crackdown on what women wore. This new approach, which was coupled with raids on clothing shops that sold "immod-est" manteaus, signaled a canny shift in tactics. Rather than provoke young people's ire by harassing them on the street or in parks, the regime would recruit civilian intermediaries, so that people could po-lice one another. That way, the hapless messenger would be the im-mediate target of resentment, rather than the state. Was it coincidence that the authorities had chosen gyms as the first locations to police? If women did not comply, was their freedom to exercise at risk?

The doorbell interrupted these musings, and I ran to greet Neda. She kissed me hello, whisked off her veil, and handed me a tin full of her famous spicy yogurt dip. Neda's parents came from the same town in Tabriz province as Arash's father, and the two families' friendship spanned most of their lives. Neda was very beautiful, with milky skin and moss-colored eyes. Her exuberant spirits and playful humor made her delightful company, and she had many suitors, all of whom she refused. She remained stubbornly unmarried at the age of thirty-five, a fact that caused her mother great sorrow.

I fixed her a drink and asked her what was new at work. Neda's days were nearly always extraordinary. She worked as a medical as-sistant to one of Tehran's premier plastic surgeons, and in the decade she had spent taking a small hatchet to the noses of thousands, she had acquired more insight into Tehrani society than most trained observers. It was only Neda who could describe the intersection of Islamic piety and modern vanity, in the tales of the faithful who sought more slender, western noses. Over and over again I asked her to repeat my two favorite stories. One concerned a young religious man who consulted his *marja' taghlid* (literally, "source of emulation," referring to an ayatollah vested with the authority to make legal decisions) over the proper disposal of the leftover bits of his formerly bulbous nose. The *marja'* held that they required proper burial, and so Neda gathered the shards of bone in a zip-lock bag and carried them out to his mother in the waiting room, who gathered them into the folds of her black chador. Neda's second best tale concerned the mullah's daughter who was so grateful for her pertly chiseled nose that she asked her father to pray each week for the health of Neda and the surgeon. When the family went to Mecca for pilgrimage, the mullah called the surgeon to say, "Doctor, we have prayed here for your health, as well as that of Miss Neda."

Neda and I sat around the table, the air perfumed by a vase of white tuberoses, and began shelling pistachios. "Thank God I don't have a mother-in-law," she began. In Iran, even prospective mothers-in-law, not yet the real thing, could blacken one's days. The St. Bernard, Geneva, trotted over, and placed a paw on Neda's leg, gazing up adoringly. He was all cuddles, a fluffy bonbon of selfless affection. London the beagle was sequestered under a couch, gnawing on a chicken bone in greedy privacy. Neda went on to describe a young woman who had come in that day for a consultation, explaining that her current nose had been rejected by her boyfriend's mother, and that her suitability for marriage depended on her correcting it. "Doctor said he wouldn't operate for such a reason," she said. "He told her, 'Why would you want to marry into such a family anyway? My prescription: keep the nose, get a new boyfriend.' But she wouldn't listen. 'Make it pretty,' she kept begging."

"How bad was the nose?"

"It had the Persian bump, but I liked it. It had character, and it matched her face."

I retreated to the stove, attempting to de-salt the curry. Neda followed me. "Forget the nose. The nose is not interesting. You will never believe what is happening to my English class," she said, hands propped behind her against the cabinet.

For the past two years, Neda had spent two afternoons each week learning the basics of English grammar at a government-run language institute in central Tehran. The fifteen men and women in her class had befriended one another over time, trading tips about language entrance exams that would enable them to study in the West. The previous week, the institute announced it would divide men and women into separate classes, held on separate days of the week. "As if that weren't awful enough," Neda continued, "the female staff began arriving at work dressed in chador." Plans were under way to move the women's classes to a separate building altogether, to eliminate the possibility of illicit mingling in the hallways.

"A third of the class dropped out," she said. "I suppose they were partly just there to meet people. But that's not criminal, to socialize alongside learning. It's so disrespectful. As though we're all just depraved, and need to be regulated at all times. Just in case. In case of what? You should see our class. We are mind-numbingly normal. Ali just sharpens his pencils and fixates on prepositions, Niloufar shows off her weird BBC accent—what do they think we are going to do?"

"I guess what's really irritating is that you're not used to this kind of thing anymore, right?" I was flinging spices into the steaming pot indiscriminately, no longer deriving much satisfaction from cooking for my guests. I wondered whether we could just order pizza, so I could fix myself a drink and enjoy its coolness on the other side of the house. The only reason we had invited people over in the first place was because as a pregnant hostess I would be spared the guests smoking indoors. At most parties, everyone smoked regardless, lamely pretending to wave the smoke in the direction of a window cracked open a centimeter. Even Iranians educated in the West, who knew better, were guilty of this.

"I mean, you're studying English to improve your future, which makes you feel productive and sort of linked to the rest of the world.

And then you're suddenly resegregated, which just makes you feel like some laboratory mouse in an experiment on the state and Islam."

"Something like that," Neda said, running to answer the door. By around eleven, most of the other guests had arrived. I served the over-spiced curry at eleven-thirty, early by Tehran dinner-party standards. The conversation, led by Neda, centered around the creeping restrictions everyone had noticed in their respective corners of city life.

Arash had invited Majid Derakhshani, his *tar* teacher, and Majid had brought his orchestra's *ney* player, and the *ney* player's wife, who played the *kamancheh*. They had all just returned from a concert in the town of Sari, in northern Iran.

"So the official comes up to me, and asks, 'Can your female musicians play behind a black curtain?' " Majid said. "I told him, 'Why would they fly here all the way from Tehran, to play behind a *curtain*?' "

The *ney* player said, "It's better than the concert in Tabriz. Remember? They asked if the females could just not play. Not behind a curtain. Just not at all."

"I myself am horrified," announced the wife of one of Arash's MBA classmates. She wore a silk scarf patterned with a designer logo around her neck in a sort of ascot, and I shifted nervously, wishing I had not tried to pay off my dinner party debt all at once by inviting people who would not ordinarily find themselves in one another's company. I hoped the musicians, who were all straining to meet their rent, would not be offended. "I met friends this morning for coffee, and we were told women could not smoke anymore in cafés. And, afterward, I went to the beauty salon and I asked my manicurist, 'What happened to all the photos on the wall?' She said the police had come and demanded that they be taken down, because images of unveiled women are illegal."

My first impulse was to tell the woman that there were far graver examples of the growing campaign of repression to worry about. Did anyone really care if the coiffed women of Tehran could smoke their European airport duty-free cigarettes with their cappuccino? I felt mortified, until I looked around and realized the other guests were listening to her respectfully. I detected no censure in their understanding expressions. They seemed to absorb her anecdotes as just another instance of the new and worrisome restrictions. There was no regime that would limit its violations to the affluent; a Taliban outlook would target musicians and schoolteachers, not only the well-heeled. Iranians, accustomed for three decades to the vagaries of the Islamic regime, understood that very well.

"The problem," concluded the only western guest, a diplomat trained in summing up our daily travails under the mullahs in clever, brief formulations, "is that your old regime viewed religion as an obstacle to modernity, and this regime views modernity as an obstacle to religion."

We all chewed on this for a while in silence. He continued a moment later, explaining that layered identities were richer, and that Iran's government should try to harmonize society's westernized and religious elements, rather than excising the parts deemed destructive or threatening. This was wise, measured thinking, but I wondered when, if ever, it might become Iranian reality. The revolution, as is the nature of such upheavals, took bloody revenge for the years in which Islam was marginalized by the secular Pahlavi monarchy. The revolutionaries murdered secularists, and even religious Iranians it considered opponents. Part of the reason the regime today brooked no opposition was, I imagined, fear. The authorities worried that if they loosened their grip even just a tiny bit, all those whom they had wronged—secular intellectuals, Muslim modernists, technocrats— would rise up together and seek their own revenge, as well as their right to participate in government.

These were heavy musings for two in the morning. Unable to think of any insight to add, I poured another round of tea in slim-waisted cups. The *ney* player blew into his flute, the notes dispelling the conversation with their own melancholy beauty.

CHAPTER 14

A Turn for the Soviet

"Mr. Hashemi would like to meet you today at one o'clock." The tone was polite, but it was quite evident that I was being summoned rather than invited. I had never met Mehdi Hashemi, the son of former president Rafsanjani and could not fathom why he would want to see me, let alone with such urgency. I canceled my lunch date with a girlfriend, and redirected my taxi toward Hashemi's office at a private university complex in north Tehran, opposite Niavaran Palace. I was wearing a longish button-down shirt, ankle-length linen trousers, and sandals, an outfit that wasn't suited for such a meeting, but I figured that wasn't my problem. I had not, after all, been given ample notice to prepare myself. At the door, a security guard scanned my attire and told me curtly that I wasn't "going anywhere at all, dressed like *that*."

I adjusted my scarf, trying to decide what to do. Clearly, the guard believed I was a college student dressed inappropriately for an institution un-ironically called the Islamic Free University. If I imperiously announced myself as a correspondent for *Time* magazine going to see the former president's son, I would likely be treated with a bit of respect. I was spared that when a moment later, the man who had set up the meeting appeared, assessed the situation, and brushed off the security guard. "She's a foreigner! Of course she's not dressed properly . . . but she's a visitor in our country—we must be hospitable! You know how they are."

He ushered me into Hashemi's private office immediately. Usually Iranian officials make you wait for at least half an hour as a way of underscoring their influence, but Hashemi's influence was so vast that it required no such airs. Over the years, he had held positions in various state bodies active in the oil and energy sectors, but his real power came from being Rafsanjani's son.

He wanted to chat about my profile of Ayatollah Khamenei, which had just recently been published. Although he did not say so directly, I presumed he was displeased by the scantness of the space devoted to his father, whom many people considered the preeminent power player in Iranian politics. My article had alluded to the lavish lifestyles of certain corrupt clerics, and it seemed Mr. Hashemi had taken the reference personally.

"People say the silliest things about us," he said, smiling defensively. He smoothed a hand over thick black hair, and leaned his softly sloped shoulders back in his chair. His appearance surprised me. Unlike his sister, who was notorious for wearing Chanel suits under her chador, and unlike the daughter of that sister, known for parading through Tehran's jet-set parties in designer clothes, Mehdi Hashemi did not look like Islamic Republic royalty. His white shirt was neatly pressed, but apart from his tidy grooming, he resembled an ordinary, mid-ranking official. "They say we have ranches overflowing with Thoroughbreds. The Supreme Leader rides; how come no one mentions that?" A popular joke that captured the extent of the Rafsanjani wealth had the former president discussing how he had amassed his fortune: "We had this bit of land in the family. A country called Iran happened to fall within its borders."

We talked seriously for the next half hour about President Ahmadinejad and the implications of his foreign policy. It remained unclear, to the outside world as well as to many Iranians, whether Ahmadinejad devised policy and had any real influence, or whether he was a marionette executive controlled by powerful ayatollahs who ruled from the shadows. Mr. Hashemi's real opinion of the president was impossible to deduce; he seemed to consider him both contemptible and effective, a phenomenon that simply needed to be waited out. He said the president's defiant stand had paid off, and that Iran was now ahead in its nuclear confrontation with the West. He predicted that Tehran would not accept the most recent European proposal.

After the meeting I climbed into the waiting car. Almost immediately my phone rang, "1111111." Mr. X had not called in a month, and it could not possibly be a coincidence that he should ring at that precise moment. I began looking out the window, wondering if I might spot him hiding behind a bush, or directing traffic, concealed behind a pair of dark glasses and an officer's hat.

"Che khabar?" he asked. What's new?

My first instinct was to say nothing about whom I had just met, but I figured he must already know. "I'm doing well, thank you! . . . How are you? . . . May you not be tired. . . . You should know that I have just met Mr. Hashemi, but that the meeting was at his request, not mine, and that nothing of great sensitivity was discussed."

"What right does Mr. Hashemi have to summon you for a meeting? And why did you not consult with us before agreeing to see him? What use is our consultative relationship if you only alert us to such matters after the fact, when our sentiments can no longer bear any weight on your decisions?"

Mr. X always referred to himself in the first-person plural. In Farsi, the formal "we," usually the prerogative of kings, is also used in conversations that demand particular correctness. According to strict Islamic norms, it was deeply inappropriate for Mr. X and me—neither relatives nor husband and wife—to consort with each other so familiarly, to be in regular phone contact and meet sometimes in the absence of a third party. This impropriety called for an excessive formality in our speech, the extra distance afforded by "we," rather than the intimacy of "I." Of course, Mr. X also intended his plural to signify the institution of the state. "We," as in "my ministry," "the government," "the totality of the Islamic state," disapprove of little, singular "you."

"I was made to believe the meeting was very urgent," I said. "Had I been informed in advance, you can be certain that I would have consulted you." This was a lie—I would never have asked Mr. X's permission to meet anyone—but after the fact, it seemed harmless to suggest otherwise. I regretted telling him about the meeting. Perhaps he had not known, after all; perhaps the timing of his call *had* been coincidence. Certainly he would have found out eventually, since my mobile phone was surely tapped, but I could have worked out at my leisure what to tell him.

He made some reply to the effect that I was being disingenuous and that I had better start to recall in much more vivid detail the content of my conversation with Mehdi Hashemi. I wished desperately for the line to cut out. The Tehran mobile network was barely functional. It often took several attempts to make a call, and even then the connection often died. Once I rang an Interior Ministry official back repeatedly in the course of a phone interview; picking up after the fourth interruption, he exploded, "A curse upon the fools in this government, who can't even fix something as elementary as a mobile network!" That day, however, the reception was crystal clear and the line never wavered. Mr. X chastised me in severe tones, and I could tell from his displeasure that he would soon request a meeting to hector me in person. Once he hung up, I paid the taxi driver and decided to walk part of the way home so I could stop at Juice Javad and console myself with an extra-large pomegranate slushie and a pomegranate fruit roll. The morning's events signaled growing tension within the political establishment; the infighting was growing more serious. I fretted over how this might affect my life, whether I might now be considered a tool or a favorite of Mr. Hashemi, and therefore a reporter whose work required more scrutiny.

In the last month, Ahmadinejad's dwindling popularity had for the first time become the subject of people's daily conversations. After nearly a year in office, he had failed to deliver on any of his economic promises, and the prices of basic commodities from cigarettes to tomatoes to butter had risen 20 percent. Though inflation was a longstanding problem of the Iranian economy, most experts blamed the sharp and sudden rise on Ahmadinejad's fiscal policies. The president continued to flood the economy with cash (a tactic known to economists as increasing liquidity) in the form of loans promised on his trips to the provinces. He intended these measures to stoke his popularity among the provincial poor, but he was ignoring the pleas of the nation's economists, who warned he was imperiling an already debilitated economy.

In particular, fruit—as central to the Iranian diet as bread—had grown prohibitively expensive. Many of our comfortably middle-class relatives had stopped buying fruit regularly, and so had we. Our weekly fruit bill had grown to around the equivalent of $25, outrageous by local standards. We either shopped at the discount Hajji Arzouni fruit shop, which sold bruised fruit in bulk, or, when we grew tired of bananas, pilfered from the fruit bowl at Arash's parents'.

The nuclear negotiations with the West had stalled, and the government's defiant position was beginning to look more destructive than heroic. This created an opening for Ahmadinejad's opponents, most importantly Rafsanjani, to begin forming an alliance against him. At such times of shifty maneuvering, the regime felt itself less stable and monitored all sorts of activity with an even more paranoid degree of vigilance than usual. This did not bode well for my hopes of leniency from Mr. X. I crossed to the other side of Niavaran Street, threading between the moving cars, confident, for no reason besides local custom, that at the last moment they would brake or swerve.

I knew I would regret it later, but when the police skipped our street one day during a swoop to confiscate satellite dishes, I was gleeful. Of course at some point they would come for ours, too, and in the interest of karmic solidarity with those whose dishes had been taken away I should have felt more sympathy. But short-sighted, naked self-interest is an unpleasant habit of people who live under dictatorships, and I was no exception. "Lucky, lucky us!" I told my sister-in-law, Solmaz, happily that evening, settling into her couch and reaching for a slice of cheesecake. Like many women in Iran, Solmaz devoted much of her free time to cooking. The two of us had a standing date to watch *The Perfect Dinner*, a German cooking–cum–reality TV show, and without it the fall evenings would have loomed bleak indeed.

Back in 2000, as part of President Khatami's drive to keep the state out of Iranians' private lives, the police had stopped carting away people's satellite dishes regularly. Iranians had grown accustomed to this laxity and had gradually begun setting up their dishes in more conspicuous places. More and more people acquired satellite dishes, until by unofficial estimates the majority of the country owned one. The recent sweeps were a disagreeable reminder that until such rights were enshrined in law, they could be plucked away at the whim of a mid-level bureaucrat. But given how adept the regime had become at jamming signals, especially of networks airing programming by opposition groups, I had a difficult time understanding what there was to gain by such heavy-handed tactics. When I met with Mr. Tabibi, President Ahmadinejad's relative, later that week, I put this to him.

"Don't you think rounding up people's dishes is so 1999?"

"No. It is a sagacious and timely move."

"Is it sagacious to cut off people's access to the outside world?"

"Television is trouble. Nothing but trouble. Don't look at yourself. For someone like you, educated, who has lived abroad, you have an appropriate context through which to filter what you watch. But for people with no education, whose world before satellite was limited to state television and their local neighborhood, it's corrupting. Suddenly, right there in your living room—women! expensive cars! vacations! appliances!—all this stuff you can't afford. None of this bothered you when you didn't know it existed, but suddenly Hassan Ali from Karaj is comparing himself to the people he sees on the screen. His expectations are tripled, quadrupled! . . ."

"Quintupled?"

"Exactly! So you understand!"

"Of course I don't understand. The answer is not to deny Hassan Ali CNN and Persian music videos, but to improve the economy so he can buy his wife the Korean refrigerator that the channels advertise, and additionally benefit from exposure to global culture."

"You are very idealistic," he said soberly. "You do not speak as someone who feels responsible for the welfare of the nation."

Mr. Tabibi, though by no means a perfectly reliable instrument, reflected the broad preoccupations of the Ahmadinejad administration. And right now, the impatience of ordinary Iranians with inflation and unmet promises of redistributed oil wealth weighed heavy. Although I disagreed with Mr. Tabibi, he was not exactly wrong. Our doorman, Yehya, who lived in the basement with his family, embodied the plight of the hypothetical Hassan Ali. Two years prior, in hopes of better wages, he had moved his family from a small village in the province of Khorasan to Tehran. Plowing the family farm in his village, where satellite dishes were uncommon, he had been unexposed to the wicked ways of city people. But in consultations with the other doormen on the block, he discovered that most of his urban colleagues had such devices, and he asked the building if he could run an extra cable from the dishes on the roof to his television.

The cable transformed Yehya and his wife, in the short space of six months, to urbane Tehranis modern in appearance and expectations. She doffed her floral village chador and began wearing a city manteau; he bought a motorcycle and started wearing black for religious holidays. She began going to the beauty salon for threading and blowouts; he began knocking at our door late in the evenings for buckets of ice and *aragh*. Such a couple would naturally develop material aspirations that when unmet would turn into discontent. On satellite television, they would get the news in Persian on *Voice of America*, always critical of Ahmadinejad's nuclear policy, as Iranian commentators linked the troubled economy to his defiant stance. In six months, bucolic contentment blossomed into urban resentment.

To prevent the metastasis of the urban Yehya phenomenon, the president preferred Band-Aid solutions, such as the confiscation of satellite dishes. Though it deserved much criticism for such shortsighted policies, the clerical regime had left itself no other way out. The only genuine solution to the Yehya problem would be to repair the economy and create real jobs, steps that in turn required Iran to address its political problems. It would need to fix its ties with the West and in general desist from behavior that angered the international community. For this to happen, the revolution would need to sort itself out. Would the pragmatists prevail? Would the ideological sacred cows finally be slaughtered? The history of revolutions teaches us that they take decades to mellow and settle into coherent forms of new governance. If historical precedent held, then Iran's problems would not be solved soon.

My latest dilemma, a light prelude of all that was to come, involved choosing a baby name. The government, it turned out, had long ago compiled a list of names it considered unsuitable for Iranian children. I hadn't known such a list existed until I began throwing out suggestions like Alessandro and Luc, and Arash informed me that foreign names were categorically forbidden. "Isn't there some way around this?" I asked. I had looked forward to picking a name with such excitement, only to find an entire world of possibilities now off limits.

The names the regime forbade included those of Zoroastrian gods and goddesses, commanders of ancient Persian armies, and other such tainted figures linked to the country's pre-Islamic past. The religious extremists who had purged that history from textbooks sought to build model Islamic citizens, preferably all with Muslim (and therefore Arabic) names. In the early years of the revolution, the authorities merged this ideological project with the need for masses of soldiers to fight in the war with Iraq. They encouraged families to have ten children and name them all after Islamic figures such as Mohammad, Ali, and Fatemeh. In time, they hoped, Iran would be cleansed of its shameful Persian history. Persian names like ours, Azadeh and Arash, were approved, but were considered inferior by the radical religious. The banning of some names, like Maneli (meaning Mermaid) or Veesta (Knowledge), seemed to have no rationale at all.

European names, Arash said, were so utterly out of the question that no one even bothered trying to bribe the clerks at the local government records office to allow them. Like me, not everyone was aware of this in advance. An unsuspecting friend of ours had tried to register his newborn daughter as Juliette Farah (a choice negotiated with his Dutch wife) and was told this was "impossible." After a frustrating back-and-forth during which only the word "impossible" was repeated, he finally asked the clerk, "Don't you know that Juliette was Imam Reza's mother?" This mocking invocation of a revered Shia saint was not appreciated, and my friend was asked to leave the building. His daughter ended up simply Farah.

Along the way, other names found themselves on the forbidden list by dint of their association with political challenges facing the regime. Wishing to quell an uprising by ethnically Kurdish Iranians in the north, for example, the government banned Kurdish names. The *ney* player at our recent dinner party, an ethnic Kurd, told us his friends typically managed to secure Kurdish names for their children by bribing the clerk at the registry office.

Fortunately, some time investigating the acceptable-name and banned-name lists revealed that the government had mellowed somewhat in recent years. A number of previously forbidden Persian names had been restored to acceptability, which explained why every few years there was a sudden profusion of antique-sounding names. After all, there was something edgy and rebellious in giving your baby a name that had until just recently been forbidden. I didn't know yet whether the names we were considering were banned or not. I suggested we drop by the local registry office to check, but Arash reasoned that if they found the name was on the list they would likely remember us when we returned, and demand a bigger bribe. This seemed like a tactic more suited to bargaining for a silk rug at the Tehran bazaar (feigning indifference to secure the best price), but I agreed that it made sense not to draw attention to what might be a special case beforehand. As we debated the wisest course, it occurred to me how ironic it was that my own name, which only became popular on the eve of the revolution, means one who is free.

One ordinary weekday afternoon, I sat drinking tepid coffee with an Iranian academic in the lobby of a Tehran hotel. We didn't talk so much as whisper, all the while eyeing the felt-covered furniture around us, half expecting that a bearded agent would pop out from behind a fake plant or that the waiter would slip a listening device under the sugar bowl. Instead of what I had ostensibly scheduled the interview to discuss—how Iran could avoid a nuclear confrontation with the West—we talked about how we could avoid being labeled enemies of the state. "Do you think you're followed?" he murmured, barely audible over the air-conditioning. I had to stop crunching on my butter cookie to hear him. "Hmm, maybe. But I don't think so," I said, wishing for a James Bond gadget-watch that would beep if I was under surveillance. The phone call from Mr. X after my meeting with Mr. Hashemi suggested I was being followed, but in the absence of other evidence I chose to believe I was not. My answer must not have been reassuring, because when it came time to leave, he avoided walking out with me. "I'll just wrap up here," he said, pretending to shuffle some papers with a wary smile.

As I rode home from my interview, I remembered with sadness how relaxed such meetings used to be only a few years earlier. It was difficult to pinpoint exactly when the authorities had begun asserting an increasingly heavy presence in our lives. Although President Ahmadinejad was now openly reviled throughout the regime's bureaucracy, his influence had strangely grown, as though in inverse proportion to the regard of those supposedly in power, as well as to the quality of his performance. The wife of his chief of staff published a book declaring his presidency a miracle, a reflection of his own controversial habit of ascribing divine qualities to his rule. Shortly after its publication, the book mysteriously disappeared from bookstores. Did the authorities disapprove, or were they trying to protect the president? That the senior ayatollahs in Qom frowned on this stoking of lay religiosity made the book a liability to him. In the end, no one knew. The political sands of the Islamic regime were shifting as noiselessly as ever, and it was unclear to whose advantage and in what form they would settle. What was evident, however, was that the regime faced a new menace that had it frightened to its very core: the threat of the United States plotting its overthrow.

Earlier that year, the Bush administration had launched a $75 million program tacitly aimed at changing the Iranian regime. Although its planners did not discuss the program in such explicit language, preferring vague terms such as "advancement of democracy," the end of the Islamic Republic (or its transformation into a moderate, normal state, which was pretty much the same thing) was quite clearly their goal. Promoted through an array of measures—expanded broadcasting into the country, funding for NGOs, and the promotion of cultural exchanges—the democracy fund was intended to foster resistance to the government. With such support for the opposition, it was hoped, the clerical regime would collapse from within, taking care of what had become one of America's largest problems in the Middle East. The average Iranian, at least the average city dweller with satellite television, was made aware of this by Persian-language news broadcasts from abroad.

Since the Bush administration's removal of Iran's most dangerous enemies (the Taliban in Afghanistan and Saddam Hussein in Iraq), Tehran had naturally emerged with more influence in the region than ever before. The prospect of Iran becoming a major political power in the Middle East unnerved Washington. The Bush administration could have responded by bombing the country or by engaging it diplomatically. Unable to countenance either option, Washington chose instead to foist its problem onto the people of Iran.

In the short months that had passed since the launching of the U.S. democracy fund, the Iranian regime, relieved to discover that its paranoia about the Great Satan was well founded, had reacted with predictable severity. It set out to systematically crush any tie, however legitimate, unthreatening, or frail, between Iranians and the West through an expansive campaign of harassment that targeted even its own officials. It began arresting scholars on trumped-up charges of plotting a "velvet revolution," rounding up activists for allegedly receiving money from abroad, and labeling writers (and even one sculptor) as subversive. Suddenly people such as me, whose careers involved contact between Iran and the West, found themselves vulnerable to harassment, facing the threat of prison for activities previously considered benign.

Many Iranians tried to communicate to the administration in Washington that the campaign had swiftly achieved the opposite of its stated objective—that activists and scholars, the people who were toiling in their respective fields to make Iran a more open society, were being targeted as a result. The Bush administration was unmoved, and one official answered that dictatorships needed no excuse to crackdown. Although this wasn't untrue, anyone who had dealt with Iran in the past decade knew the regime was skittish, and that this sustained and exceptionally severe round of repression had been provoked by what became known as the notorious $75 million.

My tense meeting with the academic was just one example of how my life now began to constrict, taking on the flavor of a Cold War spy novel. Obsessed with the American plot, the regime began considering everyone (more than usual) agents or lackeys of the West. I say "more than usual" because Iranians have believed for generations in a British (or American) plot to destroy their country, a fantasy so pervasive that it inspired the best-loved Iranian novel of the twentieth century, *My Uncle Napoleon*. Like most Iranian children, both inside the country and in the diaspora, I grew up watching the television serial based on the novel. The Islamic regime banned the serial, but we had just recently bought the complete series on DVD from a sidewalk film vendor and watched an episode each evening. With farcical humor, *My Uncle Napoleon* captures the real legacy of western interference in Iran's politics: a chronic, irrational suspicion of foreign manipulation. Even many educated Iranians believe that their leaders are secretly directed by the Americans and British. The character of Uncle Napoleon illustrates how such paranoia debilitates Iranians, deterring them from taking responsibility for the state of their country.

I could devote my evenings to dear Uncle Napoleon because, by September, I was scarcely working anymore. I still reported news stories on the nuclear crisis and domestic political squabbles, but I had to avoid sensitive subjects and I dropped altogether the myriad of projects and professional relationships that had once filled my time. I avoided meeting activists, and many avoided meeting with me. As a result, I could no longer tell you, or report on, how Iranians were challenging their government. All the people who once supplied me with such information—student dissidents, bloggers, women's movement leaders—had been branded by the United States as potential agents of "peaceful" change, and in consequence were identified as security threats. The fear that our meeting—a western journalist with an activist—would be considered a plot was mutual. In August, the government banned the Center for the Defense of Human Rights, Shirin khanoum's NGO, a clear message that it was no longer interested in putting up with her. When she called, I babbled about my dogs, anxious to hang up the phone.

I stopped attending seminars and conferences in the United States, because the government had concluded that those were the venues where the velvet revolution was being planned. On my return, I would be forced to debrief Mr. X, and would need to mention that U.S. officials had been in the audience (the Iranian government might have had a watcher or an agent at such events, who could verify my account). I might as well have had a bull's-eye painted on the back of my headscarf. I stopped appearing on western radio and television shows, because in the present climate I knew I would need to soften my analysis, and in that case I preferred to say nothing at all. I gave up meeting western diplomats, who were considered the local spymasters. I used to help Iranian journalists who were applying to various fellowships or internship programs in the West, because I believed they would return to Iran and share such valuable experiences with their colleagues, bringing professionalism and global perspective to what was still a field full of propagandists. But no more. The minister of intelligence had recently accused the United States of exploiting Iranian journalists as part of its conspiracy, so editing someone's application essay or tutoring in interview skills would be viewed as abetting espionage. Worst of all, perhaps, I had entirely given up advising the countless American individuals—documentary filmmakers, academics, aspiring journalists—who wanted to visit Iran and help change its bleak image in the United States. Cultural exchange broke down age-old misconceptions, but the practice was now being referred to as a Trojan horse.

Unlike previous moments in Iran's tense history with the West, the repressive climate showed no sign of easing; instead, it became clear that this would be the new Iranian reality for at least the duration of Ahmadinejad's tenure. This was the second time I had moved to Iran as an adult with every intention of building a life here, and the second time that grand politics and the twists of Iranian-U.S. relations were undoing my purpose. Back in 2001, in the aftermath of the September 11 attacks and President Bush's labeling of Iran as part of an "axis of evil," I had been forced to leave when Mr. X made my reporting untenable by demanding to know the identities of my anonymous sources. I wondered whether most Americans had any idea how the actions of their government influenced the lives of those across the world. Iranians had a long, sophisticated tradition of conducting their own opposition to autocracy. When would Washington realize this, and allow Iranians to resist their tyrants in the manner of their own choosing?

I discussed this and many similar matters one morning with the editor of *Shargh,* the most prominent independent newspaper still permitted to publish. A crew from Fox News sat morosely in his office, frustrated by their inability to find analysts willing to speak on camera. It was a terrible time for print journalists, and even worse for broadcasters, who had a tougher time reporting stories with anonymous sources. The telephone rang, and the editor uttered a few terse replies, then looked up and informed us all that the newspaper had just been banned. The Fox News crew did not hide their delight (they now had a story), but I could not have been more sad. Although Iranians were accustomed to having their favorite newspaper summarily shut down, *Shargh* was the last independent publication of real quality. Even in this intimidating media climate, it had been running powerful investigative features on various social ills, and editorials that challenged Ahmadinejad's foreign policy. Among the reasons offered by the authorities for shutting down *Shargh* was that the newspaper had published an "insulting" cartoon, which depicted a black donkey facing off against a white knight on a chessboard.

Compared with what was being said about the president in the halls of the regime's own bureaucracy, the cartoon was tame. But Ahmadinejad was notorious for not caring about his establishment critics; he deliberately stoked their resentment, going so far as to toss Khatami and Rafsanjani out of their offices on the presidential compound (traditionally, as ex-officeholders they were permitted to keep their quarters). What he did fear was that his core supporters would eventually cease giving him the benefit of the doubt. They felt he was sincere, that he truly wished to tackle corruption and the rich establishment mullahs. The president reached out to his low-income constituents with emotional speeches, often spending days in the provinces talking with ordinary people in the street. Their allegiance to him was likewise emotional, based on the "feeling" that he cared about justice and egalitarianism. Like all emotions not grounded in reality, it was thus prone to quick evaporation when other sentiments like frustration set in. In such a fragile environment, the last thing Ahmadinejad needed was to be portrayed as a black donkey. Sooner or later, his supporters might begin to ask themselves: If he is a donkey, then what am I?

CHAPTER 15

The Logic of Mr. X

I can no longer recall on what pretext Mr. X convened our meeting one sunny, temperate afternoon in August. Perhaps he gave no reason at all; often, he just asked whether a given afternoon was convenient. He suggested we meet at Hotel Esteghlal, which had been a Royal Hilton before the revolution but now offered, like all the big government hotels, the surly, indifferent service of an overcrowded ministry. It was not typical of Mr. X to inform me of our meeting place so far in advance. Usually, he called an hour or so before the appointed time to disclose the location, thus adding to the sense of secrecy that surrounded these assignations. This uncharacteristic openness made me uneasy, and in the hours leading up to the meeting my unease grew into full-blown dread. I had a feeling he was displeased, and that this small compromise on his part heralded a grave development of which I was still ignorant. I feared it meant that he was dispensing with me altogether, the same way you know a bad relationship is over, when one side no longer bothers to persecute the other.

In the weeks that had passed since I broached Arash's disapproval of our meeting place, I had consulted far and wide regarding my situation. Did I stand a chance of success in challenging Mr. X over such a matter? Shirin khanoum thought so. Others with previous experience in government agreed. Even the head of the government's foreign press office, which ostensibly had final say over such matters, thought so. "Just explain your husband's sensitivities, and without a doubt he will understand," the director had assured me, twirling a Montblanc pen. I wondered if Mr. X knew about the director's fondness for pens that cost more than his own monthly salary, and if so, whether this helped explain Mr. X's hostility to the press office. With so many people discussing our meetings, it was evident they were not truly secret; Mr. X's obsession with secrecy seemed more than ever simply a pretext to harass me.

During our very first meeting in 2000, he had insisted that I never disclose our interactions to anyone. At the time, that had not surprised me; it seemed the obvious thing for a secret agent to say, and even as I mechanically agreed I knew I wouldn't obey. Only later did I realize the stricture's true purpose: to make it impossible to challenge Mr. X. Once, back when the reformists controlled government, an influential vice president had tried, at my request, to get Mr. X to treat me more gently. When I told Mr. X that the vice president disapproved of his manner, he ignored this indirect censure and instead badgered me for months about my disclosure of our meetings: "Ah. So this means you have revealed we are in contact. After you expressly agreed not to. What a pity, that you are so untrustworthy. How can we work with you, if we cannot trust you?" I argued that if our meetings were confidential for the sake of national security, a point he had previously made, then surely Iran's vice president could be trusted. He found some cunning way to refute my logic, and for a very long time my "untrustworthiness" became a theme of our contact. It was after this exchange that I realized I was up against a professional deftly trained in psychological intimidation, and that I, an ordinary civilian, stood no hope of besting him in an argument. Only Mr. X's own logic could defeat Mr. X. I found myself a coach—a friend who happened to be an intelligence agent for an Arab government—to train me in the art of counterinterrogation. This had helped considerably, but I was still no match for Mr. X's most dishonorable techniques.

That day I wore a loose manteau to our appointment, purposely concealing my pregnancy. So many officials I met, even reformist types, chastised me for working while pregnant that I had stopped mentioning that I was expecting, nodding shamefacedly when they mentioned that I had gotten fat. Somehow I especially did not want Mr. X to know that I was pregnant until absolutely necessary, as though by withholding this information I was safeguarding my non-existent right to privacy.

I arrived early and sat in a far corner of the lobby of the hotel, a grand place that had been designed by a court architect under the Shah. I had brought along Proust's *Remembrance of Things Past* to help calm my nerves, escaping into a world as distant as I could imagine. I so lost myself in its pages that I stopped looking at my watch altogether, and only when my cell phone rang did I realize I was late. Having lost ground in the meeting before it had even begun, I walked across the lobby to where Mr. X and a new partner sat waiting at a table off to the side, near a series of vaulted windows facing onto a landscaped garden.

The appearance of the new partner unsettled me. Unlike both Mr. X and his previous colleague, whose grooming, manners, and neat pressed attire gave one the encouraging impression that they were not from the goon branch of the ministry, the new partner was altogether more worrisome in appearance. His stubble, outmoded glasses and shirt, and shifty bearing made him resemble the men who ordered people beaten up at demonstrations. He appeared sullen and never once met my gaze, instead dipping into his bowl of ice cream with studied concentration.

"As you can see," Mr. X began, "this is hardly an appropriate venue for us to be conducting our business. At this very moment we could be noticed by anyone in this lobby, which is hardly acceptable." He had previously made the same point on the phone, as though to suggest that in meeting privately he was actually doing me a service by protecting my public reputation. I responded that if our meetings bolstered the security of the nation, I would not mind at all if anyone noticed them. He brushed this aside.

He made a show of waiting long seconds for the waiter to stride away after taking our orders, and spoke in an exaggeratedly low voice that made it difficult for me to follow his bureaucratic language.

"The only thing that remains is for you to work on convincing your husband," he said. "This simply cannot be a regular option. If you continue to insist, this meeting will be our last. If you cannot cooperate properly, it is better that you do not work at all."

He was as chilly as I had ever seen him, the increasing assertiveness I had noticed over the previous months evident in the way he held his stocky frame. I had often wondered, during in-between moments, whether he derived satisfaction from threatening me. Did he have a sadistic personality, or was he just a decent man stuck in a particularly unpleasant job? Having watched him drive away in a faded Peykan, that sad, boxy vehicle of the Iranian working class, having spoken to the chirpy young daughter who sometimes answered his cell phone, I had felt the latter. Sometimes he even displayed flashes of humanity in our discussions. Once, exasperated and angry, I stopped circling around what I wanted to say and just blurted, "How can you expect me to trust you with the identities of my sources when your ministry just two years ago was *murdering* people?"

Unprepared for this, he responded as though hurt, his brown eyes taking on an expression of sincere distress. "Don't you think we've also had to live with that black history? Tainted by association in the eyes of the people in our neighborhoods?" That exchange softened my view of him, for his character had peeked through his interrogator's clinical civility, and the glimpse suggested that he had a conscience. Even when Shirin khanoum warned me never to let down my guard, never to believe that an agent might act in my interest, I reserved judgment. Mr. X, I reasoned, was a human just like any other. Surely he felt remorse, had some sense of fairness. But now I was not so certain. After years of watching me, of stuffing my intelligence file with useless notes about my comings and goings, he knew full well I was no security risk. The waiter returned to offer more coffee. I fantasized that he could guess the nature of our meeting and that he felt a deep, silent sympathy for my position, thinking, "What a tragedy that this gentle, ladylike young woman must consort with the henchmen of this villainous state." I gazed at him imploringly, but he walked away to refill the sugar cubes. I desperately turned to my last card, carefully saved for just such a moment.

"Perhaps you do not wish to know about an American organization that is seeking to establish cultural ties with Iran?" To satisfy Mr. X's unquenchable thirst for information to scribble in his wire note-pad, I often memorized bland news items that were widely available to the public, but that sounded just interesting enough to merit inclusion in his reports. Most Iranian officials do not speak or read English, so they lack immediate access to much of the world's media. Very often when I called officials for quotes immediately after a major incident affecting Iran, they pressed *me* for information, eager to know how the world was responding. The state's translators included only small doses of information in Farsi-language bulletins, and often officials heard about important stories, press releases, or commentaries a full week or two late. I could tell Mr. X was learning English, but I still managed to share many items of news that sounded fresh to his ears.

He nodded for me to continue, but did not appear impressed. A few minutes later, surveying my half-full cup of coffee, he inquired, "Does its quality not meet your standards?" This was of course unkind, for it implied that I was the sort of person who imposed "standards" on mass-produced instant coffee. Like many Iranians, Mr. X harbored a serious class resentment toward those more comfortably off. He should have directed the feeling at the state, whose policies cemented existing class divides, and at the officials who spoke disparagingly of the "low-class" Iranians who had voted for Ahmadinejad. (One actu-ally used this term with me, uttering it in English as if to underscore his contempt.) But instead, he often took it out on me. "The coffee is fine; I've just had enough."

Once I had exhausted whatever innocuous tidbits I had stored in hopes of tempting him to compromise, our session drew to a close with Mr. X shuffling his notepad importantly and asking whether I had any final concerns to discuss. I bade him a mumbled, hasty good-bye and hurried out of the hotel, eager to feel the autumn air, to close my eyes in the solitude of the taxi ride home.

It occurred to me that perhaps Mr. X's intransigence reflected an institutional tightening of the journalistic reins in Iran. Other re-porters I knew had had their press credentials revoked, and foreign journalists were finding it harder than ever to get visas. Only a small cadre of Iranian reporters for western organizations, composed of those who had been working in Tehran for years and whose track records met with overall approval, were still working regularly. It was clearly a time when the regime would prefer to see no coverage at all of domestic discontent, but the authorities were practical enough to know they could not shut down the media entirely. As I belonged to this group of old hands, my credentials could not be easily revoked. My work was considered balanced, and there were officials at the Ministry of Culture and Islamic Guidance who would advocate on my behalf. But should I voluntarily endanger my clearance by making what Mr. X would paint as an inappropriate request—well, that would be a different story.

Back at home, I quickly wrote an e-mail to the director of the foreign press office: "I don't understand why they are being so difficult. I think my request is reasonable, to meet in an official or public location. Why do they refuse me this? I will discuss it with my husband and see what he thinks. I think in an Islamic country where I wear hejab and follow the rules of Islam, it is unfair that those rules apparently don't apply in the one case that I actually need them."

In preparation for my fast-approaching due date, I spent an hour each morning wobbling through the neighborhood, hoping to prepare my body for labor. Though I hadn't gained much weight, I was usually winded after fifteen minutes. Traveling at a leisurely pace allowed me to pay more attention to the area than I ever had before. I lingered near the leafy intersection where the last century's foremost female poet, Forough Farrokhzad, was killed in a car crash. I examined one of the neighborhood's few remaining traditional houses dating from the 1930s, a crumbling brick villa where a reclusive older woman, an ex-dissident who had been imprisoned under both the Shah and the mullahs, now taught yoga.

One morning, as I turned left from the store where I bought soy milk, I caught sight of a new billboard looming above a busy intersection. It was an advertisement for Dolce & Gabbana, featuring a rather exquisite espresso-colored handbag and a pair of pointy alligator-skin heels. It seemed an odd location for such a billboard, since that stretch of Shahrzad Boulevard usually hosted demonstrations protesting the latest "Zionist-American" injustice. Bearded Basiji types held sit-ins, chanted, "Death to America," and painted American and Israeli flags on the street, watching with satisfaction as cars drove over them. But the billboard remained untouched by graffiti or other vandalism, as though it were the most natural thing in the world for Italian designer marketing and Islamic militants to share real estate.

The marketing of designer goods was not new to Tehran. The city's ubiquitous street vendors sold "Jogio Armani" sunglasses, and fashion billboards hung over parts of the city inhabited by upper-class Iranians. This privileged caste included senior civil servants and those connected to the regime and in a position to receive its special, wealth-enabling privileges, from import licenses to unmolested passage for smuggled goods. Their habit of conspicuous consumption made their streets the appropriate place to advertise Louis Vuitton luggage.

For those connected to a regime that proclaimed a revolutionary ideology of championing the dispossessed, flaunting financial status by way of European fashion labels was at best awkward. It also ran contrary to the tradition of conservative *bazaari* families, who did not allow their lifestyles, apart from their spacious houses, to reflect their bank accounts. Our neighbors across the street, for example, though inhabiting a spacious villa easily worth $4 million, lived ascetically.

Dolce & Gabbana were soon joined by Escada, which debuted over the local square, advertising "casual luxury look" accessories. The billboard hung next to a full-size plastic palm tree, which glowed at night in the square's central patch of lawn. According to rumor it jammed the neighborhood's satellite dishes. The next week, a full-scale Benetton boutique opened nearby. The first day, as they hung up the Benetton sign and filled the windows with satin flip-flops and beach totes, I stood outside gawking, wondering what the Afghan day laborers waiting on the corner thought of the giant posters of blond women dancing. I incorporated the Benetton shop into my daily route, and each day found myself surprised that it still stood. It was not, for the most part, a Benetton sort of moment in Tehran. But the blond women did not last the week. On Friday, I saw that the tops of their heads had been chopped off (presumably as punishment for not wearing veils). Though they had been decapitated from the nose up, their frozen smiles still beckoned shoppers into the busy store.

In the course of my walks, I recalled Shirin khanoum's memories of Tehran on the eve of revolution, in particular how the uprising was fueled by working-class and middle-class resentment of wealthy Iranians' opulent lifestyle. She had recounted how she and her girl-friends, conscious of the underlying injustice, used to linger outside expensive French restaurants where they could not even afford dessert. Such experiences politicized her generation, sparking a revo-lution that punished and purged the wealthy elite. The Islamic Re-public had reproduced the very same conditions: one caste lived in superlative comfort while the vast middle and working classes strug-gled. And while this certainly provoked indignation, the feeling was tinged less with a sense of injustice or politicized anger than with cov-etous entitlement. The young female equivalents of Shirin khanoum and her friends did not begrudge those dining inside gracious restau-rants their privilege; they simply aspired to sit on the other side of the glass.

Because young people were disenchanted with politics and thor-oughly cynical about the possibility of change through political ac-tivism, their desire for a better life remained an inchoate longing. It never occurred to them to redress the situation by organizing and speaking out against the status quo. As they saw it, that was what their parents had done in 1979, and look what they had accom-plished. Instead of protesting, the young turned to pyramid schemes and shady real estate transactions. As long as my generation remained concerned with achieving the upper class's material success, rather than somehow challenging the corruption that enabled it, I did not see how very much would change in Iran. Though particularly vile, Is-lamic plutocracy had never seemed so well entrenched.

I spent an entire weekend lost in such thoughts, as Arash was away on a business trip to Tabriz. The night he was meant to return, he called to tell me Iran Air was running a Tupolev aircraft on the flight back to Tehran, where it usually used Airbuses. The Tupolev is a shoddy Russian plane with a worrisome record of plummeting from the sky at the slightest mechanical malfunction. Because American sanctions bar Iran from purchasing Boeings (or even European Airbuses, which contain American-made parts), the country's fleet of aircraft grows more decrepit each year, and the government has no option but rickety Russian planes. It had become almost commonplace for passenger planes to crash, leaving no survivors. I told Arash I preferred him to take the bus rather than risk his life on a Tupolev. The bus took fourteen hours, and he called every two or three to complain at its slow progress.

That same evening, the retired colonel's son upstairs threw a party. Sometime just before midnight, plainclothes police, or perhaps Basij, arrived to break it up. I heard the click-clack of heels and frantic whispering in the stairwell. The guests were hiding between floors, frightened of arrest. I wondered whether I should open the door and let them hide inside our apartment. But what if the police found out and came pounding on our door? Would I then be arrested as well? I chose not to let the guests in: I heard no scuffling from upstairs, so I preferred to believe the party was being broken up peacefully. Having just prevented Arash from flying on a deathtrap, with my delivery just a few short weeks away, I had no wish to expose myself to whatever authorities were raiding the party. I turned the lights off, telling myself there was no shame in my decision.

The beginning of that October marked the start of Ramazan, the Muslim month of fasting. I could not fast because I was pregnant, but I would have been disinclined to do so anyway, so thoroughly disenchanted had I become with Islam. I knew I could not blame Islam itself for the laws that had made getting married so complicated, the opium-addicted mullah, the polygamy references in our marriage contract. Nonetheless, I felt they had worn away at my ties to the faith, leaving me more detached than ever before. Perhaps with time, I could heal this rift, demarcating my own private Islam as separate from the state's punitive caricature.

I tried to read books written by reformist Muslims, channeling my resentment into intellectual engagement. But the books failed to move me, and I found it significant that most of these reformers lived in western countries. Free from coping with Islamic realities each day, they could devote their energy to refashioning the faith from afar.

I visited fasting relatives over *iftar* (the meal that breaks the day's fast), hoping to observe something in their behavior and outlook that might suggest how they managed to preserve their faith. But nothing in the way they broke their fast with dates and tea and discussed the day's headlines revealed this inner, spiritual calculus. I remained estranged from the festive time of year I had once so keenly enjoyed; only four or five years ago, in Beirut and in Cairo, I had flitted from *iftar* to *iftar*, a veritable Shia socialite. This felt like the distant past of another person, so wide a gulf had opened between me and the religion I once absorbed in my grandmother's lap.

On an overcast day toward the end of Ramazan, Arash and I went stroller shopping on Vali Asr Boulevard, threading through the crowds in line for *halim*, a turkey and wheat stew that is traditional fare during the month of fasting. It seemed to me that everyone paused to observe my waddle down the sidewalk. "Haven't they ever seen a pregnant woman before?" I whispered to Arash. As my stomach expanded, I often searched for other women in similar stages of pregnancy on the street, wishing to feel less alone in my new, spherical form. But as my pregnancy advanced I saw fewer and fewer, until it became evident that very pregnant women simply did not go outside much. Although the Islamic revolution stressed motherhood as the central role of women's lives, although it described in lofty terms the sanctity of bearing children, somehow the physical presence of an extremely pregnant woman was not quite appropriate.

At the Eskan Shopping Center, famous for its café where teenagers flirted over ice cream desserts, we examined sleek hydraulic strollers. I had insisted on buying a stroller—it seemed essential somehow—though I did not know where it would be used. Since 1979, when the

Tehran municipality began renaming each street and freeway after war martyrs, the city's sidewalks had fallen into disrepair. Sidewalks had formerly been maintained by the city, but now the owner of each building was responsible for the stretch of sidewalk in front of it. As a result, sidewalks now varied in quality, appearance, and most unfortunately, height. Yards of rustic cobblestone might suddenly drop several inches to a path of aging asphalt. Walking down a basically flat side street, one stepped up and down, up and down; it was impossible to use a stroller (or a wheelchair or a walker) in most neighborhoods. Even had it been possible, it wasn't safe, because the authorities had also permitted sidewalks to become de facto motorcycle lanes.

After we settled on a fancy stroller that appeased my pregnancy consumption needs, a model that unfolded automatically in a color called Capri, we drove to Mehr Hospital for my first weekly fetal monitoring session. Mehr, one of the city's older hospitals, was never mentioned when people were discussing where in Tehran one should receive treatment, but it was one of the few hospitals in the city to own and use fetal monitors (acquired at Dr. Laleh's insistence).

As I took off my shoes to enter the maternity ward, the nurse told Arash to wait outside in the hall. I supposed allowing him to be present during my actual labor was generous enough, and that it was unreasonable to expect him to be admitted to the weekly checks. I waved goodbye cheerfully, following the nurse to a bed where I would lie perfectly still for twenty minutes to ensure an accurate reading. I inspected the area minutely. It was clean, though it resembled a hospital room from the 1950s. Even though this was the maternity ward, there was no pastel wallpaper, no plants, no curtains patterned with fuzzy sheep, none of that cozy baby aesthetic that is meant to offset the clinical hospital setting and create a "natural, family-centered experience." The nurses all wore forest green tunics, *maghnaeh*s, and beatific smiles, lending the ward an alien atmosphere, as though it were part of a hospital for science fiction characters.

Once I was strapped down and the machine began beeping, I turned to greet the woman occupying the other bed in the room. I assumed, because she was attached to similar equipment, that she was also undergoing a routine check, but from her frantic phone conversations ("Traffic? I don't care about traffic. Get here *now*!") it became evident she was in labor. Her nails were freshly manicured and she wore ample mascara: in the view of Iranian women, childbirth is no excuse for lax grooming. She must have been in an intermediate stage of labor, I couldn't tell exactly, but it was clear she was in an epidural-induced haze. She spoke incessantly and without inhibition about how she felt neglected by her mother, who had stopped by the previous week only four times with home-cooked meals, about the husband who had insisted on attending a business meeting and was now caught in traffic. The chief source of her distress, however, was the fear that her chosen baby name was in jeopardy.

"I had chosen Som, which is a *beautiful* name, don't you think? . . . A *Shahnameh* name that sounds modern . . . and can you believe it, my brother-in-law, two nights ago, he tells me that it is banned, because it is too close to Sam, like Uncle Sam. . . . Banned! My Som! I cried for two whole days, because, you know, I've been calling him that for months, he is Som to me, he can't just become something else. . . ." She continued in this manner for ten minutes, her voice rising in hysterical peaks.

I kept trying to summon the nurse to return, as I could no longer bear lying on my back. I had read in my pregnancy books that one should definitely, positively never lie on one's back after the first trimester, and here I was, supine, at the instruction of medical professionals who should have known better. My arms ached from propping myself up into a reclining position, but the nurse never walked past and there was no call button. I considered yelling for help, but I wasn't sure what I would yell and I was afraid of being impolite. My heart was racing, thudding in my chest as though it might burst, my arms trembling, the sweat trickling down my forehead. The epidural woman wouldn't stop chattering, and suddenly I wasn't sure I could breathe anymore. That's when I realized I was not just very, very upset, but having an actual panic attack. This awareness helped calm me down, and I relaxed my arms, reclining limply on the rough cotton sheets.

I don't know whether it was the woman's neurotic prattle or my own unacknowledged fear of giving birth in an atmosphere that still felt somewhat alien that had overwhelmed me with such a sudden, intense anxiety. What I did know was that I felt suffocated. Was there no point where such conversations would end? Can my husband come in or not, Can we pick this name or not, Can I wear this scarf or not, Can I enter this building or not? Of course, the fact was that there was no such point. That was the nature of totalitarian regimes. Previously, I had believed that this need not define my experience of life in Iran. This perspective was the key, I believed, to not living as a victim. But I was having difficulty maintaining it in the face of repeated violations. Perhaps under the moderate Khatami this attitude was progressive and empowering; under Ahmadinejad, it amounted to self-delusion. I emerged from the maternity ward wan and stiff, and Arash canceled his afternoon meeting and took me for a walk in Sayee Park. We bought steaming beets from a street vendor and ate them quietly on a bench, the sweet flesh staining our lips. He told me that in the hallway he had seen a sign announcing that the hospital admitted unwed mothers. Was this even legal? Did other hospitals practice such lenience? It was impossible to know.

That evening, the news announced that the four-hundred-person state committee that had fanned out across the country in search of the new moon had reported a sighting. This meant that starting that evening, the entire country would commence a three-day holiday on the occasion of Eid-e Fetr, the holiday that marks the end of Ramazan. In Arab countries, everyone in advance knew exactly when Ramazan was ending. This made the final day of fasting pass more quickly, the thirsty hours easier to withstand in the knowledge that they were the last. It also enabled people to plan holiday travel ahead of time. This was the way of sensible countries, but not Iran, which preferred to announce three-day holidays at nine o'clock the evening prior.

Sometime during the days that followed, I decided it was time to alert Mr. X that I would be having a baby. He needed to know that I would be on leave from work, that I would be turning off my mobile phone, and that I would not be calling with minute updates about my next story. I harbored a slim hope that this news would end our relationship. A close friend of mine, a reporter for an important American newspaper, had received a permanent dispensation from her dealings with Mr. X on the occasion of her first child's birth. Upon discovering she was pregnant, he bade her farewell, asking her to *halal* him, to forgive him for any trespass or distress he had caused. She had never heard from him since. I somehow doubted this would be my fate, but one never knew. He received the news cordially, offering congratulations and making no reference to our recent contretemps.

CHAPTER 16

Journey to Shiraz

Our baby boy, Hourmazd, was born on a November day so extraordinarily clear that the great peak of Mount Damavand, usually obscured by brown haze, loomed with ethereal dignity. You could actually see how it sloped into the Alborz range, which merges into the mountains of Anatolia and the Caucasus. It was on such a morning centuries ago, according to ancient Persian myth, that Arash the archer shot an arrow all the way across the plains of central Asia, establishing the boundary of Iran to the east. Iran had lost in battle to its archenemy Turan, and the Turanians, instead of imposing a boundary on the defeated nation, proposed to limit its territory to the radius of an arrow's flight from Damavand. The mountain was considered the very heart of the Persian empire, and is endowed in Persian mythology with almost sacred status. It is for the heroic archer that my husband is named.

The hospital did not permit men to enter the regular maternity ward, and though Dr. Laleh and the nurses smuggled Arash in for my delivery, it would not have been possible for him to linger. He was allowed, though, in the wing reserved for foreign diplomats, so I stayed there overnight. The room cost twice as much as one in the regular maternity ward, and there was nothing fair about our ability to buy our way around the rules. By lunchtime the next day, flowers crowded the floor and every surface. A couple of my relatives called to congratulate us, but whispered that they would wait a few weeks to share the news with others, so that an appropriate amount of time would elapse between our wedding and the baby's arrival. I privately considered them cowards, but said nothing.

My friends in America sent urgent e-mails asking about the experience, still in disbelief that I was having a baby in Tehran. I told them that once I was within the antiseptic confines of the maternity ward, my delivery followed the routine procedures standard across the modern world. I can only recall two exceptions. One, I was forced to wear a long, thick, billowing hospital gown with puffed sleeves, meant to preserve the modesty of a woman being delivered by a male doctor. My one irrational moment during labor was to refuse this gown, and it took Arash ten minutes to convince me to put it on. Besides being hot, uncomfortable, and ugly (in photos I resemble a Soviet nuclear scientist), it, unbelievably, did not open in the front. For the next twenty-four hours I repeated to every nurse, in a daze, "But why not? How am I supposed to breast-feed?"

The second exception involved the nurse's chatter as she guided me through the extremely intimate procedures that are performed on a woman's body ahead of delivery. I expected she would maintain a respectful silence, but instead she chided me in a thick Rashti accent for being in Iran. "But I cannot understand why you have chosen to live here. In America, is there not freedom? Here we have none. Why didn't you just stay there?" According to my American pregnancy guides, the nurse should have turned on a relaxation CD or suggested I soak in a bath, not probe my choice of theocracy over freedom. I had not bothered to read any Iranian pregnancy books, and I wondered whether they catalogued all the small details of comfort that should be provided to a woman in labor. People in Iran, like all people living under authoritarian regimes, were usually preoccupied with big ideas. Whether waiting at the bus stop or preparing a woman for labor, they contemplated hypocrisy, ethics, and personal responsibility with the focus people in America devoted to the minutiae of eating, exercise, and *The Sopranos*. In the past, I'd found Iranians' political engagement exhilarating, had seen it as a richer, more thoughtful way of being. But it was starting to feel too intense, the burden of people who, given the option, would have preferred the luxury of conversations spent vilifying gluten.

Hourmazd is the Middle Persian form of Ahuramazda, the Zoroastrian god Iranians worshipped before they were forced to convert to Islam. My father was greatly irritated by this choice of name; believing that it would be unpronounceable outside Iran, he felt that we should have chosen something easier on the western tongue. I considered Hourmazd easy enough to say (Hūr, like "tour," mazd with a short *a*, like "jazz"), but for his generation, such compromises of identity were a natural part of acculturating in the West. But that trend would soon make endangered species of any Iranian names considered too long or challenging for non–Farsi speakers, I told him. Indian immigrants in America seemed to have no qualms about bestowing complex, long names upon their children. Why were Iranians so quick to shape their culture to the West, rather than push the West to adapt?

Arash and I faced no problems registering our son's name, though we took a giant box of pastry to the registry office just in case. Everyone smiled and cooed at Hourmazd and wished him a long, healthy life. He acknowledged their attentions with a tranquil yawn, and I privately felt thankful that the first bureaucratic encounter of his life, the registration of his name, had not required bribery. On the way home, I gazed at the murals and billboards of turbaned ayatollahs as though seeing them for the first time, and almost felt the urge to cover Hourmazd's eyes. I asked Arash how we would explain them, when the question arose years down the line. "We will say they are eastern Santa Claus," he said.

December 2006, the month after Hourmazd's birth, was a deeply satisfying time for those Iranians disappointed in Ahmadinejad's performance, a sizable and ever-growing percentage of society. In the eighteen months since he took office, the president had managed to weaken Iran's frail economy, provoke U.N. Security Council sanctions, elicit the threat of American military attack, alienate members of his own party (who broke off and started a front against him), offend the ayatollahs of Qom, and trigger the first serious student protest since 1999. Fifty activists burned an effigy of the president during his visit to Amir Kabir University; they set off firecrackers and interrupted his speech with chants of "Death to the dictator!" Their outburst reflected the widespread frustration also displayed during that month's city council elections. Millions turned out across the nation to vote against Ahmadinejad's allies in what amounted to a major, unequivocal setback for the president and his policies. Reformists, having absorbed the lessons of their presidential defeat, fared well throughout the country, capturing twice as many seats on Tehran's influential council as Ahmadinejad's supporters.

I did not vote in the election; I was so crushingly exhausted from the sleepless nights of nursing Hourmazd that I couldn't even make a cup of coffee without burning something. I delighted in the election results from the confines of our apartment, where we were preparing Hourmazd for his first visit to the pediatrician.

It was an overcast morning, and we left early to reach Qaem Magham Street on time. The pediatrician, Dr. Abtahi, one of the most respected in the city, practiced at Tehran Clinic, a hospital that claimed to be modeled after the Mayo Clinic in Minnesota. Though she had trained in Iran, Dr. Abtahi was half German, and her fluency in German and English made her as popular with foreigners as Iranians. In her waiting room, Iranian grandmothers in floral print chador sat alongside the impeccably dressed wives of European ambassadors, pointing to the same fuzzy lobster mobile to distract their screaming children.

In the examining room, I gingerly peeled off Hourmazd's bodysuit as Dr. Abtahi began lining up glass vials of vaccine. I mentioned that we were flying to Germany the following week and asked for advice on how to protect the baby's ears from the fluctuating cabin pressure. "You're flying *next week*?" she asked, putting down the needle and turning toward me. "If so, why are you getting him vaccinated here?" She proceeded to explain that Iranian vaccines were of an outmoded type liable to cause fever. And whereas in advanced nations several vaccines are combined in a one-shot cocktail, Iran's were one vaccine per shot, so Hourmazd would have to be stuck with needle after needle. I *had* wondered why there were several vials, but it hadn't occurred to me that all of them were going to be serially injected into my tiny, nine-pound baby.

Dr. Abtahi suggested we have Hourmazd immunized in Germany and bring back the remaining doses for her to administer in Tehran over the course of the year. He would be spared fever and the unpleasant impression that doctors were needle-bearing tormentors in white coats.

Dr. Abtahi had not overtly criticized the government on that score, only remarking that "Iran, along with Bangladesh and Afghanistan, is the only country left in the world to still be using such vaccines." Afghanistan is a destitute country ravaged by war, with a GDP of $22 billion; Iran is an oil-rich nation with a GDP of $600 billion. It was simply staggering that despite its vast resources, the Iranian authorities could do no better for their children than the precarious government of a virtually failed state. The regime's inadequacy at this most basic level was what made the majority of Iranians despise it so. They saw, in each toman spent on groups like Hezbollah, a toman not spent on modern vaccines.

We swiftly agreed to her suggestion, determined as most parents would be to spare our baby bouts of fever when it was within our means to do so. I dressed Hourmazd and watched with relief as the vials disappeared back into the refrigerator. It was only the next week in Cologne that we confronted the monumental complexity of our decision. Arash spent two days shuttling between doctors and pharmacies, explaining our rather irregular need to buy and transport vaccines. We learned that, to retain their potency, vaccines must be kept within a precise temperature range at all times from the place of manufacture to the point of administration. They are vulnerable to damage from light as well. Tranportation requires what is called a "cold-chain system," involving special monitors, insulated containers, and dedicated trucks and refrigerators. To secure Hourmazd's vaccines, Arash and I would need to devise and execute our own improvised cold-chain system.

As though this were not difficult enough, after our second day in

Germany Arash needed to attend to work, the ostensible purpose of our trip, so the remainder of the search fell to me. I do not speak German, and Cologne numbers among the German cities with a militant Islamist problem. It was the seat from where a radical onetime associate of Osama bin Laden, a Turk known as the Caliph of Cologne, had organized followers to wage holy war. It was, in short, one of the last places where you could comfortably stride into a pharmacy and say, "Hi, I'm from Iran and I'd like a year's worth of live vaccines to take on a plane!" In the end, by deploying much charm and many introductions from local friends, we succeeded. A foam ice chest and some ice packs constituted our picnic version of a cold chain.

The next challenge lay in getting our ice chest home. We needed to take a train to Frankfurt, and from there a direct flight back to Tehran. Before departing, we calculated the total length of our journey and worked out precisely at what times the cooler would need to be placed in the on-board refrigerators of both the train and the plane. Although we both held non-Iranian citizenship, we were Iranians flying to Tehran on our Islamic Republic passports, demanding to carry live germs aboard crowded means of mass transport. With every additional minute it took to explain our situation to security officers and transportation staff, our anxiety mounted. The ice packs melted, Hourmazd screamed out of boredom, and the people behind us in line inched back as though we had confessed to carrying Ebola virus. We finally managed to board the plane, handed the vaccines over to the flight crew to refrigerate, and collapsed in our seats, elated at having carried out a seemingly impossible mission. But as the plane began its slow descent to Tehran, a flight attendant thrust the cooler into my lap, half an hour early. She flounced up the aisle before I could tell her the vaccines needed to remain cold until landing, and each time I attempted to stand an irate flight attendant barked at me to take my seat. We stared miserably at the glowing "Fasten Seatbelt" sign as the plane descended, coping with the situation as most couples would, by arguing.

"I told you this was a bad idea. You just can't live in a country like Iran and perpetually conduct your life with the standards of the West," Arash said. "This was a mistake. We should learn from it."

"How can you call it a mistake? We're providing the best for our son, protecting him from *fever*." I looked at Hourmazd asleep in my lap, tranquil and innocent, and imagined him wailing from a fever, his little body burning. "You're horrid to suggest we should let him suffer."

"You're wrong. Right now, as far as we know, these vaccines are spoiling. Unless there's some way of checking their potency, we're going to use them at our own risk, hoping that Hourmazd is protected from various awful diseases. If we had just used the Iranian vaccines, he would've had a night of discomfort. But at least we'd know for sure he wasn't at risk of contracting polio."

"But that's only because we had bad luck and because this stewardess is a rude German who can't be bothered to listen to an Iranian passenger."

"Azizam, listen to me. My sister is just like you. For years I've watched her try to live in Iran with German sensibilities. It has taken over her life. When she travels, all she thinks about is filling her suitcase with the right shampoo, cereal, child medicine. She sends her son to the German school because the Iranian ones are terrible. Don't you see how dangerous it is, getting used to things whose availability is precarious? When she runs out of the German muesli, he refuses to eat Iranian cereal. If one day the political situation turns ugly, the diplomats will send their families home and the German school will close. If you want to live a German life, you need to live in Germany. If you're going to live in Iran, you need to live as everyone else does. The same cereal, the same schools, the same vaccines. You can't live like an alien in your own society."

What Arash said made sense, though I was too stubborn to admit it at the time, and reluctant to acknowledge the wider implication of his reasoning. It meant, of course, that we would eventually need to decide whether to raise Hourmazd in Iran or move abroad. I had imagined the question would arise years down the line, once we had his schooling to contend with, but it suddenly loomed closer.

The next day, we took our perhaps potent, perhaps spoiled vaccines to Dr. Abtahi, who assured us they were fine and pointed out that we could always have Hourmazd tested later for the antibodies to the relevant diseases. The rush of relief we felt pushed aside all the uncomfortable considerations of our plane argument. With lifted spirits, we cocooned the un-feverish Hourmazd in blankets and drove out to the footsteps of the Alborz Mountains to walk amid the snow-frosted pines. We stopped along the way to eat steaming bowls of *ash-e reshteh,* a velvety soup thick with legumes and noodles, topped with minty whey. Hourmazd, generally too squirmy to permit us to eat in peace, scrunched up his face at the sun's glare and fell asleep. The memories of our harried moments in Europe faded, and we felt, fleetingly, triumphant.

"How can you be a journalist if you don't dress like Tintin?" Aryo, Arash's five-year-old nephew and my new primary companion, eyed me suspiciously through long eyelashes. It had occurred to him one afternoon that he didn't know what I did in life, apart from breast-feed his cousin every hour. "Journalists don't have uniforms; they wear normal clothes," I said, handing him a waffle covered in quince jam. We then discussed the feeding practices of killer whales, propped Hourmazd up on a doughnut pillow, and danced to the lemur song from the cartoon film *Madagascar.* This was my new life.

As the mother of an infant, I was no longer able to meet for coffee in smoky cafés or attend parties that started at eleven. All the hours in my life previously devoted to conversation, work, and fun were now spent changing diapers and fiddling with the electricity converter on my American breast pump. In time, my single friends slowly disappeared from my life, excusing themselves with gifts of stuffed animals and that frozen, pitying look reserved for those lost in the pastures of motherhood. I began spending time with other mothers, a special caste in whose company my ungroomed eyebrows and wrinkled clothing did not seem so out of place. The venues of my new life—home, other people's homes, and fast food restaurants—were overrun by children under ten, in whose company I rediscovered the appeal of chocolate milk and gummy candy, and became acquainted with SpongeBob SquarePants, in his Farsi and German incarnations.

I soon noticed that, despite their innocent pursuits and diminutive size, young children in Iran lived lives of extraordinary complexity. Before I began socializing with the under-ten set, I believed that life in Iran posed intricate and unhappy quandaries only for teenagers and adults, people of an age to contemplate love, work, and higher education, all of which were seriously compromised in the Islamic Republic. But life in a theocracy imposed its pressures on very young people as well. They learned from earliest consciousness to exist in two separate worlds.

This unhappy reality dominated that afternoon's conversation, between me, Solmaz, our friend Neda, and Neda's sister Mina, who lived in the same building. We were visiting them in their neighborhood, Tehran Pars, a middle-class district in east Tehran, on whose outskirts the Revolutionary Guards owned vast tracts of land. The residents of Tehran Pars were typically of average income, which meant they had to save carefully to afford rare vacations or the toys their children demanded. As a rule they were not as deeply traditional or religious as those who lived in south Tehran; they could be described as secular—not that they were necessarily westernized or irreligious, but that they believed in a separation between religion and government. The government knew its unpopularity in such quarters was a major weakness, that it could not forever get by on the support solely of pious, low-income Iranians in south Tehran and the provinces. It sought to reach out to Tehran Pars, dispatching mobile libraries with "Messenger of the Sun" emblazoned on their sides, a name that meant nothing in particular but that signaled cheerful intent. Smiling women in powder-blue chadors handed out Martha Stewart–like books, many of them free, to housewives and students, but the residents were not won over. Instead, they stood in the street and complained that the library was a waste of money and that they never received help of real significance. It would take far more than free cookbooks to capture the support of Tehran Pars's residents, so calcified was their resentment.

We reclined on sofas drinking tea and peeling tangerines, immersed in a discussion about Dr. Holakoee, an Iranian-American therapist whose advice many Iranians followed avidly. Because he belonged to the Baha'i faith, whose members the regime brutally persecuted, he might never be welcome inside the country. But he still managed, via television broadcasts, to educate Iranians about sibling rivalry, the implications of birth order, and other such concepts that many therapists inside the country either did not believe in or explained poorly.

Mina's two-year-old daughter twirled about the living room in a tight embrace with her beloved plastic Elmo, as yet unconfiscated because the Mattel toy recall still lay in the future. Her nine-year-old brother, Koorosh, burst in through the door, flinging off his backpack and rushing over to tickle his sister. He then watched an hour's worth of French cartoons (he was determined to learn the language, having been convinced by a summer trip to Paris, his first time outside Iran, that France was a superior country). Later he pulled a DVD out of his backpack, a collection of highlights from his third-grade class. Mina popped it in and I hid a yawn, expecting playground scenes and close-ups of elementary school artwork.

The first minutes captured the class making ritual ablutions before prayer, followed by scenes of the children actually praying together in the classroom, and, finally, a lively segment of them practicing the call to prayer. Koorosh didn't seem to be attending an Iranian elementary school but one of those scary Pakistani-type madrassahs, where rows of boys sit on the floor memorizing the Koran and names of the alumni who have died at Tora Bora. I was horrified, but wasn't sure what to say. I looked at Solmaz, who sent her son to the German school to prevent precisely this sort of Islamic indoctrination. Mina noticed my expression. "Public schools are much better these days," she said. "Now they get an hour of music lessons each week, and their textbooks have color pictures."

In earlier years, elementary school classrooms, she said, had supplied an opportunity for the authorities to terrorize Iranians who did not abide by religious codes. In the midst of a lesson, for instance, the teacher might craftily say: "Raise your hands if your parents drink alcohol at home." These days, schools only rarely exploited children's reflexive honesty this way, but they did send home checklists that asked parents to sign off on their kids' dutiful attention to homework, grooming, and of course, daily prayers. "Of course, I just sign that he's prayed," Mina said.

"But that sends the message that lying is okay," I said. "How do you get around that?"

I imagined trying to teach a third-grader the philosophic argument that breaking the rules or lying might be all right if the rule or the question posed was unjust. Such moral shades of gray required a capacity for ethical and intellectual reasoning far beyond the abilities of someone that young.

"You know, he's never really brought it up. We just model the values and behavior we believe in and hope for the best." Mina said that was the most natural way for them to grow up, by absorbing these kinds of adult intricacies slowly, without too much instruction from tense parents.

"That's interesting," I said. "So you don't actively teach lying. You just leave it to Koorosh to sort out why you're committing what is technically an untruth."

"He just told his teacher last week that his parents don't pray, so it might just be that he hasn't paid attention."

I wondered whether I could be so circumspect in Mina's place. My instinct, probably a foolish one, was to share with children precisely what I thought of the country's laws. Once when Arash and I took Aryo out for lunch, I let my headscarf slip. Hourmazd constantly tugged it off anyway, and instead of readjusting it every other minute, I sometimes left it around my shoulders. Aryo reminded me twice, and the third time his voice rose nervously. Like many children, he followed rules assiduously, at least in public. You couldn't even get him to drink from a bottle of water in a store without paying for it first. Unthinkingly, I told him that it was unfair that I had to wear the veil, and that it was all right for it to sometimes fall off.

Arash later chided me for this. Aryo was too young to understand, he said, and although I thought I was doing the right thing, instilling tolerance and the belief that women had the right to choose whether to cover their hair, I was actually confusing him in a way that might be dangerous. If the wrong person heard him repeat that it was unfair for women to have to wear the veil, he could be punished. Though he attended the German school, there were a hundred other places—the doctor's office, government buildings—where Aryo accompanied his mother on her daily business and where such a comment would make trouble.

In most cases, you simply couldn't measure the future cost of teaching your kids liberal values. The difficulties only grew in proportion to a child's age. For espousing their real beliefs openly, they might one day be punished by a teacher, expelled from school, arrested by the police, fired from a job. This grotesque dilemma—allow your child to be brainwashed, or teach him otherwise at some risk—was perhaps at the heart of why so many hundreds of thousands of young Iranians emigrated each year once on the cusp of parenthood. They could face the East–West divide in cities such as Toronto or Los Angeles, but at least they would be spared the Iran–Iran divide inside their own country. While Arash's warning made sense, I still felt that since the regime had no compunctions about brainwashing children, we had the right to counter with our notions of what was right. I said so to Mina, who was calling her mother into the living room to watch the DVD.

"But then how are we any different from them?" Neda asked. Surely Koorosh had the right to choose for himself the values he wanted to uphold.

I considered Neda's position ridiculous. It might make sense in Sweden, but here it amounted to sending your kid off to Jonestown with the Kool-Aid folks, hoping he would emerge an independent spirit. Of course you had the right, perhaps the responsibility, to intervene in the brainwashing of your children.

Arash and I had understood full well that we would be raising our child with two cultures. Having both grown up in Iranian families living in the West, we were familiar with identities anchored in two disparate worlds. But I hadn't realized that really we had three worlds to deal with: the West; fundamentalist, public Iran; and tolerant, inside-the-house Iran. Coping with the gulf between Iranian private and public life was an intricate skill that most adults I knew managed with varying degrees of success. Wearing masks or lying when required, all while keeping your core identity intact, was the daily business of adults who lived in authoritarian societies.

But Mina was right when she said you could not teach children these skills. I began to wonder whether it was even possible to raise an open-minded, healthy child in a culture that was fundamentalist and anarchic. That I had plenty of tolerant, sane friends who had grown up here—witness Neda and Mina sitting next to me on the couch—was proof that it could be done. But I wasn't sure they reflected a success rate so much as a success story. The very idea that I would be competing with my child's teachers and other role models over basic values (the role of religion in daily life; whether or not western culture was corrupt) was intimidating. What if they won out, even for a phase? Alongside Neda, Mina, and my other friends, I could also think of cases where the environment had bested the family.

Take the case of one of my cousins in Tehran, a young man I scarcely saw anymore since he joined a weird militant-spiritual cult. When we first met, he wore polo shirts, studied engineering at Sharif University (whose engineer program was among the best in the world, feeding whiz kids to graduate programs at Stanford and Harvard), and seemed destined to follow in the footsteps of his parents, moderate people who fasted during Ramazan but drank alcohol and kept a residence in Paris. Within a year he grew a beard and started looking like a Basiji, with gaunt cheekbones and untucked shirts. He stopped kissing me on the cheek when we met, and began talking about fighting "the infidels who were occupying Palestine." He wasn't the only person I knew who had undergone such a transformation. I could think of friends in Beirut and Cairo from whiskey-drinking, bikini-wearing secular families who, seduced by the militant mood of their societies, went through full-blown fundy periods. These transformations sometimes passed, but in many cases they became permanent, or left indelible marks.

I suppose the difference was that Iranian society was not in a fundamentalist mood, only the Iranian government, and cases like my cousin were exceptional. Even if he grew up in Iran, it was rather unlikely that Hourmazd would one day grow a beard and contemplate jihad. But the siren call, however muted, of militant Islam was not my only fear. There was the emotional burden of needing to deceive all the time, of having to be constantly vigilant to protect your family and their private world. The behaviors expected of children in Islamic theocracies resemble those of children from abusive or disordered families. We know that such environments deform children's thoughts and personalities, making them vulnerable to shame, depression, and anger. Indeed, Iran often felt like one vast dysfunctional family. Rates of depression and suicide climbed after the revolution, and young people tended to become either full-blown overachievers or unmotivated depressives. Neda and Mina were examples not just of people who had escaped brainwashing, but also of those who had survived an Iranian youth with their mental health intact. What if Hourmazd turned out particularly sensitive, and lacked the extra layers of skin needed to practice deception each day?

There was also peer pressure to contend with. The neighborhood boys whom Koorosh played with, for example, might never coax him to go pray at the mosque. But they celebrated religious festivals, wore black, and participated in the street culture of Islamic kitsch that the regime had successfully instilled. These included invented commemorations like Fatemieh, which had no precedent in classic Shia observance. Mina couldn't keep Koorosh holed up inside, when the boys on the block were dressed in black and raring to go. Would Mina be able to shape the role Islam played in Koorosh's life? She would do her best. He had already compared France and Iran, and rated secular Europe superior. But the rest seemed to me a matter of chance, in the end—a roll of the dice. Both family and the Islamic state had proved themselves capable of defying each other; you might end up with a freethinker like Neda, or a lost soul like my cousin.

While Mina, in my eyes, left a great deal up to fate, other mothers took a more proactive approach to the public-private divide. A friend of mine, an Iranian-American who was raising her twin boys in Tehran, had invented the "keeping secrets" method. She taught her sons that the behavior they practiced at home—drinking alcohol in moderation, watching satellite television—belonged to a special, private world of which they should never speak outside. This in turn made a value out of privacy and sidestepped the delicate task of explaining why it was okay to lie in certain situations, but not in others. In the case of this friend, however, the approach had not warded off the day when her son came home from school and informed her that she was immoral in not wearing a full black chador. "You're disrespecting our culture!" he told her, biting hungrily into the chocolate cupcake she had baked. Not long after, he ran home from school weeping after his class chanted "death to America" at an annual school protest rally. His classmates, being young and therefore casually cruel, told him that because he had been born in America, he would need to die too.

Solmaz coped by sending Aryo to the German school, bypassing school protest rallies and the Iranian education system entirely. In the process, she also bypassed Iranian reality. While no one disagreed that in the short term, Aryo was receiving an education far superior to Koorosh's—Aryo's teachers exposed him to world history and no one forced him to chant *"Allaho Akbar, Khamenei rahbar!"* ("God is great, Khamenei is our leader") during recess—the choice carried its own set of constraints. For one, the tuition was equivalent to that of an elite private school in the West, far more than Solmaz could afford without help. As a divorced single mother, she could not work full-time; she needed and received her parents' financial support. Since Arash and I both worked, however, it was expected that we manage our own lives. Though Arash's salary was generous by Iranian standards, it could not hope to cover tuition priced for western incomes. A school like Aryo's would be beyond our means.

Cost aside, there was also the uncertainty involved. The German school existed to educate the children of diplomats and expatriates, whose numbers would immediately dwindle should Iran's political relations with the West turn rocky. In that event, the school would close, and Aryo would be forced to attend regular Iranian school. His teachers would not be warm, enthusiastic, unveiled women, but dour, bored men with beards who used microphones to call the children to order. He would need to learn to read and write in Farsi and to socialize with children from vastly more diverse backgrounds. They would not be called Joschka and Fabian, but Hossein and Mohammad, and they would taunt him mercilessly, in the classic fashion of Iranian schoolboys.

As it was, Aryo was growing up a stranger to his own society. One recent afternoon, as we were baking his favorite marble cake, he casually looked up from the mixer and asked, "Maman, where is the nearest church?"

"Why do you ask?"

"Since we're Christian, we should know where the church is."

Solmaz explained that they were not, in fact, Christian. He could be forgiven the assumption, since most of his friends and classmates were, since he had played the part of a Wise Man in the school nativity play, and since in his secular family no one had taught him anything about Islam. We strove to keep serious expressions at the time, but after he went to bed we howled with laughter. It was almost as funny as the time he had asked his mother in the shower, "Maman, did you have a penis before the revolution?"

Apart from misleading him about the family's religion, we anticipated that a German education would later complicate Aryo's social life as a teenager outside the circle of his classmates. Iranian men educated in western environments, for example, usually lacked the requisite machismo to flirt with Iranian girls. But for the time being, Aryo seemed equally at home with his school mates and his Iranian friends. That afternoon, he and Koorosh stormed about the house making helicopter noises and fielding armies of Lego action figures, occasionally passing by to snatch piroshki, cream-stuffed dumplings, off the coffee table.

Koorosh's grandmother called for him to start his homework. She had taught elementary school for three decades in the Shah's Iran, and controlling the damage wrought by Koorosh's schooling now consumed her life. She spent evenings completing his art assignments for him, filling in the color-by-numbers book of the Shia imams' portraits ("Who ever heard of color by numbers at this age!") so that he could let his imagination roam with watercolors on blank paper. To her perpetual dismay, there was nothing she could do about the core third-grade textbook, which followed the devout Hashemi family through the course of their pious lives, from the meals they ate on the floor to their road trip across Iran. The father in the textbook, Mahmoud Hashemi, was a bearded civil servant who enjoyed taking his family on outings to seminaries, Shia shrines, and martyrs' cemeteries. When he took them to the city of Shiraz, he showed them many minor tourist sites but neglected to stop at Persepolis. This was something like going to Rome but skipping the Forum and the Colosseum. The task of Koorosh's grandmother was to teach him that Mr. Mahmoud Hashemi, the character at the center of his education, was a raging fool. As we gathered our things to leave, she closed the textbook with a long sigh. "Before the revolution, I used to dislike people who left Iran and chose to live abroad," she said. "I used to think, What is wrong with you that you prefer other countries to your own? But not now, not anymore."

CHAPTER 17

Under Investigation

On a cold, clear day in January, a relative, Laila, came to visit us with her five-year-old daughter. Hourmazd was almost three months old, and we were still receiving visits from friends and female members of our extended families. Laila brought a hand-knit pair of pajamas for the baby, and an apple pie with saffron crust for us. We gossiped for about an hour about mutual acquaintances, and Laila mournfully complained about her family's imminent move to Tabriz. Tehran had become too expensive under Ahmadinejad, and her husband felt that they could have a better quality of life in a smaller city. After drinking our tea and eating pie and a plate of grapes (Iranian socializing requires fruit, and the quality of your fruit bowl is a key measure of your hospitality), Laila prepared to leave. Her little girl proudly pulled out a cherry-red scarf from her purse and tied it over her hair with an innocent flourish. Only the most religiously extreme families force girls that young to cover their hair, and we all looked at her mother inquiringly.

"She insists on wearing it," Laila said, shaking her head. "I've tried to discourage her, but she thinks it makes her look like her mommy." The girl beamed beneath her scarf, imagining herself quite grown-up. She did not realize, of course, that her mommy wore the scarf because it was mandatory, and that if given the choice, she would do otherwise. The sight of them together depressed me, and I trudged downstairs thankful that Hourmazd was a boy. As I prepared him for bed, I lost myself in thoughts of the little girl, wondering whether she would be doomed to wear the veil without having had the chance to truly choose.

Hourmazd was wakeful that night, and I paced the room trying the sleep-inducing maneuver my baby books called the milk shake. It did not work. As I paced, I compiled a mental inventory of all the girls and women in my social circle whom I had observed during my years in Iran. Laila's little girl would grow up in the society in which these women had come of age, a society whose middle-class value system was being transformed. Because laws enforced religious observance, one might expect faith to grow out of a lifetime's habit rather than conviction. But in practice, this seemed true of a startlingly small number of women. Paradoxically, rather than turning out uniformly devout or predictably rebellious, the Iranian women I knew were more independent than any generation before them. They negotiated their way through society, and around hejab, with the assurance of true individuals, rather than like the model Islamic subjects the regime wished them to be.

Instead of allowing themselves to be simply oppressed by hejab, they treated it with an instrumentalist practicality. Like so many seemingly fixed or imposed beliefs, hejab could be tinkered with for the sake of an attractive marriage proposal, for instance. In Iran, where "marrying up" in social or financial standing was more imperative than in a Jane Austen novel, women commonly adjusted their head covering to match their prospective partner's degree of religiosity. Was this fluid morality or resistance to subjugation? Perhaps both.

I thought about one of Arash's cousins, a doctoral student we had seen the previous week on one of her visits home from Canada. Born into a secular family, to a mother who did not cover her hair, she started veiling to marry a more religious man she deeply loved. Her mother was mortified at first, and the extended family reacted a bit snobbishly, but with the passing of time the young woman's hejab became very ordinary. Then take the case of one of my own family acquaintances, a young man from a wealthy and devout family in

Mashad, Iran's shrine city. He ended up being snared by a young woman of little religious conviction, who happily adopted greater propriety and more conservative dress to cement the match.

Most recently, we had met the girlfriend of a bohemian but pious painter at the opening of one of his gallery shows. From the moment we shook hands, I felt there was something peculiar about her—the bright turquoise scarf and Doc Martens that peeked out from under her chador, the easy way she looked Arash in the eye and engaged him in conversation. As everyone in the gallery admired her boyfriend's art, a playful series of whirling dervishes in tribute to Rumi, she and I chatted. I learned that she had spent half her life unveiled in London and had only donned the full-length black chador to satisfy what she called his "aesthetic conception of the feminine." This sounded to me like paternalism wrapped in painterly abstraction, but she seemed entirely at ease in her new reincarnation, chirping "Ciao!" as we left the gallery.

I could easily think of other women whose marriages had necessitated a turn in the opposite direction. I knew a young chadori photographer, Fatemeh, from a deeply conservative family. Even on reporting trips to the border with Iraq during the roasting days of high summer, Fatemeh wore layered chador, dexterously managing her multiple cameras from within its nylon folds. She had married a similarly religious man, then divorced him when he objected to the long hours she spent working around other men. When she married a less strictly devout colleague, she of the tri-fold chador downgraded to a simple headscarf.

In short, many women developed a malleable attitude toward the veil, despite being forced to wear it since adolescence. This showed how dramatically the revolution had failed in keeping women subordinate to families and husbands. Iranian women now saw themselves as individuals who could challenge their families' traditions, whether liberal or conservative, and chart a wholly independent course. The other fascinating thing about such marriages is that they would have been unlikely in the Iran of my parents' generation, where social classes were impermeable; people mostly married within their religious and financial caste, and hejab was an inherited, fixed custom within spe-

cific groups. Back then, the daughters of veiled women learned to veil,
the daughters of secular women learned to go bareheaded, and each
group was taught to regard the other as, respectively, backward or immoral.

Such attitudes, as you might imagine, were not conducive to peaceful coexistence in a country that comprised religious traditionalists,
westernized secularists, and everything in between. That these days
women chose their life partners from a broader range of candidates,
and felt confident enough to tailor their hejab accordingly, suggested
an erosion of social boundaries that could only be healthy for a country whose revolution had broken out partly over class stratification
and the role of religion in daily life. Paradoxically, authoritarian laws
had somehow made Iranian society more tolerant. There was a perverse pluralism in today's Iran, where the moral weight of the family
was removed in questions of religiosity, and young people, all exposed
to the same restrictions, grow up freer to choose and change.

In the early months of 2007, American and Iranian analysts, European diplomats, and the West's media elite collectively predicted that
the United States might soon unleash a military attack on Iran. I will
forever recall that time as the winter of "Do you think America will
attack us?" dinner parties, during which everyone debated the likelihood of a bombing campaign. The previous fall I had reported a story
for *Time* the editors called "The Coming War with Iran," and in the
intervening months similar breathless anticipation of a conflict dominated the American media. At the nervous dinner parties, friends
often commented that the media frenzy amounted to psychological
warfare—that it was an American tactic to keep the mullahs uneasy
and undermine how ascendant they felt in places like Iraq and
Lebanon. While this might have been true, the saber-rattling could as
easily have signaled a serious intention to attack, or at least a serious
ambition on the part of neoconservatives to push for a military confrontation. My editors set about ensuring that I would be prepared in
case of an attack, dispatching a Thuraya satellite phone for me to use

in case the aerial campaign targeted communication and electricity infrastructure. I unwrapped the heavy phone with a sense of foreboding. The last time I had received such equipment, just before the war with Iraq, it had also been sent "just in case."

In December of 2006, the U.N. Security Council had unanimously passed a resolution imposing sanctions on Iran over its nuclear program. Not long after, American troops in Iraq arrested several members of the Iranian Revolutionary Guards, and a top official in Washington accused them of being "engaged in sectarian warfare." Most worrisome of all, though, was the January State of the Union address, in which President Bush lumped Iran together with Al Qaeda and claimed that "the Shia and Sunni extremists are different faces of the same totalitarian threat." This statement was dangerously, and some said deliberately, misleading. European diplomats argued it was Washington's way of seeking a more "robust" position ahead of negotiations with Iran, but to me it just sounded like more scary justification to bomb.

With the world so focused on the emerging threat of a U.S.-Iran confrontation, my editors pleaded with me to resume work. Though they had agreed to allow me three months of maternity leave, they convinced me to return after just two months, to help them consider making Ahmadinejad "Person of the Year." In the end, they did not bestow the president that distinction, but I was caught up again in the whirl of news and somehow back on my editors' radar. That was why, even before I'd managed to teach Hourmazd that he should sleep at night rather than during the day, I found myself riding a taxi to central Tehran to interview a university professor who was also a prominent political analyst. America wanted to know whether Tehran had the jitters, and it was my mission to find out.

It was my first full-fledged outing without three-month-old Hourmazd; I felt a rush of exhilaration, closely followed by panic. I had planned the meeting with great precision, making the appointment for an hour when traffic was at its lightest so that I could be back within three hours, the longest stretch Hourmazd, who still refused to take bottles, could go without being nursed. I prayed that there would be no unexpected accidents clogging the freeway and no collapse in the mobile phone network: that the first outing of my career as a working mother would go smoothly.

Usually the guards at the front of the university waved my taxi through the gates. But that day, they gestured me out of the car. I impatiently collected my purse and rushed up to the guardhouse, calculating the stop would entail about five minutes of lost interview time.

I explained to one of the guards who I was, whom I was there to see, but he just stared at me glacially.

"You can't enter looking like that," he said. "Your manteau has too few buttons." He used the formal pronoun for "you," the equivalent of the French *vous* in Farsi, but his tone radiated scorn.

I looked down at what I was wearing, confused. It was one of my more conservative overcoats, loose and olive green, and it was held together in the front by little hooks, not buttons. I wasn't sure if he took issue with my having hooks in lieu of buttons, or with the insufficient number of those hooks. I told him I was a foreign correspondent on my way to an interview, and that I should not be held to the dress code for female students. He shook his head, and turned his back to me. In a raised voice, I said that my attire was perfectly appropriate, that I had visited this professor numerous times without any such hassle. These protestations failed to move him, so I called the professor on my cell phone. Surely the security guard would not be screening the guests of such a prominent academic.

The professor asked to speak to the guards. I passed them my mobile phone. "Sorry, Doctor," the shorter of the two said, pronouncing the title with a sneer. "But you cannot imagine how this lady is dressed. . . . No, it is not possible." He handed the phone back to me.

"I truly apologize for this, but it seems they're not going to let you in." The professor sounded embarrassed. "When they're intent on picking on you, there's nothing that can be done." He used the Farsi verb *gir dadan*, which means to pick on or harass for no discernible reason. The term became popular after the Islamic revolution to describe a form of behavior that had not existed previously. I resented the professor for not coming out to defend me in person, as challenging them on the phone from the warm confines of his office seemed a bit unchivalrous. But I politely said that I understood, and hung up. I tried one last time with the guards.

"Please reconsider. I've left my baby at home, and he still nurses. I don't have time to go home and come all the way back."

"Lady, I don't care if you have a baby," said the shorter guard. "I don't care if you're double-parked. I don't care if you've left food on the stove. You are simply not entering the university like this. You look . . . you look *appalling*."

I felt as though I had been slapped. "How *dare* you speak to me that way?"

The taller guard rebuked him for addressing a "sister" so disrespectfully, but he continued to gaze at me with brazen contempt, relishing his petty power over the gate, over me.

I burst into tears, humiliated and angry over the loss of my interview and the deadline I would now miss. I despised myself for losing control before the guards, and ran back to the taxi. Once inside, I wept openly.

The taxi driver looked up from his newspaper, astonished. "What has happened, madam?"

"They said . . . they said . . . that I didn't have enough buttons," I cried, wiping my eyes with the sleeves. "They wouldn't let me inside."

"*Lanat bar hameshoon, khanoum, lanat bar oon Khomeinishoon!*" "A curse upon all of them, a curse upon their Khomeini! It was now my turn to look up in shock. The taxi driver had invoked a Koranic curse against the guards, and upon the founder of the Islamic Republic. *Lanat kardan,* meaning to deprive someone of God's mercy, is often used to curse the enemies of God and to curse the devil. Even I, from the very depths of my rage, would never have uttered such words in public. The cabbie spent the length of the ride home recounting tales of clerical malfeasance, some more outlandish than others, in an effort to cheer me up.

."You, madam, you are the proper human. They! They are trash! Thieves!"

I remained silent throughout, telling myself it had been an awful but edifying experience. It gave me a taste of what Iran must have

been like in the early days of the revolution, when Islamic ideologues
took over universities, purging women and secular teachers. I told
myself the professor should be excused his failure to rush to my defense, because he was lucky to still have his job. One of the first steps
Ahmadinejad had taken as president was to appoint a mullah as
chancellor of Tehran University. It was the first move in what many
called a second cultural revolution, as administrators forced scores of
secular-minded professors into early retirement. Even after the purge,
which occurred in the early months of 2006, Ahmadinejad told students during a campus appearance that they should "shout at [him]
and ask why liberal and secular university lecturers are present in the
universities."

    I told myself that being turned away from an interview, in the hi-
erarchy of misfortune one could suffer at the hands of Islamic radicals, scarcely mattered. I couldn't understand why I was so terribly
upset. I had been turned away from many places in my years of reporting in Iran—from universities, mosques, and seminaries, usually
on some sartorial pretext that masked the institution's hostility to females and journalists. It had become a simple nuisance, like getting a
parking ticket. What had happened to me? Was this the same me who,
after being beaten by police during a demonstration, stopped at a
party before going home? The same person who had endured a night
of Basiji detention with dry eyes?

    At home I took a long shower and curled down next to Hourmazd
on the bed. I set his Sleep Sheep, a fuzzy creature intended to induce
drowsiness, on its "ocean wave" setting, and pulled the cool sheets
over us. For a long time I stared at the shadows on the ceiling. Arash
brought me a cup of orange blossom tea, and even though it was
past midnight, I could not sleep. Normally I would have taken a sleeping pill, but I was still nursing. Many Iranian women stopped breastfeeding after just a couple of months. Perhaps this was because they
could not imagine spending a year or two without sleep aids, anti-
depressants, or whatever medication helped them cope with their overwhelming lives.

After a phone interview with a politically connected family friend, I finished my story the next day. The magazine, desperate for any reporting with a Tehran dateline, posted it on the website almost immediately. Only then did I realize I had not informed Mr. X of my return to work; perhaps I should contact him before he thought to call me. I considered this an act of goodwill on my part, because I was only obliged to keep him generally briefed, not report my every movement.

He answered the phone on the second ring with a curt greeting, as though irritated. I began to explain why I was calling, and wondered why he didn't sound more receptive.

"I just wanted to tell you that I've started working again, that I've already written a story."

No reply. Not even perfunctory congratulations on Hourmazd's birth, despite the fact that Mr. X and I had known each other nearly a decade. He sometimes acted, infuriatingly, as though he couldn't fathom why I was calling. It was one of his strange tics, perhaps meant to throw me off guard so that I would splutter to fill the silence.

"I thought by telling you I would be keeping our lines of communication open, ensuring there are no mistakes."

"You are far, far beyond the realm of simple mistakes," he said, his voice taking on that tone of casual malice I had grown to fear.

"What do you mean?"

"There has been a review of your articles, and it has been concluded that it is no longer appropriate for you to work."

"Oh."

"Yes; in fact, your file has been transferred to the judiciary. Proceedings will shortly be under way against you."

"Proceedings?" I whispered.

"It has been concluded that your articles are guilty of propaganda against the regime, undermining national security . . ."

He mentioned a third offense, but I was numb with terror and ceased to process what he was saying.

"But how can this be? We've been in regular contact. You should have said if something was wrong."

"You know very well the risks involved in working in Iran. You have been doing so of your own free will."

I felt betrayed by Mr. X, whose hideous presence in my life I had tolerated precisely to ward off such a day.

"Please, can you clarify? Is it a *possibility* that this will happen to me, or is there an actual process under way?"

"It is already happening," he replied breezily. "But you can be certain you will have a chance to attend the court. You can come, defend yourself, make a case. Perhaps the judge will rule in your favor."

The chances of the prosecutor general of Tehran ruling in my favor were comparable with those of a comet changing course. Once someone was charged with such offenses, the last thing they received was due process. They were inevitably incarcerated for long periods, often in solitary confinement, and were subject to interrogation as well as to psychological and sometimes physical abuse. Zahra Kazemi, an Iranian-Canadian photojournalist who found herself in the custody of Iranian authorities in 2003, did not have the chance to "defend herself." She died in prison of blows to the head, inflicted during interrogation.

There was nothing left to say. I choked out a goodbye and hung up, in disbelief that I had ever given such a vile person the benefit of the doubt.

Arash was playing with the baby. I ran to him, hyperventilating through my sobs. All I could think of was Hourmazd and how he would suffer in my prolonged absence. He was only three months old. They would come for me soon, and he would cry until he was sweaty and red, waiting for me to return. He couldn't eat or sleep without me. He still refused the bottle. He would think I had abandoned him. But surely they wouldn't take me away if they knew I had such a small baby? But of course they would. Mr. X knew I had just had a baby. All these thoughts flitted rapidly through my head, and I couldn't compose myself. Arash put his hands on my shoulders to calm me. He kept asking me to explain what had happened, but I couldn't speak. In the end he put Hourmazd into my arms. He waved his little arms around as though caressing the air, swiped at my nose, and it was only by watching these delicate movements and feeling the warmth of his body through his pajamas that I could slow my breathing and describe the nightmare that Mr. X had unleashed.

We stayed up that night until almost three. My first thought was that I needed to escape immediately, before I was summoned. "Do you think your dad could use his Tabriz connections to smuggle Hourmazd and me across the border in a truckload of sheep?"

"Why sheep?"

"It seems like a smart place to hide. Who's going to check the back of a truckload of smelly, woolly sheep?" My great-uncle, according to family lore, had escaped the country in this manner after the 1953 coup, when the reinstalled Shah began persecuting the ministers of Mohammad Mossadegh, the popular prime minster he had deposed.

In the days that followed, I grew so skittish that I would snap to attention at the sound of pigeons scuttling over the window ledges. One morning a man whose voice I did not recognize buzzed our apartment from the street, asking me to come down to receive a piece of mail. This is it, I thought, they've finally come to take me away. I began to cry and dashed toward the back of the house, passing Arash on the way. "He's here, I mean they're here. . . . Tell them I won't go! . . . I'm not sure who it is, but I think it's *them*. . . . Tell them we have a baby, that I can't leave him!" I ran into the farthest corner of the bedroom and slammed the door behind me, as though somehow the distance would protect me from the mysterious man. I lapsed into thoughts of what my cell in the Evin prison would be like, filling my imagination with details I remembered from working on Shirin khanoum's book. The vomit-encrusted carpet, the metal toilet that was never cleaned, the bacteria-infested well water piped into the women's ward (only male prisoners enjoyed clean city tap water).

"Prisoner Azadeh, will you please come out?" Arash tapped on the door.

I opened it a crack, eyeing him suspiciously. He did not appear too upset, in the manner one would expect if a van were waiting below to cart off his wife.

He handed me a manila package. "The postmark is from California, so for now you're still a free woman."

I tore it open impatiently, and pulled out a jumper with little airplane designs. It was a gift for Hourmazd from one of my relatives, and I smiled weakly. "How was I supposed to know it was the postman?"

Besides skulking about the house and falling apart every time the doorbell rang, I *was* taking active steps to do something about my predicament—trying to, anyway. I immediately stopped working and told my editors about Mr. X's threat. It was unwise for us to talk over the phone, as it wouldn't make any sense to plan an escape or chart our course of action on a tapped line. The authorities likely monitored my e-mail as well, so I talked with my editors on the satellite phone, which had turned out useful after all. Each evening I climbed the stairs to the snowy rooftop, pacing until the phone connected to the satellite, gazing over the winter skyline.

My editors wanted me to fly to Dubai immediately, but if Mr. X's threat was real, then an attempt to leave the country would invite a confrontation. I would likely be arrested at the airport and thus be detained all the sooner. Since the conversation with Mr. X, Arash and I had recalled an incident at the airport upon our return from Germany that we had given little thought to at the time. The passport officer, upon scanning my documents, had looked curiously at his screen, and turned to inspect me. "They didn't say anything to you as you were leaving the country?" he asked.

"No, why?" Arash had replied.

"Never mind. If they didn't say anything, then I guess it doesn't matter."

That exchange now seemed weighted with dark meaning. Both of us feared the screen had announced that I was barred from leaving the country, that the officer was puzzled that I had been let out at all.

Although leaving might be risky, sitting in Tehran waiting for the worst to unfold hardly seemed a better option. I decided to contact a highly influential senior official, a man of great integrity whom I had known for years and trusted implicitly, to ask for help. It was the only way to find out whether the judiciary was actually building a case against me, or whether Mr. X was bluffing—a coldhearted, sinister bluff designed to scare me away from working, perhaps forever. The official kindly agreed to investigate, promising to let me know what his inquiries turned up.

As the days turned into a week, and then two, it became apparent we needed to be patient, and that an investigation into the nature of a threat emerging from a government with multiple institutions with overlapping mandates and conflicting intentions took a measure of time. We told ourselves that until we knew more, we should not torture ourselves by assuming the worst. Actually, Arash told me this, and I tried to listen.

As though none of this were enough, precisely this time I learned that my mother in California had been diagnosed with metastatic breast cancer, a recurrence of the disease that had been in remission since I was in junior high and that we had thought had been cured forever. I did not tell her about the troubles I was facing, because she would be powerless to help and needed all her strength to cope with chemotherapy. Though she didn't say anything, I knew she wondered why I wasn't flying out to see her. I made vague references to "special circumstances" that required my presence in Tehran, but a gulf seemed to open between us. The geographic distance was magnified by how little I knew about her condition, and I stayed awake late into the night, trying to research her cancer on the Internet. I figured it would be easier to learn on the Web what the prognosis was for metastatic breast cancer than to ask her directly. But including the word "breast" in my search terms ran up against the wall of the government filters, and I continually met the maddening, final "Access to this site is denied" page of the service provider. As I had discovered when pregnant, the censors blocked searches of almost every body part, cutting off Iranians from a wealth of medical information. They denied each part of the body its vast array of rightful associations—medical, athletic, literary, sartorial, artistic—and reduced it to its crudest form, a sexual object.

I abandoned my Internet search and resolved to speak directly to her doctor, who only took calls after lunch, California time. For an entire week I stayed up until past two A.M., begging his nurses to put my call through. Eventually, I gave up trying to speak with him, and settled for the vague replies of his assistant. Those nights, weary from lack of sleep, from the unknown threat that might be stalking me, from the "special circumstances" that prevented me from seeing my sick mother, I began to feel that the life I had so lovingly created in Iran had turned into a nightmare. For the time being, at least, I no longer had a career, or even the assurance of personal safety. Nor could I take solace in the idea that I alone stood to suffer. Arash and Hourmazd were vulnerable as well, and I could do nothing to protect them.

With my toe, I gently traced the pattern of the rug, following the vines that formed its border. Those who make it their life's work to understand Persian rugs can immediately spot a carpet of poor quality. Though the designs are meant to be symmetrical, the fingers of tribal weavers tire after laborious months of knotting from sunrise to dusk. As they reach the rug's bottom, their concentration wavers, the knots loosen, the design grows less precise. That was how I felt, as though the strands of my carefully woven Iran life were unraveling.

CHAPTER 18

The Suitcase Bride

Compulsory retirement was not without advantages. Before the fateful phone call to Mr. X, I perpetually lacked time. Now I had long, luxurious days full of nothing to do. Though the warning still preyed on my mind, I found myself unable to keep up the intensity of my loathing for Mr. X and the cruelty of the Islamic government, my dread that what he told me was true. Slowly I became preoccupied again with mundane matters, like whether Persian Gulf shrimp were back in season, or whether I had dry cleaning to pick up. I walked along Shariati Avenue, Hourmazd snuggled in a sling carrier, and sipped pistachio milk shakes topped with mulberries. I haunted the Golestan Gallery, around the corner from our house, which that month was exhibiting the work of a young woman on death row. I lingered around the bookstalls near Tehran University, whose dusty stacks contained relics of a past Iran, back when there were enough Americans in the country to merit multiple copies of books by Helen Gurley Brown. Along with Arash and his friend Houshang, I spent days in south Tehran, exploring the shrine of Shabdolazim, and the pilgrimage site of Bibi Shahrbanou, one of the daughters of the last Iranian king, Yazdgerd III, before the Islamic conquest. Attracted to a myth that fuses Zoroastrian Iran with Shia Islam, many Iranians believe that Princess Shahrbanou became the wife of Imam Hossein.

Scholars have long disproved this legend, but the ordinary, often illiterate women in chador who climb the tan-colored hill to the shrine do not know this, and make their reverent pilgrimage anyway.

At other times, Hourmazd and I spent the day at my parents-in-law's home in Lavasan, curled up under the *korsi,* an electric brazier tucked beneath a table covered with quilts. We watched the birds alight on the snow-laden branches, and when it was sunny we ventured out onto the terrace, watching Geneva cavort in the banks of snow. We had moved the dogs to Lavasan, partly because Geneva had grown too large for the apartment, and partly because it was safer for them. As part of their "anti-immorality" drive, the authorities had stepped up their harassment of Iranians with pet dogs; by some reports, they had even established a dog prison to detain pooches caught walking illegally (for a dog, this seemed to mean walking in the capacity of a pet, rather than as an independent, nameless four-legged creature).

Were we to be lost in a blizzard, Geneva would have been capable of saving us, in the long tradition of the St. Bernards who rescued stranded travelers in the Alps. I told the Lavasan gardener this, hoping it might mitigate his dislike for her. Like most devout Muslims, he considered dogs ritually impure, and disapproved of us keeping them as pets. As a result, he also skimped on her meals and denied her sufficient time outside her corral. When she lost weight, her coat hanging too loosely on her frame, we reprimanded him and asked that he feed her as we instructed. But as was his maddening way, he offered her more food only when we were in residence, reasserting his pious neglect when we returned to Tehran. The knowledge of her noble lineage as a rescuer of lost travelers made no difference to the gardener, who continued to glower in resentment as she trotted after him with a goofy, drooling smile.

When Hourmazd slept, I listened to the relaxation CDs my mother had sent from California. She had just started a course of radiation therapy, and over the phone at least, she sounded as though she had already given up. I focused each day on not taking my situation, the temporary annulment of my career, personally. The instinct that rose up each day from deep inside was to somehow punish those responsible, to blast them with my generalized contempt, to write caustic essays in which I derided them (they had, of course, taken on the abstract, monolithic object status of "them") as backward, smelly, evil. There was a genre dedicated to this sort of reaction, revenge lit you might call it, comprising books like *Not Without My Daughter* and other volumes that took one person's misfortune and fashioned out of it an assault on a nation, a culture, its people, and, often, their religion. It took all my concentration to beat down this angry impulse, to view what was happening to me dispassionately as a political process. The fact that I was currently a victim did not mean all women in Iran were suddenly victims.

The most profound change inside me, one that I could not control or reverse, was the final evaporation of my spiritual regard for Islam. I did not begin to resent or disrespect the faith. I was already well acquainted with the dangerous, puritanical ways in which it could be interpreted, the premodern complexity of its jurisprudence. But my passion for its qualities subsided. Before, I had been quick to defend Islam whenever I felt it was attacked or portrayed unjustly. I remembered how determined I used to be to ensure that *Time* cover Islam fairly, even once waking up a respected Islamic scholar in the middle of the night to help me correct what I knew was a distorted reference parsing the Koran.

I would always cover Islam diligently, but I could no longer imagine myself throwing all my energy and soul into the task. Why should I, when the grand ayatollahs of Qom could not be bothered to defend the rights of Iranians against Mr. X and the regime he represented? Once, I would have argued that the ayatollahs were moderates at heart, but that a long tradition of political quietism prevented them from stepping into the fray. Now that reasoning did not satisfy me. If they were indeed moderates, let them come out and defend moderation. Islam could not be constituted only of the liberal reverence and interpretations of a handful of reformist Muslims who accepted western humanism and universal values. Islam was the sum total of its many million believers, their behavior and outlook. And at this point in time, that majority had not come out in favor of change; they did not accept the liberal reformists, or even know of them. These were intellectual conclusions that I could easily have arrived at before, had my spirit been willing. Though it is the most commonplace thing in the world for faith to cloud reason, I had always applied that truth to extremists, such as the Israeli settlers and Muslim suicide bombers in their perpetual standoff. It had not occurred to me that *my* attitude toward Islam might also be vulnerable to such emotional distortion. I wasn't at all pious; I had attended university; I had grown up in California. Was it Mr. X who had taught me otherwise, or simply living in Iran, years of living right up against Muslim hypocrisy? Though I could not be sure, and though I missed the easy pride and sense of belonging my previous views had afforded, I considered myself cured—and free.

That spring, news spread that a new director had been appointed to the government office of the foreign press. The official who had promised to investigate my case had still not contacted me, and the uncertainty was growing unbearable. I decided to seek a meeting with this new director. If what Mr. X said was true, I reasoned, the new director would surely have been apprised of the proceedings, and that would be evident in how he received me. Though the precise nature of the link between Mr. X and the press office was ambiguous at best, it was evident that they cooperated to some extent. At previous tense junctures in my relationship with Mr. X, when he was displeased and withheld security approval of my work, the director of the press office had refused to see me, communicating through his unavailability that my credentials were not in order. He seemed to resent having to obey a security agent's dictates, and he chose, in situations when he had an unpleasant message to convey, to convey no message at all.

In what I took to be a promising sign, the new director granted me his very first meeting with a foreign journalist. With no information about the man's political background, I had no idea what to expect. Out of caution, I dressed conservatively in head-to-toe black, in a Gulf-style abaya. Unlike an Iranian chador, which is basically a large square of cloth that you clutch together with your hands or teeth, an abaya includes arm holes, so it is much more wearable.

I took a taxi to the Ministry of Culture and Islamic Guidance on a weekday morning for the meeting. The form of his greetings suggested that the new director was a traditional official, unlike his suave, westernized predecessor. "I would like to felicitate you on your marriage," he began, speaking softly, as though not yet at home in the new position. "We consider the family of your husband noble and respectable in the extreme, and are very pleased at your union."

How excellent: the Islamic state approved of my marriage.

"My father-in-law's example is truly inspiring," I said. (Mahmoud Agha, Arash's father, was renowned for his business ethics—he refused to buy property that had been appropriated by the government after the revolution, or to boost his profits with black-market trade; officials who were above neither of these practices nonetheless respected him for his principles.)

We proceeded to discuss the noble duties of motherhood and the wildly exaggerated images of Iranian women in the western media. Once tea was served, our conversation warmed up, and we moved to matters of Shiism. I tended to shine in such meetings, as my experience reporting in the Arab world provided endless material. Iranian officials enjoyed debating gossipy points of Shia religiosity, even Shia intrigue (Who *really* killed the Lebanese-Iranian cleric Musa Sadr in 1978?), and Shia clerical gossip (the feud between Iran's Supreme Leader and the top ayatollah of Lebanon, Sheikh Muhammad Hussein Fadlallah).

The director glanced at his watch, noting with embarrassed surprise that we had been chatting for nearly an hour although he had allotted only half an hour for our meeting. He then turned the conversation deftly to the matter of my press credentials. While the press office generally approved of my work, he said, he would be "best able to advocate" on my behalf if I spent some time working on stories that were "easy to defend." This meant that for the time being I should avoid subjects the government deemed provocative and instead focus on more neutral topics, such as film and women's high rates of university attendance.

Although this fell short of an explicit denial of Mr. X's threats, it was encouraging. It was unlikely that the ministry would push me to work while at the same time the judiciary prepared proceedings against me. That evening, I wrote to the official who had been looking into the matter, to inform him of the meeting. He wrote back to say that he was pleased and that his own investigation had turned up nothing. Taking this together with the result of my meeting, it seemed plausible that Mr. X had been making an empty threat, intended to discourage my work or to cow me into freezing all my connections with non-Iranian institutions and people.

This was, of course, speculation, but it was informed speculation, the best anyone could hope for in such matters. When dealing with an opaque, secretive system, there is no such thing as "inside information" or real political analysis. This holds as true for journalistic analysis as it did for my dilemma. Every year or so, some American publication runs a political analysis that can be broadly described as the "Who *Really* Runs Iran?" story, the answer being the Supreme Leader, the president, the Revolutionary Guards, or unelected clerical bodies. But the reality is that no one knows, ever. The closest approximation of the truth is that many people run Iran, but that at no given moment is it entirely clear who has the upper hand and why. We can guess at this clique's broad motivations and at the internal dynamics that shape their behavior. But to go beyond that was just speculation. I knew this because I had spent years writing such pieces, and, that experience aside, I was a Farsi-speaker with better connections and sources inside the regime than most. Along the way, I had honed my detective skills, culling information from as broad a range of sources as possible, trying to devise an interpretation that would, I hoped, hint at the regime's reality. I never imagined I would be applying these skills to my own life, and in doing so I was forced to confront what a hack job it was, this fumbling effort to determine the contours of what lurked behind the curtain.

Arash and I talked at length about how to proceed. I could remain in retirement, thus suggesting to Mr. X that I was intimidated and obedient, that his scare tactics had worked. I could start working again as before, and risk whatever repercussions this might entail in the new, more hostile climate. I could work gingerly, on tame features that would not cause offense, or dry news stories that recast what the wire services reported. In the end, we agreed the last option was the most responsible. It would give me a chance to better appraise the situation—to see whether the new press director would be an ally and what befell other reporters.

After years of reporting aggressive, boundary-pushing stories, the kind of coverage to which family and friends responded with e-mails saying "This is the one that's going to finally get you in trouble," I felt somewhat squeamish about my new resolution. But caution was the only wise course.

In my new incarnation as a soft journalist, I no longer tried to brainstorm stories that fired up my investigative instincts. Instead, I just reacted to what was happening around me. I wrote about people's indignation over the blockbuster American film *300,* which they felt insulted their proud, ancient history. Using as a springboard the weddings I attended, I wrote about how modern marriage offered rich material for understanding contemporary Iran. Fortunately, the news that spring was livelier than the usual back-and-forth over the nuclear program. In March, Iran took captive fifteen British sailors in the Persian Gulf, and a mini hostage crisis ensued, taking over international headlines for nearly two weeks. I filed dispatches recounting what the foreign minister and president said at press conferences. I became, in effect, a human tape recorder.

Once that crisis passed, I went searching for more stories, and discovered that when I made a point of trying to produce "neutral" or even positive coverage, many legitimately fascinating subjects occurred to me that might not have captured my attention otherwise. In a way, the combative, investigative journalism that I felt was the only real kind tended to lead me only to stories that highlighted everything that was wrong in Iran. When dealing with a government as obviously nasty as that of the Islamic Republic, it is very easy to consider this impulse noble, in the tradition of the great muckraking of people like I. F. Stone. Various forces also combined to focus me exclusively on the Next Horrible Thing story—the appetite of editors; the "pickup" factor of certain stories. Once I had put this mentality aside, my consciousness found room for other topics. Everyone knew that Iran forced women to cover, but who knew that it also ran the most progressive HIV program in the Middle East, ahead of other Muslim countries with less puritanical images? Who knew that many of its undergraduate university programs numbered among the best in the world?

The next thing I learned was that there were no "neutral stories." In covering even the most benign subject, there was no avoiding mention of the regime's flaws. I wrote a story about the renaissance of Persian classical music, but then had to detail how for years musical instruments had been illegal. When I reported an essay on people's taste in reading, censorship asserted itself as a theme throughout the story. It reminded me of the days when I toiled over the ending of *Lipstick Jihad*. I confessed to Lily, my publisher friend, that despite all my efforts it ended sorrowfully. "I want so badly not to write a grim Iran book," I told her. "Why is it turning out this way?"

"It's not your fault," she said with a knowing smile. "You can't write the sadness out of Iran's story."

And so I could not will away the paragraphs that detailed what was still unacceptable, unfair, extraordinarily awful. With each story, it grew more apparent to me that at least for now, remaining in Iran as a journalist meant risking my safety. Though I trudged through each week, guiltily corresponding with my editors and plotting the next article, I knew the situation was unsustainable. Sooner or later I would need to decide what mattered more, being a mother or being a reporter. This wasn't a real choice, of course, but Arash and I had not properly contemplated other options. We would need to soon enough, and meanwhile I sought to console myself by reading about the history of journalism in Iran.

Censorship predated the mullahs; in a book written before they took power, I learned that the media "intended to conceal facts that might hurt those in power." In 1961, many newspapers refrained from covering the country's election riots, and authorities jailed the resident *New York Times* reporter for five days. That same year, Abdol Rahman Faramarzi, the founder of one of the country's most influential newspapers, described the Iranian media as "often monotonous, useless propaganda."

Though it did nothing to alleviate my current plight, it helped to know that even Iran's secular rulers had bullied the media. Unlike their successors, they did not murder journalists and nearly annihilate written culture with censorship. But every now and then it is instructive to remember that Iran has a long tradition of autocracy, and that while the present Islamic tyranny feels terribly foreign, it is undeniably *Iranian.* Even though Iranians resent their government, there is almost always a degree of complicity between rulers and the ruled. Something in our culture nurtures tyranny, and has for centuries. I felt I finally understood the poet Simin Behbehani, when she writes: "If the snake is domestic / I will give it shelter / I will be fond of it still / even if it does cruel things."

The sound of loud crashes on the roof carried all the way down to our third-floor apartment. They startled Hourmazd, who had been reluctant to sleep and now rolled over to attention with a look of satisfaction. At barely over five months, he spent much of his time reclined on a doughnut pillow observing our living room, one arm propped in a Caesar-like pose. I scooped him up from the bed and headed toward the elevator. It was family custom to gather at Arash's parents' apartment during thunderstorms, power outages, and other troubling, extraordinary circumstances.

Arash's mother, Eshrat khanoum, opened the door, and I entered to find Arash's nephew Aryo perched on a chair, knees clutched to his chest, sobbing. "They're knocking down the satellite dishes on the roof," Eshrat khanoum explained.

I climbed up the stairs and peered onto the roof through the tiny window in the stairwell. A dozen soldiers were bent over kicking at the dishes' cement bases, while two officers stood aside chatting. Back downstairs, Aryo remained inconsolable. His life revolved around the hour on Wednesday afternoon when the German cartoon channel broadcast *Power Rangers,* and the thought that he might miss it had reduced him to panic. "I want to complain, I want to call the police!" he kept howling.

"The police are the ones who are taking them away," Eshrat khanoum told him. "That's the law. Do I cry because the law says I have to wear a headscarf and a manteau?" She looked to me for assistance.

"Yes, it is the law," I said solemnly. "We live here and we must respect the laws."

"Let's buy a ticket *right now* and go to Germany," he said. "I want to go to Germany."

We tried to explain that we could not leave the country, that he could watch a DVD instead, that it was not the end of the world. But these assurances only frustrated him more, and soon he crunched up again in the chair, and began wailing *"Dish! Dish! Dish!"* without pausing for air.

I felt sorry for Aryo, for his wounded sense of justice and his inability to comprehend what was happening. "Poor kid, what a world he has to grow up in," I said, pressing my hands around a cup of tea, and surveying naked rooftops in the the rest of the neighborhood.

Eshrat khanoum was less moved. "Azadeh, what have you seen? Things are so much better now. Before, they would show up, insult you, treat the doorman horribly, and charge you a huge fine for having the dish in the first place. Now they arrive respectfully, kick over your dishes, and cart them off."

It was the perennial matter of perspective, emerging as it always did, revealing the difference in expectations I found so painful. I had grown up in a world where policemen did not kick down people's satellite dishes, either respectfully or brutishly, and I expected it not to happen at all. The same gulf separated me from other young mothers in Tehran. Once, when the wait at Hourmazd's pediatrician was exceptionally long, several mothers began talking about the difficulties of raising children in Iran. I listened to their conversation stupefied. They complained about the poor quality of Iranian diapers and about how challenging it was to find well-made baby products in general. Of course I, too, found Iranian diapers plastic heat traps and had to hunt to find all-cotton pajamas, but these things hardly occurred to me as grievances, compared with the fact that I couldn't take my baby out for a walk, because of the pollution, the uneven sidewalks, or the hooligans overrunning the parks. Women who had grown up in revolutionary Iran were accustomed to public space being hostile. They had no particular expectations of a park and they did not imagine the city should provide them with play centers or playgrounds or well-stocked children's libraries. What disappointed me, in short, often did not even occur to them, and vice versa.

By noon we had managed to coax Aryo out of his gloom with promises of ice cream and cartoon DVDs. Once his mood brightened, he suggested we buy one of the new dishes he had heard about at school, tiny ones that could connect to the satellite from the balcony and were thus immune to police sweeps. We walked to the square nearby to buy the promised ice cream, and heard from the produce seller that the police had confiscated the mobile phones of local merchants who had filmed trucks rumbling out of the neighborhood. The building witnessed another bout of tears later that afternoon as the doorman's son, Saeed, returned home from school to discover the dishes were gone. His mourning revived Aryo's despair, and they roamed the stairwells morosely, shuffling their feet and refusing to play soccer outside. It was one of the special moments in their friendship: the regime had just leveled their status—Aryo as the grandson of a successful textile manufacturer, Saeed as the doorman's son. They were just two boys desolate at the loss of their cartoons.

In the course of the evening, as Arash, Aryo's mother, and Mahmoud Agha all drifted in separately to hear the news, our pretense of respecting the law crumbled, and we complained openly about the backwardness of censorship in the twenty-first century. Aryo appreciated being admitted into the confidence of the adults, and repeated, with a conspiratorial glint in his eye, "Yeah, what jerks!" His mother cast him a stern look. I tried to imagine the day's lessons from his six-year-old perspective: Our family deliberately breaks the law. The law is senseless. We have been punished for breaking the law, but we intend to do so again. This time, however, we will spend more money on a smaller dish so as not to be caught. Money protects us from the unfair law. Money is good. Germany is good. Iran is bad. Long live the Power Rangers.

~

Solmaz was walking Aryo to school one morning when three police officers in pine-green uniforms stopped a car that was idling in traffic. The woman behind the wheel wore a fuchsia headscarf and Jackie O sunglasses, and the officers motioned for her to pull over and roll down her window. One leaned over to inspect her appearance, informed her she was "badly veiled," and proceeded to issue a formal warning for violating the Islamic dress code. When the woman protested, they told her she could either sign the warning or be detained. Solmaz, who was also wearing a bright-colored headscarf, grabbed Aryo's hand and hurried across the street.

It was not the most terrible incident that occurred that day, but it was the one Solmaz witnessed and would recall as the moment after which everything changed. That Monday, for no apparent reason, the authorities launched the most ferocious crackdown on "un-Islamic" dress in over a decade. Overnight, they revised the tacit rules governing women's dress. The closets of millions of women across the country contained nothing but short, tailored coats, ankle-length pants, and bright headscarves. Suddenly, these styles were grounds for arrest. In the days that followed, the police detained 150,000 women for failing to abide by the official dress code. We were all afraid to leave the house, because it was obvious the authorities were out to make a point, arresting even women who were "sufficiently" covered.

When forced outside by a meeting or an appointment that could not be rescheduled, we sent each other text messages upon departure and arrival, as though commuting through a war zone, as though we were in danger of disappearing en route, which I guess we were. The broadcaster who read the state's evening news bulletin, a wolfish-looking man with puffy gray hair and an imperious voice, informed us that 86 percent of Iranians supported the crackdown. By that time, however, we had installed the new satellite dishes on our balconies, so we could see footage on foreign news channels of angry scuffles, of police forcing screaming, kicking women into their cars. During the height of the crackdown, Arash told me sales at Laico's stores dropped precipitously: women were afraid to go out to buy bed linen.

Ironically, the same problem applied to all of us who needed new wardrobes. My own closet contained the long abayas and chador I wore to official meetings and religious places, and the short, tight manteaus I wore everywhere else. I could not exactly see myself going out to buy bread dressed in an abaya, which is, after all, the national dress of Saudi Arabia, and looks it. I wrote to my best friend in California about the new campaign, complaining that the weather was getting hot and that I would be sweating in long, shapeless cloaks. She wrote back confused, having been under the impression that I had been wearing those shapeless cloaks all along. I suppose to people living in free countries where women wear what they please, the difference between a relaxed dress code and a stern one sounds inconsequential. In fact, it mattered desperately. In the years when women could wear colors, could show off the lines of their figures, what in effect became acceptable was the expression of individuality. Between the year 2000 until that April of 2007, I wore a headscarf and manteau in Tehran, but I still looked, from head to toe, like Azadeh. I did not resemble the thousands of other women on the street, but only myself. As I presume was the case for most women, this helped me to perceive the oppressive weight of the regime as lighter than it perhaps actually was.

We gathered one morning over breakfast, discussing the new restrictions. Arash's mother had invited us upstairs so that we could visit with Arash's father, who had returned from Tabriz the night before and would be leaving for the Caspian that afternoon. The Ahmadinejad government was still refusing to take back the indebted factory, and as pressure mounted on the company, he was nearly always traveling between the factories in Tabriz and the company's store at the Caspian. We lingered over breakfast, spreading fresh cream and cardamom-carrot jam over buttery rolls laced with ginger, fresh from a Tabriz bakery. Solmaz appeared, late as always, looking as though dressed for a funeral, in the loose, long black manteau that had become the only prudent outdoor garment. She poured herself tea and sat down to lecture Aryo. "If we are stopped on the way to school, you are to remain quiet, okay? Just sit there and think up a riddle for me. Remember, if you try to defend me, you might just make things worse." He nodded seriously.

The regime appeared divided over the crackdown. Conservatives in parliament issued a letter thanking the Interior Ministry and the police for their fine work and suggesting that the United States and Israel were responsible for Iranian women's immodest dress. But the same week, the head of the judiciary argued that such "tough measures [would] backfire." It seemed the Islamic Republic's institutions were at war, and as usual, ordinary people suffered the consequences. I suggested that the infighting might herald an eventual easing of the new restrictions, but everyone around the table said it was too difficult to speculate. In Iran, sometimes internal rifts produced the most unexpected openings; sometimes they produced violence and chaos. Usually I was at my busiest during such fraught times, reporting both analytical pieces and accounts of how the turbulence affected women's daily lives. This time, though, I did not write a word. The Ministry of Culture and Islamic Guidance told reporters not to "undermine" the police's "public decency" drive with criticism, and threatened repercussions for those who engaged in such "divisive" journalism.

I felt comfortable not writing about such momentous injustice. Many years ago, when I first started reporting, I believed that journalists who watched demonstrations and riots from the sidelines were somehow not the real thing. That you had to be in the midst of it all, to see the expression on the policeman's face when he raised his baton to beat a teenage girl, to smell the sweat of those running in fear, to hear the shouts of the protesters resounding in your ear. The tension between personal safety and getting up close to the story lies at the very heart of journalism, and I had long since decided I was not willing to risk my life. I had stopped reporting in Iraq once the terrorists began beheading their captives, and while I respected my colleagues who continued, I knew I could not live that way. Covering wars changed many reporters forever. Once you consciously begin risking your life for journalism, the knowledge that you are doing so can disfigure your personality. You become enchanted with the romance of your sacrifice, dependent on the adrenaline-laced theater of close escapes, and emotionally walled off from those who do not inhabit the same charged, dangerous world. The safe repose of everyday existence begins to feel oppressive, and you begin to feel alive only when death lurks in the background. While no one can question the sheer nobility of reporting in hostile places, chronicling unimaginable evils, I did not want to be that reporter.

Having long ago made peace with my decision to put safety above the story, I sat back and observed the crackdown unfold with the same trepidation and dismay as those around me. Several days later, however, in early May, I learned of an occurrence that shook my measured convictions. The call came in the afternoon.

"Hi, this is ABC. We were wondering if you could talk to us later today about the implications of the arrest of Haleh Esfandiari."

"What arrest? . . . Are you sure? . . . When?"

He told me that Haleh, an academic at the Woodrow Wilson Center in Washington, D.C., had been taken to Evin Prison earlier that day. She was one of the few Iranians I knew who had successfully risen to prominence in the United States and still made a point of nurturing the careers of young Iranian-Americans. I had met her when I was a reporter at the *Los Angeles Times,* and since then had enjoyed her warm support and advice. I often consulted with Haleh about projects and story ideas. When my first book was published, she had invited me to give a talk at the Wilson Center. I still remember how proud I felt at being introduced by such an accomplished, impressive Iranian woman, how much it meant when she squeezed my hand after the talk and whispered that I had done well. The news that she was now in Evin left me cold. I asked the reporter twice again whether he was certain. Such rumors were not unheard-of in Iran.

"I know her," I repeated numbly, waiting for the reporter to acknowledge what upsetting news he had relayed.

Silence. He was waiting for me to say whether I would agree to the interview.

"She's my friend. I'm in shock."

"Do you know anyone else who might be willing to talk about it?"

I said I didn't, and hung up. My very first thoughts, after I read the wire stories over my agonizingly slow dial-up Internet connection, were of what I could write in her defense. It was odious that the authorities were arresting academics on baseless charges, but to target Haleh was also exceptionally obtuse. She was one of the most respected, influential voices in Washington, arguing for a moderate Iran policy, convening conferences and hosting speakers who advocated engagement and a recognition of the two countries' mutual interests. If those in Washington who wished to bomb Iran had one formidable foe, it was Haleh. Now the mullahs had put her in prison. As I imagined how I might say this in a story, I also felt, with growing dismay, how unwise that would be. The authorities had arrested her on the grounds that she used the Wilson Center as a base from which to plot the regime's overthrow. Having spoken there more than once myself, in defending Haleh I would only draw attention to the association. The charges against her were precisely those Mr. X said were being prepared against me. Clearly, the safer course would be to stay silent, but to say nothing was also unbearable. I knew that if the situation were reversed, if I were the one sitting in Evin, Haleh would use the full force of her influence and connections to help me. How could I sit in my Tehran living room, doing nothing? I asked Arash what he thought about my writing some sort of opinion piece. Something that focused on her activities in Washington.

"Are you forgetting that barely a month ago you had a nervous breakdown when the mailman rang?" He reminded me that we still did not know for certain whether Mr. X's threats were empty, and that, with a small baby, it was reckless to raise my profile with such a story. I knew he was upset at my suggestion.

"But I don't want her to think I did nothing."

"If she knew about your situation, she would understand. That's what makes her the person you admire."

Perhaps Arah was right. But I have never felt so small as I did that evening, preparing for bed in the comfort of my own home, imagining Haleh in a cramped, musty cell in Evin. It was loathsome to have to choose between protecting myself and my family, and acting ethically to help a friend. I began to wonder why Arash and I were still in Iran, when the present and what we could see of the future had nothing in common any longer with our purpose in life. And when did we start having a purpose in life? We had never discussed such a notion. I made a list in my head anyway: doing work we believed in (and hoping that work somehow made a difference to the country we both loved); raising our son in a reasonably stable environment with decent schools; being able to say, at the end of each month, that the joy we derived from our surroundings (our family and friends, the mountains and the city, the intimacy of the produce seller noticing we were buying less fruit) outweighed the petty nuisances (traffic; pollution) and the emotional burdens (the nervous tension; Mr. X).

We were not bound to stay in Iran by forces out of our control. It was a country that had for three decades inspired in millions a fierce, desperate urge to flee. It was said that back in the early 1980s, shortly after the revolution, one man resorted to packing his fiancée in a suitcase and putting her on a plane as checked luggage. She arrived, of course, in a freer land, asphyxiated. This story circulated for years throughout Iranian émigré communities in the West, a heartrending example of the lengths to which some people would go in seeking a better life outside Iran's borders. I heard it often as a child, and I brooded over the horrific last moments the suffocating fiancée, the suitcase bride as I came to think of her, must have suffered. Somewhere along the way, the story was embroidered to add bananas as the only thing she had to eat along the way. Had she even been able to peel them? I wondered with my child's imagination. Or had she lost consciousness first? I fell asleep that night haunted by thoughts of Haleh in her cell, and of the suitcase bride's hungry, tragic end.

CHAPTER 19

The Looming Mountains

On a sunny weekend morning in the middle of spring, Arash and I headed out with Hourmazd for a walk in the Alborz foothills. Several days earlier, the familiar police vans and officers detaining women for improper dress had disappeared from the streets, and it seemed the anti-immodesty campaign had eased. We were eager to resume our weekly mountain stroll, one of the few stress-free public outings we could enjoy with Hourmazd. The tree-lined, paved path to Velenjak was navigable with a stroller, and the place drew mostly families and well-behaved young people, rather than the thuggish bands of young men who tromped around nearby Darband. From between the pine trees, billboards advertised electric kettles, panini presses, and high-tech deep fryers. People strolled along the path, chatting leisurely and snacking on crepes and barbecued corn. More adventurous young men and women donned puffy uniforms and darted around the paint-ball grounds. As usual, the "Answers to Your Religious Questions" booth stood empty and unattended.

As I pushed the stroller along, a policewoman in black chador blocked my way. She could not have been older than sixteen, an adolescent fuzz of mustache above her lip. She fingered my plain white headscarf, pronounced it too thin, and directed me toward a parked minibus with dark windows. It took a full minute before I realized that she meant to arrest me. "I've been wearing this veil for over five years," I pleaded, "surely it can't be that unacceptable."

"My dear woman, it is your own fault for having chosen to wear such a thin veil, when you could have opted for a nice, thick, long shawl," she scolded.

Though I was nervous, I also had a hard time taking the teenager entirely seriously. She was underage, the thickness of my veil was debatable, and there was an infant in my stroller. Did she not notice the stroller? And why was she picking on me, when women wearing layers of makeup and more objectionable attire streamed past? Arash soon caught up with us and began berating the policewoman for harassing a young mother. Tongued-tied in my anger, I admired the perfect torrent of words. Arash used the motherhood jargon of state propaganda to admonish the girl; the language of the regime gave him full cover to attack. The girl shrank, with the deference to male authority natural in a traditional teenage female. The commotion caught the attention of a bearded superior officer, who came over to inspect me. "The problems are not few," he said, frowning at my sleeves, which fell a few inches above my unsteady wrists. He ordered me to sign a *ta'ahod,* a promise that I would not repeat my mistake. "Now go home," he said, "go home and don't come back."

We climbed back into the car, silent and furious. Hourmazd detested his car seat and had screamed and cried throughout the thirty-minute ride to Velenjak. His pale skin was still red from the exertion, and the collar of his shirt still damp with sweat. Now he took one look at the car seat and began to scream. "What do you want me to do? They won't let us take a walk," I told him. Why had I ever thought parenting in Iran would be challenging only once elementary school started?

At that moment, neither Hourmazd, nor I, nor Arash could bear another half hour of weeping. I held the baby in my lap as Arash recited the opening lines of "O mountain, today you heard my scream," a poem by Houshang Ebtehaj, an eminent Iranian poet living in Germany. Ebtehaj composed the poem in the early years of the revolution, after morality squads barred him and a group of friends from climbing the very same mountain.

We drove home, stopping to buy groceries for lunch. The produce seller was flipping the channels on his television and paused on a state-produced miniseries. Something in the drama provoked Arash. "Look at them, at all the money they waste making preachy serials for their own entertainment," he said. Noticing a middle-aged woman in black chador who was inspecting dusky purple eggplants, he added, "If my saying so doesn't offend Hajj khanoum."

"But we're dissatisfied also," she said, looking up in surprise.

The produce seller selected a few choice mangoes to cheer us up. Then he added a basket of strawberries. "They'll boost her IQ," he said, smiling at Hourmazd. Advanced in years and partly deaf, every second week the produce seller forgot Hourmazd was a boy. One of his own sons usually bellowed, "*He,* Hajj Agha, he's a *he!*" We gathered our consolation fruit and headed for the car, looking forward to an afternoon spent indoors, far from the morality police and their sixteen-year-old enforcers.

After this incident, harrowing in a distinctive way, a reminder of how casually our lives could be turned upside down, we began talking about leaving Iran. We had been circling the issue for weeks but never acknowledging it explicitly. Now it forced its way into the open. It was one thing having our security compromised by my work, which was deemed sensitive in the state's paranoid view. It was another thing entirely to come so close to arrest as an ordinary citizen, because a teenage enforcer took issue with the fabric of my headscarf.

Our conversations about leaving operated on two levels. There were the practical questions to work out. We talked about real estate and whether we could sell our apartment, about where we might move and what we might do in those places. Our choices consisted of Germany and England. We considered the United States, but only fleetingly. As much as I longed to live near my friends and relatives in California, my work required frequent travel to the Middle East and that made Europe a more practical choice. Europe also better suited Arash's academic ambitions. With his MBA now completed, he had decided to continue his undergraduate study of religions at the doctoral level, focusing on Zoroastrianism. This meant he would need to study old Iranian languages, and only a very few universities in the world—most of them in Europe—offered instruction in those ancient tongues. Rather on a whim, he had sent off an application to the University of London earlier that year, at the height of the media furor over a U.S. attack. Since we had not actively been planning to leave, he had never taken the English language tests required for admission. When he did attempt to register for the exams (standing in line overnight with hundreds of others outside the registration center), he discovered that there would be no space in Tehran for months to come. It turned out we weren't the only Iranians to have concluded recently that Iran was best left behind. Two and a half times as many young people were sitting the exams this year as had taken them the year before. Arash would need to go abroad in order to take the test in time for admission to the university.

In making my own practical preparations, I, too, encountered the desperation of those trying to leave. It was fascinating how, when you were staying, the country seemed full of those also coping, intending to stay. When you began getting ready to leave, preparing for English exams or applying for foreign visas, it seemed as though everyone else was desperately pushing against the borders, too. I went to renew my Iranian passport, and asked the clerk to change my official status to "resident of Iran." This was so that I could stay however long I wished during visits and not be bothered at the passport check at the airport (Iranian citizens registered as living abroad could stay a maximum of six months). A complete stranger who overhead me thought I was forsaking my American citizenship, and began to shriek in protest: "Madam! What are you *doing*? You will regret this forever, please reconsider!"

I spent a long morning outside the British embassy in line for an extended visa, and watched the line growing longer and more impatient. The sun scorched overhead and the embassy guard refused to let people wait in the shade. He herded old people and those with children into a narrow line, unmoved as they wilted and cursed him. Many of those around nervously wondered whether their visas would be approved, and I felt during those hours the humiliated desperation of those who were, in their own society, engineers and respected matrons, but were now abasing themselves before the haughty embassy staff of a European power. Inside, I filled out visa applications for women who could not read English but were eager to emigrate and join sons and daughters. At one point, a guard walked over and asked whether he had not seen me before at the embassy. "I used to attend parties here all the time. But that era seems rather over, don't you think?" I said. I told him the last time I tried to attend a diplomatic function, hundreds of Basij and security police surrounded the embassy, calling the guests traitors, *vatan-foroush*. Arash and I decided not to go inside, which had turned out to be wise. Several of our friends who braved the harassment cordon were arrested on the way out, charged with attending the Queen of England's birthday party or some such nonsense.

Once we finished handling our logistical concerns, we began feeling the emotional distress of leaving more acutely. Inevitably, that distress took the form of fights. Although we were in general agreement about leaving, we differed in the ranks we assigned our reasons, as well in how and whether those reasons should be shared with others. I was consumed by second thoughts that I unhelpfully aired for the first time in company. As our erstwhile therapist Dr. Majidi had discovered, friends and relatives seemed to have an oversize stake in the decision. Those who despised Iran and considered leaving themselves supported us, but those whose circumstances compelled them to stay made a sport of undermining our reasons. In the company of the latter, I felt awkward recounting our rationale. They warned that Hourmazd would grow up without close bonds to his extended family, that I would fall apart without the help and female companionship I was accustomed to. They argued that Iranian schools, the propaganda factor aside, turned out young people far more skilled in mathematics and hard sciences than graduates of western schools. I might have told myself all this, too, if I had been stuck in Iran. Arash felt blindsided when, say, during the soup course at a dinner party, I would suddenly celebrate the science curriculum of Iranian schools. "But how can I trash the school system in front of a mother—the hostess—

who has two school-age kids and will never have the chance of leaving?" I argued to Arash. "That's rude. It's unkind."

I made my case for etiquette, aware all the while that it was disingenuous. Rather than acknowledging my own doubts, I dressed them up in concern for other people's feelings. The truth was, I was torn. I knew we needed to leave, *should* leave. But I didn't particularly want to leave. I was also, strangely enough, nervous. I didn't know how my career would fare in Europe, where I had no roots, connections, or expertise. My life had for so long existed between two poles, the United States and the Middle East. Europe was a place for airport transfers and holidays. "Why do you make yourself sound so helpless?" Arash asked. "If you can handle Baghdad and Kandahar, London could not possibly be intimidating. They speak English there."

Perhaps I could conquer my irrational fear of European life. But I was most nervous about motherhood in the style of the West, because I knew from the lives of my friends precisely what it would entail. I imagined myself marooned at home with an infant who did not speak, eating my meals alone, bereft of adult company and conversation. In Iran, motherhood did not entail such isolation. Like nearly all young Iranian mothers, I lived in close proximity to relatives and in-laws, and they shared my days. The culture of proximity I had found so cloying when I was single now seemed sensible and wise.

And then there was the reluctance that lurked at the bottom of all my worries, a more abstract feeling, but as upsetting as the obvious pain of being separated from the people we cared about. "Don't you see what it means for us to leave? It means Iran wasn't livable enough. It means people like you and me don't have a place here. We're being run out, by a government that doesn't care whether its people have a future. And don't you see how it's so much bigger than just us? We're just two, but there are literally tens of thousands of people *just like us*. All of them, leaving. It means that all this talk of mending and changing and improving was a charade. That Iran is all heavy and rotten at the core. Doesn't that make you horribly sad?"

Indeed, Arash and I were joining the great stream of educated Iranians who each year abandoned (yes, abandoned) their country for better jobs and better futures abroad. Iran had one of the highest rates of brain drain in the world, according to official Iranian figures. Each year, at least 150,000 educated Iranians emigrated, taking their considerable talents with them to enrich the economies and key industries, the software, banking, and aerospace sectors, of other nations. Iranian state media lovingly, even gloatingly recounted their achievements abroad on the nightly news. Scarcely a night went by when the anchor did not intone something like "And today! An Iranian scientist in Australia decoded the human genome, a monumental breakthrough that will revolutionize modern medicine!" As though the state that ran the news broadcast with such nationalist relish were not the same state that willfully chased its most talented citizens away.

Economic instability being a hallmark of authoritarian states, the week we decided to sell our apartment real estate prices in Tehran jumped 40 percent. The swing in the market, just the latest bit of mayhem wrought by Ahmadinejad's catastrophic economic policies, frightened off buyers, overwhelming Iranians already struggling with high rent and home prices. The president, who now referred to U.N. sanctions against the country as a "piece of torn paper," did not appear overly concerned. He took his inspiration from the Ayatollah Khomeini, who once famously remarked that "we did not make a revolution to slash the price of watermelon." This nonchalance infuriated many Iranians, and the taxi driver who drove me to the doctor that week complained bitterly about the president, whose name was now synonymous with "This costs more." The driver had taken out loans and saved for three years to buy a one-bedroom apartment in Shahrak-e Gendarmarie, a district in western Tehran. In the space of just one week, his plans had been dashed.

For a whole month, I patiently stayed home in the evenings in case the local real estate agent wanted to bring over a prospective buyer. In Tehran, people often conducted their real estate dealings in the evenings, and the agent called only five minutes ahead of arrival. Just two people came to view our apartment. Though only eight years old, it was considered ancient—undesirable in a market saturated with brand-new buildings—and it had suddenly become expensive. Not surprisingly, most people who could afford such prices were either well-placed bureaucrats or those connected to them. One woman who arrived in full black chador immediately sniffed at being shown an apartment so "old." The real estate agent introduced her as a surgeon, referred to her ingratiatingly as "khanoum doktor," Madam Doctor, and tried to placate her by pointing out the building was built to western earthquake safety standards, an unheard-of feature in all the marble-encased luxury high-rise towers she was doubtless also viewing. These boasted lobbies with vaulted ceilings lined with vases of orchids, and seemed much more in keeping with her Islamic-oligarch tastes.

She strode about the apartment, eyeing Arash's instrument collection and our shabby antique furniture, curling her lip in distaste. "Your décor is so . . . so Iranian," she said, pronouncing the final word with particular contempt. She paused in front of a painting, a piece of modernist calligraphy based on the Rumi verse "Pour nothing on my grave but wine." It seemed to cause her physical discomfort. Her hands twitched around her chador and she turned to leave. "You should sell this place to foreigners. They would like such a place," she said on her way out the door.

We phoned the agent and told him to stop advertising the apartment to such people. In a building compring only five apartments, even one assertively conservative tenant could change the atmosphere. First they would demand the shared swimming pool be gender segregated. Then they might take issue with the satellite dishes and with parties. They could easily impose the culture of the regime on the building, as they had the law on their side. We couldn't inflict such neighbors on Solmaz or on Arash's parents. The real estate agent grumbled that he was doing his best; people were too skittish to buy in such an unstable market, because they expected that prices would fall again. And, he informed us, "People don't want earthquake safety. They want a sauna and whirlpool in the master bath. Your place is going to take months to sell." We told him to bring the price down. We started packing, hoping buyers would come. We finished packing. We bought airplane tickets. Still no one came.

Smoke filled the night sky, billowing through the trees and coating our windshield in fine soot. Rioters had torched the main gas station on Niavaran Street, creating a traffic jam that we had been sitting in for over two hours. It was the first night of the government's new gas rationing scheme, and gas stations across the city had been set ablaze. We were on the way home from a goodbye dinner party, and I called home every thirty minutes from my mobile phone, checking whether Hourmazd was still asleep. The government, nervous that the West might impose sanctions on its import of gasoline, had decided to withdraw the longtime subsidy that enabled Iranians to buy gas at the absurd price of about 35 cents per gallon. You may wonder why Iran, sitting atop such vast oil reserves, had to import gasoline in the first place. The answer is that the government had failed to build a sufficient refining capacity to meet the nation's consumption needs. The subsidy was unsustainable and officials had long talked of canceling it, but successive governments, wary of the short-term protest and job losses it would entail, had delayed the move. The timing now, however, was more auspicious. Officials could blame the West, claiming they were forced to abrogate people's God-given right to cheap gas because of the threat of unjust sanctions. But if the evening's violence was any indication, this calculation had backfired. In addition to torching gas stations, rioters set fire to cars, smashed shop windows, and attacked a supermarket and bank. They hurled stones at police and chanted that Ahmadinejad should be killed.

The authorities informed the nation at nine that evening, an ordinary Tuesday in June, that the rationing would go into effect at midnight. They neglected to notify the Tehran police in advance, so the force had taken no special precautions ahead of an announcement that would so obviously trigger an outpouring of anger. The regime also failed to explain to the nation's seventy million people exactly how rationing would work. Would people have access to gas at all beyond their ration? If so, at what price? If not, would the authorities offer recourse? Naturally, everyone panicked, and the country descended into full-scale mayhem. People began storing gasoline in their houses, which promptly burned to the ground. In one day, 300,000 people registered applications for taxi licenses, since taxis would be allotted a larger ration (it was common for people to use unmarked, private vehicles as taxis). The next day the authorities announced that all taxis would have to bear a taxi placard, and most of the applications were withdrawn. For days, gas stations saw five-block-long queues at all hours. We were all down to the last drops in our tanks, and even at midnight the lines were still too long. "Why do we have an SUV?" I asked Arash peevishly on our third day at home.

Taxis wouldn't come at all, and when they did, they charged three times the normal fare. The last place I had seen such astonishingly long lines for gasoline was Baghdad immediately after the fall of Saddam (though I'm told those lines persist even now), and it struck me that if Tehran was beginning to resemble Iraq, perhaps we had chosen an appropriate time to leave. Iran's uncertain place in the world had ceased to be an abstraction and become a reality disrupting our daily lives.

It was the first time I had seen the square's produce seller, usually mellow and not prone to talk of politics, unable to control his fury at the president. "He's ruined this country," he yelled, storming around a stand of figs and mulberries. "Why doesn't someone shoot him?"

I had secretly hoped our last day in Iran would be marred by another spate of gasoline rioting or an ugly encounter with the police. I wanted to depart with the memories of such hardships fresh in my mind, so that instead of feeling sad during our final hours I might think instead of the daily humiliations we were leaving behind. Instead, the day passed smoothly, and the evening was one of incomparable, poignant beauty. Arash had carefully planned the date of departure so that we might catch, on our very final evening, the opening night of Ostad Lotfi's concert series. Lotfi had not played in Iran for over a decade, and Tehran had been abuzz with anticipation and excitement for weeks. What did it mean that authorities were permitting open air performances by the nation's preeminent musicians? To Arash's keen disappointment, that summer concerts were to be held across the country, several of them including orchestras with female musicians.

It would be a summer of music, probably the richest, most diverse array of fine performances held since the revolution. Did such official leniency suggest the brutality of the previous weeks would now ease out of the foreground? Certainly not. It was just a continuation of the perverse reality of Iranian life, which fluctuated between extraordinary brutality, commonplace routine, and unexpected, fleeting instances of real openness.

As the sun set, we drove to Niavaran Palace. Built out of concrete and stone, the palace is architecturally unimpressive, but I was sentimentally attached to its bland modern lines. Here Arash and I had whispered through a concert of Indian music on our first real date. The Supreme Leader, a devotee of *tar* and classical Persian music, was rumored to live nearby, and several people in line to enter the palace joked that he could listen from his garden for free. As Solmaz handed her ticket to an attendant, a woman in chador asked her to pull her veil forward, then she whispered into her ear, "Just pull it back when you're inside, no one will say anything!"

At least three thousand people, among them many women in black chadors, mingled under a velvet sky before the palace steps, which were lined with flickering candles. The country's most distinguished poets, musicians, film stars, and directors occupied the front row, and giant video screens displayed their faces as they entered and took their seats. "It's like the Oscars!" I whispered to Arash. These celebrities sat alongside government officials and their chador-clad wives, and gazing at the scene, you could be forgiven for imagining this was a society at peace with itself, run by men who appreciated the arts, reconciled over the role of Islam in daily life. The crowd rose to its feet in excitement as Lotfi took the stage, dressed in plain white. He played with sublime beauty, even reaching for an instrument he rarely played in public, the *daf*. This is a round frame drum that Iranians have played for almost two millennia, long before the Moors introduced it to Spain, before it was adopted by Sufis in their rituals, before the mullah regime banned it from television. I gazed around me, at the faces of those I would miss lit by moonlight, and wished for them many more of such evenings.

Epilogue

Arash, Hourmazd, and I arrived in London during the late summer of 2007. We rode a black hackney cab through the drizzly, overcast morning to our new apartment, and gazed eagerly at the exotic (at least to us) surroundings—red phone booths, mail trucks adorned with a crown, pubs with names like Ye Olde Cheshire Cheese. I was excited to arrive in our new neighborhood, Kilburn, where we would launch our new English life. We had chosen to live there because it was relatively affordable, an easy walk to the cafés and health food stores of gentrified West Hampstead, and most important, truly diverse. Kilburn traces its origins to the eleventh-century reign of King Henry I, when a community of Augustinian nuns built a priory near an ancient Celtic road. I had researched the history of London while still in Tehran and was fully prepared to fall in love with the city. From short holidays and my British friends' accounts, I knew it was grandly beautiful, ethnically varied, and one of the most vibrant cities in Europe. I imagined that our neighbors would resemble the cast of *Love Actually,* the local Indian restaurant would serve delectable curries, and we would spend leisurely afternoons with our new friends at the local pub discussing Ian McEwan.

But Little Riyadh, as Arash and I quickly dubbed the area, felt altogether more like a dour Muslim village than the charming London

quarter I had expected. "We left Tehran for *this*?" I said, looking at
the grocery shop down the street from our apartment in shock. Its
sign read ASHOURA MARKET, and the words were flanked on both
sides by a crescent moon and star, the symbols of Islam. The second
time I went inside, I found the stern Pakistani owner arguing with several Muslim kids from the block. He was refusing to sell them gummy
candy on the grounds that it contained un-*halal* pig gelatin. I thought
of intervening—if their parents didn't care, what business was it of
his?—but they were already trooping out and I figured I should wait
at least a week before alienating the neighborhood grocer.

As my friends had said, the area was indeed multiethnic. Our
landlords were a Russian-Venezuelan couple, the flat upstairs was occupied by an Australian, and the street vendors on the main thoroughfare were Sri Lankan and Chinese. But the neighborhood's sizable
Muslim community seemed to exist in a separate sphere—it was as
though everyone else came from a distinct country but they were from
a besieged and borderless place called Islam. They seemed to project
this sentiment, and others reflected it back to them. "The people who
live on the corner, they are *Mooslims,*" a Spanish neighbor informed
me with a meaningful look.

The neighborhood's Muslims, I soon found, seemed to share the
Pakistani grocer's strict sensibility. One afternoon, in search of Hour-
mazd's favorite baby food, I wandered into a store called the Al-
Mahdi Market (after the occulted twelfth Imam-messiah of Shia
Islam). Al Jazeera blared from the wall-mounted TV, and when I tried
to pay, the Lebanese clerk told me to put the coins on the counter.
Puritanical Muslims consider it forbidden for unmarried men and
women to touch one another, but it takes a real fundamentalist to
cringe at the threat of a light grazing. In all the years I had spent in the
Middle East, not once had a man refused to take money from my
hand. I slammed the coins on the counter and walked out.

When I began taking Hourmazd to the nearest playground, I
found the mothers clustered according to civilization. The western
moms congregated near the teeter-totter, discussing BBC specials on
childhood, the Portobello Road market, and local museums. The Muslim women, some of whom even covered their faces and hands, as-

sembled near the swings. The subjects of their conversations reflected the separateness of their world—husbands who vetoed breastfeeding because of the risk of exposed flesh, husbands who complained about their women taking English lessons, the strain of cooking four-dish meals each day for a bevy of extended relatives. Initially I alternated sitting with each group, but eventually found myself most at home with the western moms, who were on average at least a decade older than the Muslim homemakers. In addition to not having much to say to an eighteen-year-old Bengali speaker, I found it difficult connecting through the *niqabs* (full-face masks with slits for the eyes) that some of the Muslim moms wore. The *niqab* made it impossible to smile hello, as a preliminary to conversation; it made it impossible to share kindly, forgiving glances, as our sons filched each others' spades in the sand pit. The Muslim women, and by their own accounts rigid husbands, were cleaving to a traditional, suffocating lifestyle, afraid of what might happen if the godless ways of the secular West permeated their lives.

I assumed most of the Muslim mothers must be recent immigrants, until I heard a voice emanating from underneath a full-face black veil that might have belonged to Victoria Beckham. Some of the Muslims in the neighborhood, like the face-veiled Victoria, were second- or third-generation immigrants, born and raised in England. Others had recently come from places as far away as Somalia, Nigeria, and Bangladesh.

I found the Muslim presence to be so assertive that I once even forgot I was in England altogether. One day, when I was on the tube, two women dressed in severe black, their faces concealed under imposing *niqabs*, boarded the train. They carried Korans and radiated such militancy that I thought they were morality policewomen and looked down to see whether I was dressed appropriately.

I hadn't lived in England very long and was aware that my views were unseasoned. I also knew that the problems Europe faced with the assimilation of its Muslim immigrants were very different from America's—the Muslims who move to Europe, by and large, tend to be poorer and less educated, making integration more difficult. But that reality, as I saw it, made their assimilation especially urgent. If the

Muslim women of my neighborhood were any indication, the country's Muslim community was living entirely at odds with the society
around them. And Britian seemed to be appeasing this tendency
rather than confronting it head-on.

This upset me, for I felt myself an immigrant as well—a recent immigrant from a repressive Islamic theocracy. I had deliberately left traditional, defensive Islam behind and did not wish to see it nurtured in
the heart of my new home, a western democracy whose secular values
I had come to treasure in an entirely new way. Everywhere I went,
from the doctor's office to playgroups, I saw evidence of England's
special sensitivity to Muslims' needs. Signs asked: Do you require a
chaperone while being seen by a male doctor? Do you wish to keep
your head covering on for ID photos? Do you wish to attend sermons
where radical clerics preach hatred and jihad? Of course, there was no
sign for the latter, but there may as well have been. Britain's recent
history as a breeding ground for militant Islam numbered among the
most controversial topics in Europe, and had led the French to devise
the term "Londonistan."

Of course, nurturing the veiling and sequestering of women is not
the same thing as allowing militants free rein to organize terror attacks. But they share one important aspect, and that is their willingness to accommodate antediluvian Islam rather than push the faith
into a healthy acceptance of modernity. I had no doubt that this is
what Islam needed, and living in Iran had stripped me of all my liberal
California ambivalence about imposing western values on an "other"
from elsewhere. I felt like a messenger from the land of radical Islam,
sent to shake some sense into all these well-intentioned but deluded
British people. Didn't they realize that if the situation were reversed,
if they were a secular minority in a country of deeply pious Muslims,
there would be no signs asking, Do you require a beer on the weekend? Do you wish to bare your hair and arms?

As weeks turned to months, however, my views softened slightly.
I experienced both the subtle and visceral racism of British society
toward its Muslim community, and this helped me understand part of
why Muslims clung so defensively to their traditions. Some instances
were slight, like the time I heard a well-dressed white British man

sneer at a young Muslim girl, who cowered in fear of the pug puppy he held on a leash. "Is it a dog's saliva, or what, that these people are supposedly scared of?" he asked, turning to me. "She's probably just not used to dogs as pets," I said.

Another time, while trying to maneuver Hourmazd's stroller off a crowded bus, an older white British woman rebuked me: "You should learn to say 'excuse me,' as the English do, when you get in people's way," she said, glaring with an open, disproportionate hostility. I had, in fact, apologized, she just hadn't heard me, but was too shocked to say anything. A young, veiled woman rose to help me with the stroller, and later I was struck by the rush of feelings that had overcome me—fury at the white woman (for in that instant, that is what she became to me); fear that one day Hourmazd would hear such comments; and a profound sense of gratitude for and kinship with the woman in the veil.

These experiences, and my life in England altogether, left me feeling confused and unmoored in a country whose racial and political dynamics I didn't quite understand. Was racism alienating British Muslims, causing the Muslim part of their identity to take on a defensive, oversize importance? Or was it just stoking a tendency that had its roots elsewhere, in a stuffy, paranoid Islam that was already keeping Muslims sequestered and unhappy? How had the problem changed since September 11, and July 7, 2005, when a series of bombs left by Islamic extremists ripped through London? Whatever the reasons, I grew to accept the fact that I had not left Islam's modern problems—its traditionalism, the frightening zeal of its radical adherents, its tendency to blame the West for its societies' stagnation—behind when I left Iran. In new and different ways, the religion would remain a part of my life, and a part of the environment in which we raised Hourmazd.

Regardless of what hemisphere we lived in, I would need to teach him that Islam could be tolerant as well as repressive, and that he should take ownership of the faith by dispassionately studying its history (its past glories, as well as its modern ignominy). If we had raised him in Iran, I would have tried to make him see that rejecting spirituality was no way to distance himself from the tyrannical Islam of the state. Here I would need to teach him that embracing Islam was no way to empower himself before racism. Whether he lived in London or in Tehran, he would need to grapple with these issues, which I supposed made him a citizen of the twenty-first century.

Compared to the veiled women on the playground and their aggressively bearded husbands, we eased into British life comfortably. Arash was engrossed in his graduate studies and spent most of his hours at the university or the British Library in the quiet company of ancient manuscripts. The study of Zoroastrianism essentially involved the mastery of old Iranian languages; by deciphering the texts composed in these archaic tongues, scholars sought to understand the nature of ancient Persia. Busily immersed in such scholarship, Arash did not find himself, like me, questioning whether he was altogether happier than he had been in Iran. There were days when I was grateful for everything that London and life in the West offered—stability, a fast and uncensored Internet, and the luxury of worrying about toxicity in Hourmazd's toiletries rather than in the propaganda murals on the street. On other days, usually cold, gray afternoons when the faces of Londoners rushing past seemed especially blank, I felt unbearably lonely. Just as I had suspected, being a working mom in the West was harder and infinitely less enjoyable than in Iran. In Tehran, the constant presence of relatives had meant that I had the pleasure of company, intellectual stimulation, and reassurance that was more steady than any parenting book, as well as time to shower, and even occasional moments of idleness. I was poised and rested, and I actually found both working and mothering *fun*. In London, I became the sort of woman, the sort of mother, who suddenly needed many extraneous and costly things—yoga classes, child-care gadgets, an agency-certified nanny, a housekeeper, bottled baby food—just to get through the week without becoming an exhausted wreck. Many days, as the rain splattered against the windows and the sky drew dark by four P.M., I felt that I would give anything to be back in Iran. I felt I would gladly tolerate the hell of living there in exchange for once again feeling connected to those around me.

I told Arash one night: "Do you know what I miss? I miss the produce seller. I miss buying oyster mushrooms and having him ask me, 'Now, Mrs. Zeini, how are you, and tell me, what do you cook with these strange mushrooms?' To me that's civilization, not the swiping of a club card."

"Wait until you're next in Iran again. Tell me then what you think about civilization," he said.

That next trip happened to fall in April of 2008, when Hourmazd and I flew to Tehran for a brief holiday. I had been thinking of going back for a few months, for many reasons. For one, I was curious to see how things had changed since we left. But more important, we wanted to have Hourmazd examined by his Tehran pediatrician, as he had developed a lump under his arm as a result of his tuberculosis vaccine and the doctors in London were advising it be removed surgically. Since babies in the UK receive the vaccine far less frequently than in places like Iran, I figured the Tehran doctor might offer a valuable second opinion, and perhaps an alternative to the scary-sounding operation. As added incentive to go, I also needed to visit the dentist, get a haircut, and have my eyebrows threaded, all of which in London would have cost as much as my plane ticket.

I was a touch worried about my safety going back, especially since I would be traveling alone with Hourmazd. But I figured that if we had been allowed to leave the country, returning should pose no great risk and that staying away would only suggest I had been permanently cowed. I had no intention of writing, so I would not need to let the press office know of my trip. And I refused to speak to Mr. X, that shameless emotional terrorist, ever again.

We stayed with Arash's parents, who were elated to welcome the grandson they had seen every day for nearly a year and then not at all. Hourmazd delighted in the company, finding incentive to turn his babble into near words, and was entertained enough to abandon his attention-thirsty naughtiness. Watching my transformed little son play, I wondered whether this is how it was supposed to be—big families living together, generations under one roof, a whole community of well-intentioned relatives helping raise one another's children. I believe that children show you what they need in order to be happy, and if Hourmazd's behavior was any measure, this is what he needed: cousins, aunties, honorary aunties, and grandparents to be in his life *every day*, not just twice a year for a week. Maybe I needed it, too.

That first evening we sat on the balcony and ate sandwiches of roast wild boar on crusty baguettes, delivered by a beloved local sandwich shop that even just a year ago had not served the *haram* meat of the pig. Of course wild boar did not appear on the menu, but in response to the demand of Iranians who liked ham sandwiches, the shop had begun selling them in the guise of "lamb." As I sipped my tea, gazing at the shadows cast by the Alborz Mountains, an accordion player passed by on the street below, filling the night with a croaking, familiar melody. The warm air carried the soft scent of night-blooming jasmine, and I felt so embraced by Tehran that I thought of calling Arash and telling him that our move had been a huge mistake. Instead I put on my nightgown, ate half a succulent watermelon, and read the newspaper until I felt sleepy, sometime near dawn.

Tehran had changed since we had left. The half-finished apartment buildings on the block were now completed, and new craters had appeared in other parts of the neighborhood. The city's construction boom continued despite the staggering 150 percent rise in real estate prices, which meant a two-bedroom apartment in north Tehran now easily ran over $1 million. Hourmazd was ecstatic at seeing cement mixers and dump trucks at nearly every intersection, his Bob the Builder fantasies coming to real life. He would press his face against the window for long minutes and watch the cranes bobbing up and down across the neighborhood, and then he'd flap his arms when one of them lifted something particularly impressive or heavy.

Though inflation had hit the housing market hardest, even basic commodities cost much more than the previous summer. The next day I picked up some groceries with Eshrat khanoum—a sack of potatoes, some green plums, two cantaloupes, and tomatoes—and the bill came to the equivalent of $40. "Do you realize this would be cheaper in London, the second most expensive city in the entire world?" I said.

My depressive bouts in England aside, the fact was I doubted we could even *afford* to move back to Iran.

Only the truly affluent were unaffected by Ahmadinejad's demolishing of the economy—the corrupt, upper echelons of the regime, the private sector tycoons who flew business in and out of Imam Khomeini airport. For regular Iranians, money had never been so tight. Even middle- and upper-class Iranians, like many of my relatives, were finding their material lives deteriorating. Things they used to take for granted, like vacations and keeping the house in good repair, were now becoming insupportable luxuries. Low-income Iranians, like my former babysitter, could no longer afford to eat red meat and were being forced to relocate to cheaper neighborhoods.

Before arriving, I had told my sister-in-law Solmaz that I wanted to see how Tehran had changed, especially everything that had opened since I left. She had taken this quite literally, and planned two days' worth of outings that left me astonished at how decadent this city, the capital of Khomeini's populist revolution, had become. We drank "virgin mojitos" in an exquisite garden café on the former Elahieh estate of Dr. Mahmoud Hessaby, the legendary, Sorbonne-trained scientist who studied with Albert Einstein. In the shade of the sycamore trees, matrons in Hermès scarves escaped the heat and a table full of Iranian-American entrepreneurs plotted a luxury bridal spa. We ate a proper brunch of fluffy pancakes and caviar toast, which was a first for Tehran, offered by the kabob empire of Nayyeb in a setting that evoked, well, Versailles. We dunked lobster tempura into delicate Japanese bowls at the remodeled Monsoon on Gandhi Street and enjoyed ravioli with truffle sauce at the new French restaurant La Cheminée, alongside the famous television actor Mehran Modiri and the singer Assar. As we flitted between these places, I noticed that the BMW SUV had been supplanted by another imported car of the moment: a magnolia white Mercedes-Benz with cartoonish curves.

In all my years I had never seen Tehran like this before. So urbane and openly hospitable to people with money to spend, yet so hard-edged and ungenerous to those who were struggling. After my round of sybaritic tourism, I spent a day visiting two girlfriends who had just had babies. Neither were particularly well-off, and both seemed downright nervous over the state of the economy. One had a daughter who was suffering allergies from the polluted air of central Tehran, the other a son who could only take a certain brand of expensive, imported formula. Five years ago, neither of these problems would have been such a big deal. The first friend could have moved to a less congested neighborhood, the second would have absorbed the cost of the formula. Now, moving was out of the question, and inflation meant that the formula cut into their monthly savings.

A week into our trip, Solmaz called to warn us that the police were sweeping the neighborhood to confiscate illegal satellite dishes. I climbed to the roof to remove the coding device out of my parents-in-law's dish. It was costly to replace, unlike the dish itself, and the raids of recent months had made us expert in such matters. Now accustomed to such invasions, Arash's nephew Aryo sulkily announced that "the stupid people are back," and popped in a Tom and Jerry DVD—already world-weary at the age of seven.

Our two weeks in Tehran quickly drew to an end, and I found myself satisfied only on two scores. First, Hourmazd's pediatrician had examined his underarm and concluded he didn't need surgery. Such reactions to the tuberculosis vaccine were commonplace, it turned out, and in most cases resolved themselves without such intervention. Second, I hadn't contacted Mr. X, and he had left me alone; I had already decided that I would never consent to deal with him again, and it was a great relief not being forced to enact that resolution. But otherwise, I felt frustratingly unresolved. I had imagined that visiting Iran would somehow be a corrective journey for me. I would either conclude that we had misjudged our priorities and would have been better off staying, surrounded by relatives who would give Hourmazd perhaps the strongest life foundation of all, or I would be abruptly reminded of how awful the country was, how inconvenient, poorly run, starkly divided, even dangerous. Instead, though, I felt all of these things in equal measure. Not being able to reach a well-defined conclusion frustrated me. I didn't want to go back to London with my mind rehearsing its familiar, tiring dialogue ("I don't like London . . . but Tehran is unlivable, right? . . . Remember how cars wouldn't stop when you were trying to cross the street with Aryo and Hourmazd? . . . You can't live in such a ruthless place! . . . but what if we stayed at home more?").

On our way back, something terrible happened at the Imam Khomeini airport that would silence these deliberations forever. I was rushing to reassemble Hourmazd's stroller after passing it through the second X-ray machine (he was possessive of his "car" and wept each time it disappeared, however briefly). He had placed his hand on its side when I wasn't looking and one of his fingers caught in the hinge as I pulled the stroller open. He screamed in pain, and by the time I managed to pry the hinge apart, his tiny finger was crushed. It was purple and pressed sickeningly thin, so thin I was certain he would lose at least the tip. As he gasped, screaming in short, staccato bursts, I asked the attendant to call the airport emergency line. In tears myself, I tried to distract him, but there was nothing on the walls but posters of mosques and ayatollahs. I think you can only absorb the full absurdity of these images when trying to use them as a distraction for a wounded, frantic child.

As five minutes turned to ten and no one arrived to help, I grew desperate and angry. Why did the airport need a second X-ray check? We had already dismantled the stroller once upon entering the departure terminal. Even at Heathrow, the airport of a nation that was a victim rather than a purveyor of terrorism, we had only gone through one check. When fifteen minutes passed, I became desperate. What if he needed immediate first aid to save the finger? I had given him a double dose of Tylenol already, but he still seemed in agony, writhing in my arms and drenched in sweat. I decided I had to save him, and ran toward the information desk. Along the way, I saw two men carrying a small leather box that looked like a doctor's bag from the nineteenth century *walking unhurriedly* toward the women's security check. I rushed toward them, yelling, "It was us, it was us who called you."

I was very polite. I didn't ask them why it had taken so long, and why, as emergency first-aid personnel, they had been walking instead of running or riding a trolley. One of the paramedics examined the finger and said there was nothing to worry about. "At this age, babies don't really have bones so much as cartilage, so there's actually noth-

ing you can do. He'll be fine. Just give him pain medication if he
needs it."

"That's all?" I couldn't believe that a finger so thoroughly crushed
required such little attention.

Zoned-out from the Tylenol and drained from so much crying,
Hourmazd slept all the way to London. I spent the flight consumed
with anger, raging silently at all the various historical forces and individuals who had brought about the Iranian government in its present
form. I cursed the Islamic revolutionaries, the radical Mujahed-
din who assassinated the few moderates among them, I even cursed
Yasser Arafat (the first foreign leader to visit Khomeini). I had no
doubt that the Islamic regime was responsible for Hourmazd's injury,
which shows just how irrational and stupid my anger had become.

Back at home, I dropped off our bags and took Hourmazd straight
to the doctor, who immediately sent us to the hospital for X-rays
and prescribed a course of antibiotics. Smashed fingers, it turned out,
do require medical attention. Antibiotics are required to prevent serious infections, which are not uncommon in crush injuries, and even
a slight bone fracture can retard the growth of a child's finger if left
untreated. We walked home together, breathing in the cool spring
air, past the leafy square where Virginia Woolf used to live, past
the corner where Islamic extremists blew up a bus during the 2005
bombings.

During this walk, all the doubts and longings of the past few
months seemed to fall into order. Perhaps the shock of what had happened cut through my confusion and forced upon me a preternatural
clarity. I had spent nearly a decade living in one place and pining for
others, utterly perplexed over where I truly belonged, what place
would make me truly happy. I realized, that day, the astonishingly
simple truth was that I needed to stop thinking about where I might
achieve mythical, perfect happiness and just choose to live in a country that did not make me crazy. This would probably not be the place
where I felt most at home, the most comfortable, or the most loved.
But no matter, because that place, Iran, also denied me balance.

The rage I had felt on the flight back had reminded me of how
angry I had always been in Iran. I didn't realize until we left, until a

whole continent separated me from the sources of my anger, how that corrosive emotion had become part of my experience of life. If I wasn't boiling mad at Mr. X, I resented the officials at the press office who disapproved of his invasions but did nothing to prevent them. I fumed at the censored Internet and the jammed satellite signal, and spent hours brooding over all the horrible things the regime had done through the years to people I cared about.

As though this constant outrage wasn't punishment enough, I had also found it compromised my ability to perceive life around me properly. I had blamed the government for everything—traffic, the stuffy nose I got from the pollution, boredom, my cousins' lack of motivation, my inability to show up anywhere on time, the apathy that afflicted everyone from street sweepers to engineers. At heart I had known the mullahs *were* at fault, and this conviction had sapped my will to do enough, or anything at all, about those things.

It had also encouraged me to widen the net of my blame, holding the government responsible for most of the dilemmas and challenges that befell me. Not being able to realize this properly had, I felt, lessened my person. I was smaller for losing perspective, and for not taking more responsibility for my actions. I could and should not have blamed the Islamic revolution for Hourmazd's finger, because accidents are exactly that, and bad medicine is as common in the West as it is in countries run by bearded ayatollahs. Just before I had left for Iran, I had seen a news headline about a woman who had died in Britain after a nurse incorrectly administered an epidural into her *arm*. Upon reading that, I hadn't condemned the Queen and Gordon Brown, but rather winced at the dreadful cost of human incompetence and the vagaries of fate.

Living in Iran, I had lost that kind of perspective altogether, and I knew that staying away was the only way to try to regain it. I might be lonely in London for a long while yet, but compared to permanent anger and myopia, loneliness was something I could conquer. Outside Iran I was a more composed person, and that soundness was what my life—my family, my writing, my journalism—needed the most.

On quiet evenings, when Hourmazd slept, I still gazed out the window and imagined the life we might all have had—all the Iranians in my life, in the world—living in one country, instead of scattered across the globe. It is a fantasy that all exiles indulge in, and perhaps the only recourse is the refuge Iranians have sought for centuries: literature. Persian poets of centuries past often roamed great distances, and their work traces the effect of migration on the imagination, its curious ability to both estrange and inspire. In London, I found myself reaching for these volumes more frequently than ever, grateful for the heritage in books that offers Iranians a place to retreat from the uncertainty of the present. They are a reminder that though today Iranians are diminished by the cruel laws of unjust tyrants, it has not always been so, and thus will not always be.

Author's Note

Most of the characters in this book carry their real names and identities. In a handful of cases, I have changed names to protect people. In one instance I have changed the biological details of a character whose position in Iran requires special protection. In the case of the infamous Mr. X, whose "real" name was an acknowledged pseudonym, the "X" simply veils what was already hidden.

I benefited tremendously from knowing in advance that these two years of my life would be transformed into a story. I have reconstructed most of the dialogue and events from notes, some more detailed than others. To fill the lacunae in my journal, I have relied on the help and memory of those who shared the experience with me.

Readers may be confused to find familiar Arabic words and names, for example Ramadan and Hussein, rendered a bit differently: Ramazan, Hossein. I have used the Persian transliteration of Arabic to reflect how these words are pronounced in Iran.

Acknowledgments

I am deeply grateful to the many individuals who supported my work in Iran and the publication of *Honeymoon in Tehran*.

For generously sharing time and knowledge over the years: Farhad Behbehani, Kavous Sayyed-Emami, Mohammad Ali Abtahi, Saeed Laylaz, Nasser Hadian, Hadi Semati, Hamidreza Jalaipour, Mahmoud Sariolghalam, Mohammad Atrianfar, Goli Emami, Ali Dehbashi, and Majid Derakhshani. Mohammed Reza Lotfi, for the privilege of his friendship and continual inspiration. Shirin Ebadi, whose counsel and company have enriched my understanding of Iran immeasurably.

For sharing their expertise: Farideh Farhi, Vali Nasr, Karim Sadjadpour, Shahab Ahmed, and Sohrab Mahdavi. At the Ministry of Culture and Islamic Guidance: Effat ol-Sadat Eghbali, Gelareh Pardakhty, and Farahnaz Abdi, who have treated me with nothing but kindness and respect for so many years. Muhammad Sahimi, Mohamad Bazzi, and Fiona O'Brien, for reading parts of the book and offering their excellent insights. My editors at *Time*, eternally patient with a book-writing mom-reporter: Howard Chua-Eoan, Romesh Ratnesar, Tony Karon, and Lisa Beyer. To Ambassador M. Javad Zarif, for his unstinting encouragement.

Eshrat Abedi Hayaty, my mother-in-law, for crossing continents to look after my son while I wrote. My friends in Iran, for their stories:

Nazila, Carmen, Solmaz, Shabnam, Mehrdad, Ghazal, and Ahmad. My mother, Fariba Katouzi, for her tremendous resilience.

David Ebershoff, my editor at Random House, for his wonderful enthusiasm and generosity, and for bringing his brilliant creative instincts to virtually every line of *Honeymoon in Tehran*. Lindsey Schwoeri, for additional help editing. Diana Finch, my agent, for her abundant support and keen oversight of everything to do with my writing.

Most of all, I want to thank my husband, Arash Zeini, who showed me glorious corners of Iran that I never knew existed, championed me throughout the darkest times, and nurtured my ideas and ambitions as though they were his own. Without Arash's insight, love, and tireless help, this book simply would not have been written.

Bibliography

Abou El Fadl, Khaled. *The Place of Tolerance in Islam*. Boston, MA: Beacon Press, 2002.

Ahmed, Shahab. "Hadith (i. A General Introduction)," *Encyclopaedia Iranica,* ed. Ehsan Yarshater, New York: Bibliotheca Persica Press, 1982–ongoing, Vol. 9.4.

Al-e Ahmad, Jalal. *Iranian Society: An Anthology of Writings by Jalal Al-e Ahmad*. Lexington, KY: Mazda, Publishers, 1982.

Bakhash, Shaul. *The Reign of the Ayatollahs: Iran and the Islamic Revolution*. London: Unwin, 1986.

Boyce, Mary. *A History of Zoroastrianism*. Leiden: E. J. Brill, 1982.

Chelkowski, Peter J., and Metropolitan Museum of Art (New York, N.Y.). *Mirror of the Invisible World: Tales from the Khamseh of Nizami*. New York: Metropolitan Museum of Art, 1975.

During, Jean. *Musique et mystique dans les traditions de l'Iran*. Paris: Institut Français de Recherche en Iran, 1989.

Ebadi, Shirin. *Iran Awakening: A Memoir of Revolution and Hope*. London: Rider, 2006.

Hamzeh, Ahmed Nizar. *In the Path of Hizbullah*. Syracuse, NY; Great Britain: Syracuse University Press, 2004.

Keddie, Nikki. *Modern Iran: Roots and Results of Revolution*. New Haven, CT: Yale University Press, 2003.

Khalkhali, Sadeq. *Khaterat-e Ayatollah Khalkhali,* Nashr-e Saye, 1379, 2000.

Kian-Thiébaut, Azadeh. *Secularization of Iran: A Doomed Failure?: The New Middle Class and the Making of Modern Iran.* Paris: Diffusion Peeters, 1998.

Lewis, Bernard. *The Assassins: A Radical Sect in Islam.* New York: Octagon Books, 1980.

———. *From Babel to Dragomans: Interpreting the Middle East.* London: Weidenfeld & Nicolson, 2004.

Mottahedeh, Roy. *The Mantle of the Prophet: Learning and Power in Modern Iran.* London: Chatto & Windus, 1986.

Nasr, Sayyed Vali Reza. *The Shia Revival: How Conflicts Within Islam Will Shape the Future.* New York: Norton, 2006.

Pezeshkzad, Iraj. *My Uncle Napoleon: A Novel.* New York: Modern Library, 2006.

Polo, Marco. *The Travels of Marco Polo.* London: Penguin Books, 1992.

Ramadan, Tariq. *Western Muslims and the Future of Islam.* Oxford: Oxford University Press, 2004.

Saidi Sirjani, Ali-Akbar. *Simay-e Do Zan,* Nashr-e Paykan, 1380, 2001.

Varzi, Roxanne. *Warring Souls: Youth, Media, and Martyrdom in Post-Revolution Iran.* Durham, NC: Duke University Press, 2006.

ABOUT THE AUTHOR

AZADEH MOAVENI is the author of *Lipstick Jihad* and co-author, with Nobel Peace Prize laureate Shirin Ebadi, of *Iran Awakening*. She has lived and reported throughout the Middle East, and speaks both Farsi and Arabic fluently. As one of the few American correspondents allowed to work continuously in Iran since 1999, she has reported widely on youth culture, women's rights, and Islamic reform for *Time, The New York Times Book Review, The Washington Post,* NPR, and the *Los Angeles Times.* Currently a *Time* magazine contributing writer on Iran and the Middle East, she lives with her husband and son in London.

www.azadeh.info